RESTORATIVE JUSTICE
ON THE COLLEGE CAMPUS

RESTORATIVE JUSTICE ON THE COLLEGE CAMPUS

Promoting Student Growth and Responsibility, and
Reawakening the Spirit of Campus Community

Edited by

DAVID R. KARP, Ph.D.

Department of Sociology
Skidmore College
Saratoga Springs, New York

and

THOM ALLENA, M.S.

Department of Criminal Justice
University of New Mexico-Taos
Taos, New Mexico

CHARLES C THOMAS • PUBLISHER, LTD.
Springfield • Illinois • U.S.A.

Published and Distributed Throughout the World by

CHARLES C THOMAS • PUBLISHER, LTD.
2600 South First Street
Springfield, Illinois 62704

© 2004 by CHARLES C THOMAS • PUBLISHER, LTD.

ISBN 0-398-07515-8 (hard)
ISBN 0-398-07516-6 (paper)

Library of Congress Catalog Card Number: 2004046061

With **THOMAS BOOKS** *careful attention is given to all details of manufacturing
and design. It is the Publisher's desire to present books that are satisfactory as to their
physical qualities and artistic possibilities and appropriate for their particular use.*
THOMAS BOOKS *will be true to those laws of quality that assure a good name
and good will.*

Printed in the United States of America
JW-R-3

Library of Congress Cataloging-in-Publication Data

Restorative justice on the college campus : promoting student growth and
responsibility, and reawakening the spirit of campus community / edited by
David R. Karp and Thom Allena.
    p. cm.
  Includes bibliographical references.
  ISBN 0-398-07515-8 — ISBN 0-398-07516-6 (pbk.)
    1. College discipline—United States—Case studies. 2. Universities and
colleges—United States—Administration—Case studies. 3. Restorative justice—
United States—Case studies. 4. Conflict management—United States—Case
studies. I. Karp, David R., 1964– II. Allena, Thom.

LB2344.R47 2004
378.1'95—dc22

                                           2004046061

To Gina, Julia, and Abby, who balance my labor with love.

David R. Karp
January 2004

I want to express my heartfelt appreciation to my beloved coach and guide, Larry, and to Paul, a true brother in every sense, for their continued support of this project and of me.

Thom Allena
January 2004

CONTRIBUTORS

Roane Akchurin currently serves as the Manager of Community Housing at UC Santa Barbara. Roane has been with the University of California in a variety of capacities for the past 18 years. She received her Bachelor of Science in ergonomics at UC Santa Barbara and a Master's of Education in college student personnel administration from Colorado State University. She serves as a mediator on campus and in the community and is one of the original restorative justice facilitators at UCSB.

Thom Allena is an Instructor of Criminal Justice and Sociology at the University of New Mexico–Taos. He has worked with restorative justice ideas since 1984 through his consulting practice, Innovations in Justice, and consults with police, courts, correctional systems, probation and parole agencies, and public defenders across the United States and has authored several articles on the applications of restorative justice in these venues. Some of his clients include National Institute of Corrections, American Probation and Parole Association, National Legal Aid and Defenders Association, and the Vermont Department of Corrections. In addition, Thom has consulted with several universities in the application of restorative justice to campus-related issues, including University of California–Los Angeles, University of Colorado, University of California–Santa Barbara and Association for Student Judicial Affairs. He received his B.A. from Niagara University and his M.S. in criminal justice administration from San Diego State University.

Vané Becidyan graduated from Skidmore College in 2003 with a B.A. in English literature. She became a member of the Integrity Board during her sophomore year and was a co-chair for both her junior and senior years. She currently attends Pratt Institute for her Master's in interior design.

Kristie R. Blevins is a Ph.D. candidate in criminal justice at the University of Cincinnati. Previously, she received her M.S. from East Tennessee State University. Her publications and research interests are in the areas of correctional rehabilitation, reaction to the work environment by correctional staff, fairness in the application of capital punishment, public attitudes toward and the effectiveness of gun laws, and the impact of southern culture on criminal justice.

Beau Breslin is Associate Professor of Government and Director of the Law and Society Program at Skidmore College. He teaches courses in constitutional law, civil liberties, constitutional thought, and capital punishment. He has published articles on such issues as restorative justice in the classroom, comparative constitutionalism, and the death penalty. His book, *The Communitarian Constitution*, was published by Johns Hopkins University Press in February 2004. He holds a Ph.D. in political science from the University of Pennsylvania.

Kenneth D. Butterfield is Associate Professor in the Department of Management and Operations at Washington State University. He received his Ph.D. in business administration from The Pennsylvania State University. His current research interests include managing ethical behavior in organizations, moral awareness, ethical decision making, performance appraisal, and organizational punishment. Dr. Butterfield's research has been published in *Academy of Management Journal, Academy of Management Review, Business Ethics Quarterly, Ethics and Behavior, Human Relations, Journal of Higher Education,* and *Research in Higher Education.*

Francis T. Cullen is Distinguished Research Professor of Criminal Justice and Sociology at the University of Cincinnati. His most recent works include *Combating Corporate Crime: Local Prosecutors at Work, Criminological Theory: Context and Consequences,* and *Criminological Theory: Past to Present—Essential Readings.* His current research focuses on the impact of social support on crime, the measurement of sexual victimization, and rehabilitation as a correctional policy. He is President of the American Society of Criminology and a Past President of the Academy of Criminal Justice Sciences.

Michael Dannells is Professor of Higher Education and Student Affairs in the College of Education and Human Development at Bowling Green State University. He received his B.S. (1971) from Bradley University and his Ph.D. (1978) in student development and higher education administration from the University of Iowa. He has been doing research in and writing about student judicial affairs for almost 30 years.

William DeJong serves as director of the U.S. Department of Education's Higher Education Center for Alcohol and Other Drug Prevention, which is based at Education Development Center, Inc., in Newton, Massachusetts. The Center assists colleges and universities as they develop, implement, and evaluate new programs and policies to reduce substance use problems on campus. Dr. DeJong is also the principal investigator for the Social Norms Marketing Research Project, a five-year randomized trial funded by the National Institute on Alcohol Abuse and Alcoholism. Dr. DeJong is the author of over 300 monographs, book chapters, and academic papers in substance abuse prevention, health promotion, criminal justice, social psychology, and the use of media to change social norms and behaviors. In 2000 Dr. DeJong received the College Leadership Award from the American Public Health Association (Alcohol, Tobacco, and Other Drugs Section). Dr. DeJong graduated from Dartmouth College in 1973. He received a doctorate in social psychology from Stanford University in 1977.

Bruce Duncan is Co-Director of the Office of Conflict Resolution at the University of Vermont in Burlington, Vermont. The office offers conflict resolution services and support to all member of the UVM community.

Joyce Ester is currently the Judicial Affairs Coordinator at the University of California, Santa Barbara. Joyce attended Northern Illinois University for a Bachelor's degree in sociology and a Master's in special education. In addition to her current position, Joyce is a Doctoral student at the UCSB Gevirtz Graduate School of Education with an emphasis in Child and Adolescent Development.

Bonnie S. Fisher is a professor in the Division of Criminal Justice at the University of Cincinnati. Her most recent work has examined the predictors of acknowledging rape and effective resistance for different types of sexual victimizations, and fear of rape among college women. She is the co-author of *Campus Crime: Legal, Social and Political Perspectives* and over 50 articles on the topics of college campus victimization, sexual victimization of female college students, measurement of sexual victimization, and the extent and nature of violence in the workplace.

Brooke Hadwen is the Coordinator of the Burlington Community Support Program in Burlington, Vermont. She is a professionally trained mediator and works with all members of the Burlington community providing conflict resolution services.

Donald B. Hastings is a 1974 graduate of SUNY Fredonia, where he earned his B.A. He received his M.S. in counseling in higher education from the University of Bridgeport, Connecticut, in 1977. Don has been in higher education administration for 28 years and is currently Associate Dean of Student Affairs at Skidmore College, New York.

David R. Karp is Associate Professor of Sociology at Skidmore College in Saratoga Springs, New York. He conducts research on community-based responses to crime, has given workshops on restorative justice and community justice nationally, and is a founding member of the New York State Community Justice Forum. Current projects include an evaluation of Vermont's Offender Reentry Program, the impact of the death penalty on victims' families, and restorative practices in college judicial systems and K–12 school settings. He is the author of more than 50 academic articles and technical reports and a trilogy of books on community justice. He received a B.A. from the University of California at Berkeley and a Ph.D. in sociology from the University of Washington.

Connie J. Kirkland, M.A., N.C.C., is the creator of and has directed the George Mason University Sexual Assault Services Office in Fairfax, Virginia, since 1993. Previously she was the first director of a victim/witness assistance program on a college campus in the George Mason University Police Department. Prior to coming to George Mason University, she directed victim advocacy centers in California, Arkansas, and Illinois. She has also developed model law enforcement policies for Virginia. She is a Certified Law Enforcement Instructor, a National Certified Counselor, an Internationally Certified Trauma Specialist and a George Mason University faculty member, teaching criminal justice and women's studies courses. She has been recognized by numerous state and federal agencies for her innovative work in the fields of sexual assault and stalking.

Matthew Lopez-Phillips is the Director of Judicial Affairs at the University of Colorado, Boulder. He has over 10 years of professional experience in higher education in residence life, judicial affairs, and Greek life. He received his Master's degree in counseling psychology and college student development from Northeastern University. He is a member of Alpha Kappa Phi, Archania, Order of Omega, and Phi Kappa Phi.

John Wesley Lowery is Assistant Professor of Higher Education and Student Affairs in the Department of Educational Leadership and Policies at the University of South Carolina. He earned his doctorate at Bowling Green State University in higher education administration. He previously held administrative positions at Adrian College and Washington University. John is actively involved in numerous professional associations, including the American College Personnel Association, the Association for Student Judicial Affairs, and the National Association of Student Personnel Administrators. John has a Master's degree in student personnel services from the University of South Carolina and an undergraduate degree from the University of Virginia in religious studies. He is a frequent speaker and author on topics related to student affairs and higher education, particularly legislative issues and judicial affairs on which he is widely regarding as an expert.

Donald L. McCabe is Professor of Management and Global Business at Rutgers, The State University of New Jersey. He received his Ph.D. in management from New York University. His current research focuses almost exclusively on questions of academic integrity with a particular interest in academic honor codes. Dr. McCabe's research has been published in a variety of journals, including *Business Ethics Quarterly, Change, Ethics and Behavior, Human Relations, Journal of Higher Education, Journal of Marketing,* and *Research in Higher Education.* He is founding president of the Center for Academic Integrity at Duke University. He joined Rutgers after a more than 20-year career in the corporate world.

Robert L. Mikus has served as the Director of Residence Life at Elizabethtown College for the past seven years. He earned his Master's Degree in human services psychology from LaSalle University. Shortly after arriving at Elizabethtown College, Bob co-authored a grant to establish the Community Accountability Conferencing (Restorative Justice) program. Integrating the Community Accountability Conferencing program and the Community Standards program has enabled Bob and his staff to foster a residential environment where students establish the standards for community living and enlist restorative accountability practices to deal with members who willingly compromise those standards. Bob authored the article "Restorative Practices Come to Campus: Setting the Standards for Community Development" for ResLife.Net, and has presented to higher education groups about the Elizabethtown College program. Bob and his wife, Donna, live in Lancaster County, Pennsylvania, with their two sons.

Priscilla Mori has worked at the University of California, Santa Barbara for over 30 years in a variety of administrative positions, most of which have been in academic units. She holds a Bachelor's degree from the University of California, Santa Barbara in combination social science with an anthropology emphasis. She has served as a facilitator in a number of restorative justice circles and as a mediator.

Pat Oles is Associate Professor of Social Work and Dean of Student Affairs at Skidmore College. Pat has taught at Skidmore College since 1985, becoming dean of student affairs in 1997. His professional and scholarly work has focused on abused and delinquent teenagers, reducing homophobia among social workers, and most recently student cultures on campus.

Jon Ramsey is Dean of Studies and an Associate Professor of English at Skidmore College. He received a B.A. from San Diego State University and a Ph.D. in English from the University of California, Riverside. He has over-seen academic integrity cases at Skidmore, and participated in regional and national conversations on the topic, for the past 23 years. His publications, including articles and two co-edited books, center on English literature and expository writing; he has also presented papers on academic integrity, advising, and curriculum development at various conferences, especially those sponsored by NACADA (the National Academic Advising Association). His most recent presentation on integrity occurred at a con-ference on "Information Ethics and Academic Dishonesty" hosted by Colby, Bates, and Bowdoin Colleges (October 15, 2003).

Nora Rogers is the Program Coordinator for the Restorative Justice Program at the University of Colorado, Boulder. She has three years of pro-fessional experience in student affairs and judicial affairs in higher educa-tion. She received her B.A. in psychology from the University of Colorado, Boulder.

Shannon A. Santana is a Ph.D. candidate at the University of Cincinnati. Her research publications have appeared in the *Security Journal* and the *Justice System Journal.* Her research interests include public opinion about crime and punishment, rehabilitation, gender and workplace violence, and the impact of resistance on violent victimization.

Tom Sebok is the Director of the Ombuds Office at the University of Colorado at Boulder. Between 1976 and 1990 he worked as a counselor in three different community colleges. He became an ombudsperson at the University of Colorado at Boulder in 1990 and the Director of the office in 1992. From 1995 to 1999, he served as Secretary for the Board of the University and College Ombuds Association (UCOA). He serves on the edi-torial board of *The Journal of the California Caucus of College and University Ombuds,* the only professional journal dedicated to ombuds practice. He has published seven articles related to ombudsing and has made numerous pre-sentations at regional and national conferences related to ombudsing, con-flict management, and restorative justice. He is the winner of the 2002 Stanley V. Anderson Award for Overall Service to Ombudsmen and the 1998 Service Excellence Award for the California Caucus of College and University Ombuds. He helped establish the University of Colorado's Restorative Justice Program, the first of its kind at a college or university in the United States. He holds a Master's in Education degree in college coun-seling and student personnel administration (1976) from the University of Delaware.

Jeffrey O. Segrave is a Professor in the Department of Exercise Science, Dance, and Athletics at Skidmore College. For 25 years he taught courses in sport studies and liberal studies and coached the women's tennis team. He also served as Department Chair for five years. His interests focus on the sociology of sport and his main areas of interests include the Olympic Games, women in sport, and language and sport. He has co-edited three books, published five book chapters, and published over 30 articles in scholarly journals, including *Journal of Sport and Social Issues, International Review for the Sociology of Sport, Sociology of Sport Journal, Quest, Sociological Focus, Violence Against Women,* and *Aethlon: The Journal of Sport Literature.* In 1998–1999 he was Sterling McMurrin Distinguished Visiting Professor, University of Utah.

Laura Strohminger is the Director of Greek Affairs at the Univerisity of Colorado, Boulder. She has worked in Student Affairs for over seven years in various positions in Residence Life and Greek affairs. She has a Master's degree in college student personnel from Bowling Green State University in Ohio.

Linda Klebe Treviño is Professor of Organizational Behavior and Acting Chair of the Department of Management and Organization in the Smeal College of Business Administration at The Pennsylvania State University. She holds a Ph.D. in management from Texas A&M University. Her research and writing on the management of ethical conduct in organizations is widely published and well known internationally. She co-authored a textbook with Katherine Nelson entitled *Managing Business Ethics: Straight Talk About How to Do It Right* (3rd edition, 2004) and a more academic book summarizing 10 years of research with coauthor Gary Weaver, entitled *Managing Ethics in Business Organizations: Social Scientific Perspectives* (Stanford University Press, 2003). Her current research focuses on ethical leadership, ethical role modeling, moral awareness, moral motivation, and organizational justice.

Amy Van Meter has worked for Housing and Residential Services at University of California Santa Barbara for nine years. She has a B.A. in peace and global studies from Earlham College and an M.A. in international peace studies from the University of Notre Dame. She serves as a mediator and a restorative justice facilitator.

William C. Warters is an Assistant Professor (Research) in Interdisciplinary Studies at the College of Urban, Labor and Metropolitan Affairs at Wayne State University in Detroit. Doctor Warters, a former co-chair of the Association for Conflict Resolution's Education Section, is Editor of the *Conflict Management in Higher Education Report* and Director of the Conflict

Management in Higher Education Resource Center (http://www.campus-adr.org) funded by the Department of Education's Fund for the Improvement of Post Secondary Education (FIPSE). He is the author of *Mediation in the Campus Community* (Jossey-Bass, 1999) and an instructor within the Master of Arts in Dispute Resolution Program at Wayne State University. He holds a B.A. in conflict resolution from UCSC and an inter-disciplinary social science Ph.D. from the Program on the Analysis and Resolution of Conflicts at Syracuse University's Maxwell School of Citizenship and Public Affairs.

Stephen L. Wessler is the Director of the Center for the Prevention of Hate Violence (CPHV) at the University of Southern Maine. Mr. Wessler is also a research associate professor within the College of Arts and Sciences and the Muskie School of Public Service. CPHV develops and implements programs in schools, colleges, and communities to prevent bias, prejudice, harassment, and violence and promotes research and teaching on issues relating to bias motivated violence. Mr. Wessler has conducted scores of workshops, lectures, and keynote addresses on preventing hate violence for educators, students, police officers, correctional staff, health care professionals, and community members. Mr. Wessler, an attorney, developed and directed the civil rights enforcement effort at the Maine Department of the Attorney General from 1992 to 1999. In 1996, Mr. Wessler developed with others the Civil Rights Teams Project, a hate violence prevention program conducted by the Attorney General's office, which is now in over 200 Maine middle and high schools. Mr. Wessler participated in 1998 in the U.S. Department of Justice's Working Group, which developed and piloted the National Hate Crimes Training Curriculum. Mr. Wessler is a graduate of Harvard College and Boston University School of Law. He practiced law, both in the Attorney General's office and in private practice, for over 22 years before creating CPHV in 1999. Mr. Wessler has authored a number of publications on hate crime enforcement and prevention, including *The Respectful School: How Educators and Students Can Conquer Hate and Harassment* (ASCD, August, 2003).

Christina Baker Zwerenz is the Assistant Director of Judicial Affairs at the University of Colorado, Boulder. She has over four years of professional experience in higher education in judicial affairs, student activities, and Greek life. She received her Master's degree in higher education adminis-tration–student development and enrollment management from the University of Denver.

PREFACE

Since 1996, we have been advancing the idea that restorative justice is the best approach to campus disciplinary problems. One of us (Thom Allena) helped the University of Colorado implement the first restorative program in a large university setting. The other (David Karp) helped to do the same at Skidmore College, a small liberal arts college. The settings are different, and so are the practices developed: Thom trained staff to conduct restorative conferences, while David adapted Vermont Department of Corrections' Reparative Probation Program for use by Skidmore's Integrity Board. The differences, however, are less important than the common underlying philosophy of restorative justice and its suitability to the disciplinary problems of college students, be they big 10 or little arts.

Restorative justice is a new response to criminal incidents. It has quickly become an international movement with programs proliferating particularly in the United States, Canada, Great Britain, Australia, and New Zealand (Roche 2003). It has become a dominant model guiding juvenile justice practice in the United States with substantial federal support (Office of Juvenile Justice and Delinquency Prevention 1998). It is increasingly used in K–12 school communities (Karp and Breslin, 2001; Cameron and Thorsborne, 2001). Restorative justice can be defined as a collaborative decision-making process that includes victims, offenders, and others seeking to hold offenders accountable by having them (1) accept and acknowledge responsibility for their offenses, (2) to the best of their ability repair the harm they caused to victims and communities, and (3) work to reduce the risk of reoffense by building positive social ties to the community.

Although some colleges and universities have adopted restorative practices, very little has been written about its use in the college setting (but see Karp, Breslin, and Oles, 2002; Warters, Sebok, and Goldblum, 2000). Colleges and universities are surprisingly lagging behind others in their exploration, experimentation, and institutional adoption of restorative practices. Nevertheless, enough work has been done to merit focused attention. We have assembled a distinguished group of scholars and student affairs professionals to examine the problem of student discipline and the potential of restorative justice as a proactive, educational response.

This book has four sections. The first section provides an overview of restorative justice and an evaluation of contemporary practices in student judicial affairs. The second section introduces the major restorative practices: accountability boards, conferencing, and victim offender mediation/dialogue. Each chapter that describes a practice is followed by a case study illustrating how the models have been used. The case studies not only illustrate best practices, but also identify obstacles and issues to consider.

The third section identifies particular problem areas from binge drinking to plagiarism to date rape. The authors provide an overview of the nature and prevalence of each problem, and again case studies follow for illustration. Several case studies consider particular applications such as a conference to address the misconduct of a student with a drinking problem. Two case studies look at broader policy and program questions such as the failure of speech codes to effectively address bias-motivated harassment and how restorative practices may provide an effective alternative. The second looks at the sexual assault services provided at one university and how its attention to victims' needs exemplifies the restorative justice concern for addressing the harm of an offense. The final section of the book includes an epilogue that speculates on the promise of restorative justice for the current generation of students and their particular set of assets and challenges.

We are grateful to our colleagues who contributed to this volume, and especially to the student affairs professionals nationwide who are willing to try new practices in their efforts to improve the lives of those who live, work, and study in the campus community.

David R. Karp
Saratoga Springs, New York

Thom Allena
Taos, New Mexico

References

Cameron, Lisa, and Margaret Thorsborne (2001). "Restorative Justice and School Discipline: Mutually Exclusive?" pp. 180–194 in *Restorative Justice and Civil Society*, edited by H. Strang and J. Braithwaite. Cambridge, UK: Cambridge University Press.

Karp, David R., and Beau Breslin (2001). "Restorative Justice in School Communities." *Youth and Society* 33:249–272.

Karp, David R., Beau Breslin, and Pat Oles (2002). "Community Justice in the Campus Setting." *Conflict Management in Higher Education Report.* 3(1). http://www.campus-adr.org/CMHER/ReportArticles/Edition3_1/Karp3_1a.html

Roche, Declan (2003). *Accountability in Restorative Justice.* New York: Oxford University Press.

Office of Juvenile Justice and Delinquency Prevention (1998). *Guide for Implementing the Balanced and Restorative Justice Model.* Washington, DC: U.S. Department of Justice.

Warters, William C., Tom Sebok, and Andrea Goldblum (2000). "Making Things Right: Restorative Justice Comes to Campuses." *Conflict Management in Higher Education 1.* http://www.culma.wayne.edu/CMHER/Articles/Restorative.html

CONTENTS

PART IV: CONCLUSION

RESTORATIVE JUSTICE
ON THE COLLEGE CAMPUS

Part I

INTRODUCTION

Chapter 1

INTRODUCING RESTORATIVE JUSTICE TO THE CAMPUS COMMUNITY

David R. Karp

THE DISCIPLINARY PROBLEM

Although restorative justice is a new concept, there are already dozens of empirical evaluations demonstrating its effectiveness in criminal justice (see Braithwaite 2002 for a review). Participants tend to be more satisfied by their experiences with this process as compared with traditional court processes, and recidivism rates for offenders in restorative justice programs are lower than for those who received traditional sentences. On the basis of its rapid proliferation and successful outcomes, we find sufficient grounds for its adoption in campus judicial affairs. But there are other reasons as well. Restorative justice may be particularly well suited to campus communities because of their democratic and egalitarian ethos and educational mission.

The problem of student misconduct has several interrelated dimensions. First, students arriving on campus as freshmen experience a sudden, dramatic loss of supervision. Many of these students have not developed strong internal controls to regulate their behavior. This is especially true for students coming from very authoritative homes, where self-regulation was not cultivated (Colvin, 2000). For students whose behavior has been largely dependent on external controls, the liberated college environment may come as quite a shock.

Second, arriving students, who are anxious to make friends and establish a sense of belonging, are strongly pressured by peers to "party" with alcohol and other drugs. Prior research suggests that students overestimate the actual degree of alcohol and drug use by other students and seek to conform to the perceived norm (Perkins and Berkowitz, 1986). Research also shows that drug and alcohol use, and binge drinking in particular, is correlated with reduced academic performance. Even students who exercise moderation are affected by property damage and unwanted sexual advances (Wechsler et al., 1994).

Third, student culture is at odds with mainstream society and legal codes with regard to drug use and underage alcohol consumption. Survey data from 2001 reveal that 85 percent of college students had consumed alcohol in the year prior to data collection and 36 percent had smoked marijuana. It should be noted that 65 percent of the survey sample was under age 21 (Core Institute 2003). College alcohol and drug policies, which obviously must comply with the criminal law, are accorded scant legitimacy among students. This dissensus creates an adversarial relationship between students and administration (as well as campus safety officers). Faculty members are caught in the middle and tend to remain awkwardly neutral about student extracurricular conduct. Campus life is strangely bifurcated. Students describe professors as their primary non-peer role models, yet the social control faculty exert in the academic sphere does not extend to the students' residential lives. In that realm, students largely fend for themselves.

Fourth, colleges typically rely on coercive techniques to gain compliance with college policies and the criminal law because they have had little alternative. Since college administrations cannot rely on student internal controls, and since dissensus precludes them from appealing to universal moral codes, administrators are forced to increase surveillance and punitive sanctions. This creates a conundrum because higher educational institutions in the United States often operate as cloistered liberal polities. While campuses generally repudiate authoritarian social control, they increasingly rely on the techniques of the police state to enforce campus policies. However, campus safety departments are rarely adequately staffed to accomplish coercive control, municipal police are not invited on campus, students remain largely free to consume drugs and alcohol at will, and an unlucky few are subject to increasingly harsh penalties when they are caught. Failing to achieve any deterrent effect, a common student reaction is that a few students are unfairly singled out for a punishment and call for campus officials to look the other way and leave them alone.

Fifth, because a quarter of the student body is new each year, disciplinary approaches must be educational and ongoing. Smith and Dickey (1999) describe a Milwaukee neighborhood street corner where the drug trade thrives. In a three-month period in 1996, 94 drug arrests were made, and most of those arrested were convicted and sentenced to two years in prison. Nevertheless, the drug trade continued unabated. The removal of one dealer merely created the opportunity for the next dealer to stake his claim on the corner. Just as Milwaukee police officers could not arrest their way out of the drug problem, colleges cannot effectively respond to student disciplinary problems (including the drug trade) through apprehension and removal. The continual student population turnover guarantees that individual-level solutions cannot resolve community-level problems. Instead, solutions must continuously strive to socialize students to be community members who are able to consider the consequences of their behavior on the welfare of the community (DeJong et al., 1998).

The restorative approach described here offers a communitarian alternative to liberal avoidance and conservative crackdowns. It is an approach that focuses on moral education by integrating academic learning, student participation in the campus judicial process, and restorative justice principles. The approach is a response to both individual misbehavior and campus dissensus.

RESTORATIVE JUSTICE: PRINCIPLES AND VALUES

Restorative justice is an approach to criminal offending that emphasizes values of democratic participation, inclusion, and stewardship (Clear and Karp, 1999). Restorative justice encourages dialogue among victims and offenders to construct plans of action that hold offenders accountable and meet victims' needs. This approach may be effectively extended to the college arena, where misconduct is not always illegal, but often is a violation of campus honor codes and college policies. Restorative processes help educate community members about the need for civic commitment and build student capacity for evaluating the impact of their behavior on the community. They also legitimate college policies by creating not only due process, but also consensus around behavioral standards and equitable responses to misconduct. Offender accountability is central, but it is balanced with a concern for reintegration—which is defined by an offender's ability to regain trust through demonstrated good citizenship. The restorative values of repairing harm, reintegration, and community building is reflected in Figure 1.1.

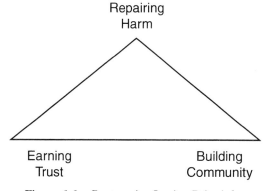

Figure 1.1   Restorative Justice Principles

Our approach is particularly concerned with the use of restorative justice in a well-defined community—the campus community. As such, we stress four principles to guide student judicial practices (Karp and Clear, 2002). First, the judicial system must be *accessible* to the student community. Students must know of the campus policies, which should be communicated clearly with a minimum of legalese. Practices of the judicial system should be consistent and respectful, but not rigidly bureaucratic.

Second, community members should participate actively in the process. On the college campus, this means that students should have active roles in the process, as should faculty, staff, and administration. *Community involvement* includes the active participation of offenders[1] in the decision-making process. Equally important is the voice of victims or "harmed parties." More generally, a mechanism should exist to recruit volunteers in the community who are interested in the judicial process. A justice system is legitimated when participants in the process believe that others who participate represent the broader community. Without democratic representation, those who are sanctioned are less likely to view the process as just (Tyler, 1990).

Third, sanctioning should focus on repairing harm. Here, accountability is defined not by the proportional harm imposed on the offender, but by the offender's obligation to make amends for the harm he or she has caused. Bazemore and Walgrave (1999) define restorative justice as "action that is primarily oriented toward doing justice by repairing the harm that has been caused by a crime" (p. 48). If a window has been broken, the offender's obligation is to fix it. It is not possible for the offender to take responsibility for all types of harm; he or she, for example, cannot repair emotional harm. Nevertheless, the obligation remains for the offender to take steps toward ameliorating such harm through apology, expression of remorse, or victim-offender mediation. Communal harm can be repaired through community service work.

Fourth, the offender also incurs an obligation to reassure the community that he or she will not cause further harm to the community. The community, in turn, must strive to *reintegrate* the offender. This reciprocal process begins with an identification of offender risk factors. If the offender needs academic tutoring, psychological counseling, or other competency needs, these should be made available. Sanctions should be guided by the objectives of restoration and reintegration so that harm is repaired and offenders can become productive community members. Accountability is demonstrated through expressions of remorse and commitment, and through the completion of tasks negotiated as part of the sanctioning process.

---

1. We use the terms *offenders* and *victims* because that is the convention of criminologists. But in practice, we use terms that are less symbolically tied to criminal justice, such as *respondents* for offenders and *harmed parties* for victims.

Consider one recent case at Skidmore College. A student was arrested for dealing cocaine. After serving time in state prison, the student reapplied to Skidmore to complete his senior year. He was readmitted, but one of the stipulations required him to tell his story to other students so they might learn from his experience. For his project, he created a 30-minute video memoir, which the college uses as a platform for discussion about the risks of dealing drugs. While it was tempting to deny his readmission, enabling the student to take active responsibility for his behavior provided the campus with a new resource for discussing drug issues with the student body.

RETHINKING SANCTIONS AND EMBRACING
RESTORATIVE JUSTICE

In a review of college judicial affairs practices, Dannells (1996) argues that the historical development of the field has moved away from retributive punishment and toward rehabilitation and the development of student self-discipline. "Throughout the 1950s and '60s, disciplinary affairs became less punishment and control-oriented, more democratic, and more focused on reeducation and rehabilitation" (p. 177). This is certainly true as judicial officers increasingly provide direct counseling or refer students to treatment. Nevertheless, the continuum of sanctions is still defined by punishment and outcasting, rather than restoration and reintegration. Students are given warnings; their privileges are restricted (such as being prevented from participating in intercollegiate sports or in other cocurricular clubs); or they are removed from campus housing, suspended, or ultimately expelled. Nevertheless, the widely adopted "model student code" generally reflects a retributive rubric (Dannells, 1997, pp. 107–108; Stoner, 1998). Thus, a student already operating at the margins of social acceptability is progressively outcast from membership in the conventional college community. The restorative justice approach promotes inclusion over social distancing, emphasizing instead sanctioning strategies that rebuild conventional social ties to the college community.

Central to replacing outcasting with reintegration is to shift the burden of sanctioning responsibility from the college to the student. While suspension and expulsion must be retained, they are anticommunitarian devices that should be minimized wherever possible. The removal of a student from the community is likely to displace the problem to another, less fortified community without resolving it. We believe that suspension should be limited to two situations. First, colleges are not correctional facilities, and removal may be necessary when a student poses a threat to campus safety. Second, when a student refuses to participate in judicial proceedings, or a student fails to complete sanctioning tasks, then the student should be removed. Otherwise, the goal should be reintegration through the development of personal responsibility.

We advocate a new conceptualization of suspension called "self-suspension." Each student is obligated to repair harm and demonstrate his or her ability to be a member in good standing. A contract with the student should be negotiated and it should clearly detail what steps the student must take to regain social standing. While a student may apply for an extension if necessary, a student generally is not allowed to register for the following semester's classes until the contract is complete.[2] Thus, a student who fails to comply with the college's expectations for responsible membership loses his or her right to participate in community life. The burden of responsibility is shifted from the college to the student. In essence, restorative justice sends a very clear message to offenders: You have done wrong, and we can agree on this by clearly identifying the damage done to victims and the community. We will now give you the opportunity to take responsibility for what you have done by repairing that harm as best you can and demonstrating to us your ability to be a good citizen.

Apology. Apology occupies a central place in restorative justice. Retzinger and Scheff (1996) argue that reconciliation is predicated on a core sequence: "This process involves the social rituals of respect, courtesy, apology, and forgiveness. . . . The ideal outcome, from the point of view of symbolic reparation, is constituted by two steps: the offender first clearly expresses genuine shame and remorse over his or her actions. In response, the victim takes at least a first step towards forgiving the offender for the trespass. The core sequence generates repair and restoration of the bond between victim and offender, after this bond had been severed by the offender's crime" (p. 316). The sanctioning process, therefore, must begin with an acknowledgment of responsibility for the offense, articulated through an apology. Our apology guidelines require that letters contain (1) an acknowledgement of responsibility, (2) a delineation of how the behavior was harmful, (3) an expression of remorse, and (4) a commitment to making amends and socially responsible behavior in the future.

From Fines to Restitution. Restitution should be distinguished from fines. Fines are imposed as a punishment to deter the misbehavior and, presumably, to generate revenue. Restitution is collected to pay for lost or damaged property as a result of the offense. The amount of a fine is determined by the deterrent need and is independent of the particular offense. Restitution is determined by the extent of harm. From the perspective of the offender, fines are likely to be perceived as arbitrary since the rationale for the amount

---

2. At Skidmore, this model works for all students except graduating seniors. For this group, failure to complete sanctions will prevent them from participating in commencement exercises and receiving their diploma.

is not transparent. More problematic, fines create moral ambiguity (Kahan, 1999). In a market society, goods and services have prices, but are morally neutral. If misbehavior is fined, the message of moral disapproval is easily obscured. Instead, we communicate that the behavior is acceptable "if you can afford it." Restitution is paid in order to make amends. By clearly identifying harm, the offender learns why the behavior is morally unacceptable.

Enlightened Community Service. Community service is widely used in college judicial sanctioning, yet it often is not restorative. Community service can be misused as a retributive device. This is the case when it is merely a substitution for another punishment, scored on a rubric of punitive commensurability (Kahan, 1999)—40 hours of community service = $400 fine = 4 days in jail = 40 lashes of the whip. The symbolism suggests it is just one more type of pain that can be imposed on the offender. This is just the wrong message to send to someone in need of community reintegration. If service is used as a punitive deterrent, why would the offender embrace it as a positive expression of community membership?

When used correctly, community service is central to a restorative approach. As restitution should be distinguished from fines, so should restorative community service be distinguished from punitive service (Bazemore and Karp, forthcoming 2004). If a student vandalizes a campus building, community service would be necessary—the student should fix the damage, perhaps working alongside maintenance staff. In a recent case at Skidmore College, two dormitory roommates had moved lounge furniture to their room. As part of our judicial process, the students learned that the violation not only was harmful to the other residents by denying them a comfortable common space, but also had broader effects on the college because visiting prospective students would only see unpleasant residential spaces. A contract was negotiated in which the two students would return the furniture and clean the lounge (renting an upholstery cleaner) in time for an upcoming event in which large numbers of prospective students would be visiting the campus. The students were encouraged not to do this alone, but to organize a dorm-wide "spring cleaning." Their leadership would serve as a demonstration of their commitment to making amends and promoting school spirit.

Community service, properly understood, is a mechanism of reintegration for student offenders because it provides a venue for making their prosocial efforts visible to others and fostering positive social ties with the campus community. It is also a means of reframing individual student misconduct as a community issue. Since the problems that appear before judicial boards generally speak to the broader issues of student culture (e.g., underage drinking and drug use), service projects linked to the offense become vehicles of community education. The student who uses hate speech might work with a diversity specialist to organize a campus event on multicultural issues; the drunk driver might work with MADD (Mothers Against Drunk Driving) to bring a relevant speaker to campus; the student who downloaded a term paper from the Internet might organize a session during freshman orientation regarding the standards of academic integrity. Community service sanctions may be endlessly creative as they seek to change the underlying social norms that reinforce individual misbehavior.

RESTORATIVE JUSTICE MODELS

Because restorative justice is an international movement and is practiced in many different settings—from elementary schools to maximum security prisons—a variety of models have developed. Each has a unique history with a different set of practices. Today, many people have been trained in multiple practices, incorporating elements of one as they use another, so it is often difficult to distinguish them. Bazemore and Umbreit (2001) and Roche (2003) identify four basic models: victim offender mediation (VOM), conferencing, circles, and boards.

Victim offender mediation was pioneered in the 1970s in Canada and the United States by secular practitioners/researchers such as Mark Umbreit (Umbreit, 1994) and faith community activists such as Howard Zehr (Zehr, 1990). Victim offender mediation, sometimes called victim offender reconciliation or victim offender dialogue, is used for minor crimes and for cases of serious violence. The goal of the dialogue between a victim and an offender may be for clarification and healing, providing victims an opportunity to convey the harm they have suffered and to ask questions of the offender that help them make sense of the crime. VOM is often also used to negotiate a restorative contract in which the offender agrees to tasks that will help repair the harm. Although campuses across the country have embraced mediation (Warters, 2000), VOM is distinct from the more common "settlement-driven mediation" because offenders must admit responsibility before the meeting.

Conferencing models, sometimes called family group conferencing or family group decision making, are similar to VOM except that they include "supporters" of the victim and the offender. These may be friends and family, and supporters actively participate in the discussion. Theoretically, supporters serve two important roles: support and accountability. First, they help create an environment in which the key stakeholders feel comfortable enough to speak openly and honestly. They also provide both support during the meeting and assistance with the completion of agreed-upon tasks. A victim might decide, for example, to return to school and a friend might offer to share an apartment. Second, supporters increase accountability, such as by moderating extreme comments made during the meeting, by challenging dishonest statements, and by monitoring compliance with agreements. Conferencing has its origins in the tribal justice practices of the Maori and proliferated as a modern practice in New Zealand, beginning in 1989, and Australia before arriving in the United States (Hudson et al., 1996).

Circles, also called circle sentencing and peacemaking circles, have their roots in North American indigenous practices, but are now used in numerous U.S. jurisdictions (Coates et al., 2003; Pranis, Stuart, and Wedge, 2003). In 1982, the Navaho Nation formally resurrected traditional circle practices to address crime problems (Roche, 2003). In 1992, Judge Barry Stuart pioneered the use of circles in the Canadian court serving First Nations peoples in the Yukon (Stuart, 1996). Circles are inclusive of all affected parties in a criminal incident, and the number of participants can be in the dozens. In traditional peacemaking circles of indigenous people of North America, participants use a "talking piece" to regulate the flow of dialogue. The talking piece is a ritual object that symbolizes the commonality and interdependence of circle participants. The person holding the talking piece may speak for as long as he or she wishes and retains the full attention of circle members. This communication technique prevents individuals from dominating the conversation, allowing all members to speak and enabling them to prepare their thoughts before sharing them. A "keeper" of the circle facilitates the process and is responsible for setting a tone of respect, hope, and support. Unfortunately, we do not know of any peacemaking circle programs operating on the college campus and do not provide case studies of this practice.

Boards, known by a variety of monikers such as integrity boards, reparative boards, and community panels, originated with the Vermont Department of Corrections Reparative Probation Program in 1996 (Walther and Perry, 1997). There are now hundreds of board programs in juvenile and adult criminal justice across the United States (Schiff et al., 2001). In this model, a small group of trained volunteers representing the community meet with offenders and victims to negotiate a restorative contract. This model is the most similar to contemporary campus judicial boards that include students, faculty, and staff. However, they differ in their emphasis on restorative dialogue and the creation of reparative agreements. They tend to differ in sanctioning philosophy and in the training board members receive.

Whichever approach is taken, each seeks an outcome that is morally satisfying to the participants in the decision-making process, particularly those most deeply affected by the misconduct. Restorative practices may not succeed in every case, but they may more closely reflect the overarching mission of higher education than contemporary judicial affairs practices.

References

Bazemore, Gordon, and Lode Walgrave. 1999. "Restorative Juvenile Justice: In Search of Fundamentals and an Outline for Systemic Reform," pp. 45–74 in *Restorative Juvenile Justice*, edited by G. Bazemore and L. Walgrave. Monsey, NY: Criminal Justice Press.

Bazemore, Gordon, and Mark S. Umbreit. 2001. *A Comparison of Four Restorative Conferencing Models*. Washington, DC: Office of Juvenile Justice and Delinquency Prevention.

Bazemore, Gordon, and David R. Karp. Forthcoming 2004. "Community Service and Offender Reintegration." *Justice Policy Journal*.

Braithwaite, John. 2002. *Restorative Justice and Responsive Regulation*. New York: Oxford University Press.

Clear, Todd R., and David R. Karp. 1999. *The Community Justice Ideal*. Boulder, CO: Westview.

Coates, Robert B., Mark Umbreit, and Betty Vos. 2003. "Restorative Justice Circles: An Exploratory Study." *Contemporary Justice Review* 6:265–278.

Colvin, Mark. 2000. *Crime and Coercion*. New York: St. Martin's.

Core Institute. 2003. *American Campuses 2001 Statistics on Alcohol and Other Drug Use*. http://www.siu.edu/departments/coreinst/public_html/recent.html

Dannells, Michael. 1996. "Discipline and Judicial Affairs," pp. 175–213 in *Student Affairs Practice in Higher Education*, edited by A. L. Rentz. Springfield, IL: Charles C Thomas.

———. 1997. *From Discipline to Development: Rethinking Student Conduct in Higher Education*, vol. 25 (2). Washington, DC: The George Washington University Graduate School of Education and Human Development.

DeJong, William, Cheryl Vince-Whitman, Tom Colthurst, Maggie Cretella, Michael Gilbreath, Michael Rosati, and Karen Zweig. 1998. *Environmental Management: A Comprehensive Strategy for Reducing Alcohol and Other Drug Use on College Campuses*. U.S. Department of Education Higher Education Center for Alcohol and Other Drug Prevention. http://www.edc.org/hec/pubs/enviro-mgnt.html

Hudson, Joe, Allison Morris, Gabrielle Maxwell, and Burt Galaway. 1996. *Family Group Conferences*. Monsey, NY: Criminal Justice Press.

Kahan, Dan M. 1999. "Punishment Incommensurability." *Buffalo Criminal Law Review* 1:691–708.

Karp, David R., and Todd R. Clear. 2002. *What Is Community Justice? Case Studies of Restorative Justice and Community Supervision*. Thousand Oaks, CA: Sage.

Perkins, H. Wesley, and Alan D. Berkowitz. 1986. "Perceiving the Community Norms of Alcohol Use Among Students: Some Research Implications for Campus Alcohol Education Programming." *International Journal of the Addictions* 21:961–976.

Pranis, Kay, Barry Stuart, and Mark Wedge. 2003. *Peacemaking Circles*. St. Paul, MN: Living Justice Press.

Retzinger, Suzanne M., and Thomas J. Scheff. 1996. "Strategy for Community Conferences: Emotions and Social Bonds," pp. 315–336 in *Restorative Justice: International Perspectives*, edited by B. Galaway and J. Hudson. Monsey, NY: Criminal Justice Press.

Roche, Declan. 2003. *Accountability in Restorative Justice.* New York: Oxford University Press.

Schiff, Mara, Gordon Bazemore, and Carsten Erbe. 2001. *Tracking Restorative Justice Decisionmaking in the Response to Youth Crime: The Prevalence of Youth Conferencing in the United States.* Ft. Lauderdale, FL: The Community Justice Institute, Florida Atlantic University.

Smith, Michael E., and Walter J. Dickey. 1999. *Reforming Sentencing and Corrections for Just Punishment.* Washington, DC: National Institute of Justice. http://www.ncjrs.org/pdffiles1/nij/175724.pdf

Stoner, Edward N. 1998. "A Model Code for Student Discipline," pp. 3–42 in *The Administration of Campus Discipline: Student, Organizational, and Community Issues,* edited by B. G. Paterson and W. L. Kibler. Asheville, NC: College Administration Publications, Inc.

Stuart, Barry. 1996. "Circle Sentencing: Turning Swords into Ploughshares," pp. 193–206 in *Restorative Justice: International Perspectives,* edited by B. Galaway and J. Hudson. Monsey, NY: Criminal Justice Press.

Tyler, Tom R. 1990. *Why People Obey the Law.* New Haven, CT: Yale University Press.

Umbreit, Mark S. 1994. *Victim Meets Offender: The Impact of Restorative Justice and Mediation.* Monsey, NY: Criminal Justice Press.

Walther, Lynne, and John Perry. 1997. "The Vermont Reparative Probation Program." *ICCA Journal on Community Corrections* 8:26–34.

Warters, William C. 2000. *Mediation in the Campus Community.* San Francisco, CA: Jossey-Bass.

Wechsler, Henry, Andrea Davenport, George Dowdall, Barbara Moeykens, and Sonia Castillo. 1994. "Health and Behavioral Consequences of Binge Drinking in College: A National Survey of Students at 140 Campuses." *Journal of the American Medical Association* 272:1672–1677.

Zehr, Howard. 1990. *Changing Lenses.* Scottdale, PA: Herald Press.

Chapter 2

CONTEMPORARY PRACTICE IN STUDENT JUDICIAL AFFAIRS: STRENGTHS AND WEAKNESSES

JOHN WESLEY LOWERY AND MICHAEL DANNELLS

INTRODUCTION

The purposes of this chapter are to provide the reader with an overview of contemporary practice in student judicial affairs on college and university campuses, to review the strengths and weaknesses of those practices, and to speculate on the obstacles to and the possibilities of restorative justice in higher education. In this chapter, the terms *student discipline* and judicial affairs are used interchangeably, although it should be noted that the former is the older and less current term, while the latter is much more recent and more popular with most student affairs professionals who work in this area.

A BRIEF HISTORY

Some historical context helps us understand current trends and the state of disciplinary/judicial practices on today's college campuses. This is particularly true today because some observers (Pavela 1992) have noted that recently colleges and universities seem to have returned to some old practices.

In the colonial colleges, student discipline was an integral part of the total shaping of the young men—boys really—who were to be the future leaders of the colonies. The religious, moral, and intellectual development of their students was the primary purpose of these colleges, which stood *in loco parentis* (in the place of the parent) in all matters pertaining to the lives of their young charges. Rules of conduct were lengthy and detailed, and punishment was swift and often harsh. The faculty, tutors (older or recently graduated students), the president, and sometimes even trustees were the disciplinary agents of the colonial college, and total regulation of students' lives was the objective. During this period, corporal punishment was a commonly used sanction for student violations. The punishments were imposed on students in front of the entire student body, including whippings and a practice known at Yale as cuffing, where the president would strike the offending student repeatedly on both ears (Birdseye, 1907). Student–faculty relations were often contentious, and occasionally were marked by violence as students chafed at the yoke of these efforts to completely control them (Rudolph, 1990).

While significant vestiges of the colonial college approach to student discipline could be found in colleges of the early Federal period, the rising tide of democracy in the new nation led to student resistance, sometimes even rebellion (Rudolph, 1990). Colleges continued to exert parental-like control, and lengthy lists of proscribed behaviors were common, but the dawn of the nineteenth century saw milder punishment, more educational responses (like counseling) emerged, and the president and faculty began to pull back from disciplinary duties. The first disciplinary specialists, drawn from faculty ranks, were appointed. Student self-government, student-run disciplinary systems, and the extracurriculum developed as student–faculty relations improved and students were accorded greater respect and freedom in keeping with the democratic ethos and growing secularism of the time.

After the Civil War, with the introduction of the German university model of focus on research and the intellectual growth of students, and with the establishment of the land-grant universities, colleges and universities increasingly loosened their grip on student behavior. Their interest in student life outside the classroom waned as faculty increasingly turned their attention to scholarship and presidents became more and more concerned with external relations. With more appointments of specialists to deal with students outside the classroom, authoritarian control gave way to more humanistic and developmental practices.

The emergence of the student personnel movement in the early twentieth century led to a more scientific and educational approach to student behavior. These new student personnel professionals were deeply concerned about the issues surrounding student discipline. Matthews observed, "The problem of student discipline is one over which administrative officers are more puzzled than over any other" (1915, p. 173).

Following World War II, colleges and universities expanded greatly as federal money and older students flowed in as the result of the GI Bill and other federal aid programs. These older, more mature students, needed—and tolerated—even less control of their lives. Student populations became increasingly diverse following the civil rights movement, and that movement spilled onto the college campus in the form of the student rights movement. In the 1960s, federal court intervention in campus disciplinary practices established students rights to due process, rendered in loco parentis dead, and ushered in a trend in making those practices considerably more legalistic than the courts ever required.

In the past few decades, most colleges and universities have returned to less legalistic, more educational approaches, while seeking to retain due process safeguards. Very recently, in response to apparently increasing crime on campus, institutions of higher education have been faced with public demands and federal legislation for more and better crime reporting, and greater intervention into the lives of students.

CURRENT PHILOSOPHY AND ISSUES

In the preamble to its constitution, the Association for Student Judicial Affairs (1989) articulated an underlying philosophy for student judicial affairs practice. The Association for Student Judicial Affairs emphasized the educational nature of the student judicial affairs process in which students play a significant role. The enforcement of the code of conduct must protect the "rights, health and safety" of the community. The association stressed that "integrity, wisdom and empathy" were the hallmarks of judicial affairs professionals, who should carry out their duties "with a sense of impartiality and fairness." The Association for Student Judicial Affairs (1998) also identified five core assumptions and beliefs at the heart of student judicial affairs practice. Of greatest significance to the topic of restorative justice, the association stressed the impact of peer culture and community on student behavior.

Gehring (2001) argued that it is vital for student judicial affairs to aid in the development and learning of students while ensuring that due process is also provided. Pavela (1996) suggested that student judicial affairs should also embrace a larger, more proactive role in creating a community of values on campus, facilitating an ethical dialogue, and identifying shared community values. One useful perspective to consider when reviewing the code of student conduct is whether each rule or provision addresses one or more of the following goals:

1. To prevent or punish exploitation and harm inflicted or suffered by students; or
2. To prevent or punish behavior that undermines the academic values of free discussion and learning; or
3. To foster a sense of moral community and mutual responsibility. (Hoekema, 1994, p. 134)

Some of the issues facing student judicial affairs over the past decade will likely continue to create controversy for years to come. In the late 1980s, a number of institutions sought to respond to the difficult problem of bigotry and intolerance on campus through the adoption of hate speech codes, which were consistently ruled unconstitutional by the courts (Dannells and Lowery, in press; O'Neil 1997). However, some institutions have continued to seek effective means to respond to bigotry and intolerance on campus. Some observers (O'Neil, 2003; Silverglate and Lukianoff, 2003) have argued that many of these recent efforts are also speech codes and no less unconstitutional. Breslin (see Chapter 19) discusses the use of restorative approaches to hate speech on campus. As previously noted, there has been a significant increase in legislative intervention into student judicial affairs practice over the past decade. This intervention has often been based at least in part on the belief that institutions are unwilling or unable to address the serious misconduct of students. It has been further argued by groups such as the Student Press Law Center that institutions use the campus judicial system "as a means to thwart public access to crime information" (2000, p. 25). Advances in technology will also present new issues for student judicial affairs professionals to address. One area of significant concern has been the claims of illegal file sharing and copyright violations by college students downloading music and movies.

The overarching issue facing student judicial affairs is the challenge of balancing the legal and developmental concerns inherent in contemporary practice. This challenge led Mercer (1996, p. 116) to observe, "The campus administrator charged with responsibility for campus discipline . . . operates as a performer on a tightrope, stealthily approaching each step of a difficult process with precision and grace. While the purpose of realizing the educational goals of the student remains constantly in sight. . . ." The best way to understand this issue is as a matter of balance. It is a mistake to view the legal rights of students and developmental goals as incompatible or at odds. Baldizan urged that student affairs professionals seek to redirect our work back to its developmental roots: "Not only must we determine how to foster the moral and ethical growth of our students within due process constraints, but we must also address empowering our professional and institutional practices" (1997, p. 32).

CONTEMPORARY PRACTICE

On most campuses, the responsibility for the administration of student judicial affairs is delegated by the president of the institution to officials in student affairs. At mid-sized to large institutions, there is often one or more mid-level administrator whose primary job responsibility is student judicial affairs. However, at smaller institutions, student judicial affairs may be but one of several responsibilities assigned to an upper-level administrator such as a dean of students (Dannells, 1990; Lancaster, Cooper, and Harman, 1993). One indication of the growth of student judicial affairs into a distinct area of specialization in student affairs was the establishment of the Association for Student Judicial Affairs in 1987 and its rapid growth (Dannells and Lowery, in press).

In 1961, the 5th Circuit Court of Appeals handed down its landmark ruling in *Dixon v. Alabama State Board of Education*. In *Dixon*, the court ruled that students at public colleges and universities have a constitutional right to notice and hearing before suspension or expulsion. The Dixon court's decision was the first of many rendered throughout the 1960s in which the courts articulated the constitutional rights of college students in this area (Ardaiolo, 1983; Bakken, 1968; Dannells, 1977). While the courts established constitutional protections for college students, the courts made it clear that the constitutional rights of criminal defendants were not appropriate in student discipline (*Esteban v. Central Missouri State College*, 1969; *United States v. Miami University and Ohio State University*, 2002). Furthermore, the due process in student discipline is best understood as a "flexible concept" (Gehring, 2001, p. 469).

In some areas, the courts have left public institutions broad discretion in the administration of student judicial affairs. For example, the courts allow institutions to determine the limits of their jurisdiction. Dannells (1990) found a significant increase between 1978 and 1988 in the number of institutions electing to address off-campus student behavior. The courts have also allowed institutions considerable flexibility in determining the appropriate types of sanctions to impose. The courts have supported the use of punitive, educational, and environmentally targeted sanctions (Dannells, 1991, 1997). Rowe (2003, p. 3) argued, "Effective sanctions can be both aversive and developmental, and rationally related to the severity of the violation, the individual student's needs, and community standards."

Private colleges and universities are not required to meet the due process requirements applied to public institutions. At private colleges and universities, the rights afforded to students are primarily determined by the various institutional documents that courts treat as contracts (Kaplin and Lee, 1995, 1997). Although not required to do so, many private colleges and universities developed student judicial systems that afford students the same rights as those afforded to students at public institutions, and then those private institutions have a contractual obligation to follow their own rules (Stoner, 1998; Stoner and Cerminara, 1990).

STRENGTHS AND WEAKNESSES

Some commentators (Dannells, 1990, 1997; Gehring, 2001) have expressed concern about a "'creeping legalism' or proceduralism" (Dannells, 1997, p. 69) that undermines the educational focus of student judicial affairs. Travelstead (1987) argued that the blame for this proceduralism does not rest with the courts. He noted, "much of this complaining about excessive proceduralism and legalism is hollow. The excessive proceduralism, where it exists, has been largely caused by the institutions themselves" (15). The concern rests not with the rights that the courts have afforded to college students, but rather with various additional rights or procedural elements that institutions have added on their own. Even as the trend toward increasing legalism has abated, many within student judicial affairs continue to call for simpler, less legalistic systems that preserve basic student rights (Dannells, 1997).

The primary weakness resulting from these overly legalistic student judicial affairs systems is the creation of an increasingly adversarial environment (Dannells, 1997). Within this environment, the educational focus of student judicial affairs is often lost. Gehring (2001, p. 478) warned, "Adversarial procedures that pit one antagonist against another, like criminal procedures, are complex, but even worse, do not provide the support necessary for personal and social development."

Another potential consequence of the adversarial system is an environment in which many violations of the code of student conduct are viewed primarily, if not exclusively, from the perspective of the primary participants. Within this adversarial environment, it is difficult to look beyond those primary participants to consider the impact of a student's behavior on the larger campus community. Without a more educational perspective, it is difficult to develop sanctions that respond to and make use of the community impact that is inherent in almost every case.

Although this concern about legalistic systems is significant, several new approaches to addressing student behavior have also emerged in recent years. In the 1990s, Alternative Dispute Resolution, most typically mediation, became increasingly popular as an effective means to respond to some campus conflicts (Zdziarski, 1998). The development of creeds and community standards are also powerful antidotes to excessive legalism. The University of South Carolina and a number of other institutions developed creeds or other documents to serve as a positive expression of institutional values. The community standards approach empowers a group of students, such as a residence hall association, to establish a set of shared expectations for life in the community. Once the community has established its standards, the students then hold one another accountable for living within these expectations (Lowery, 1998).

POSSIBILITIES AND OBSTACLES

Several developments over the past decade have suggested that a large segment of the higher education community is ready to embrace restorative justice as an alternative approach to enhance, or perhaps reclaim, the educational nature of student judicial affairs. One example of an alternative approach is "resolution by agreement," whereby the formal adversarial hearing is avoided when students accept responsibility for their actions and reach an agreement about appropriate sanctions (Wilson, 1996). Another indication that opportunities currently exist has been the rapid adoption of other alternative dispute resolution systems by student judicial affairs professionals over the past decade (Zdziarski, 1998).

Some student judicial affairs professionals are prepared to embrace the possibilities that restorative justice offers for enhancing the core educational function of judicial affairs and the community development role. But some critics of campus judicial affairs (Silverglate and Gewolb, 2003) have argued that public college and university students should essentially be provided the same rights as criminal defendants and are likely to oppose alternative approaches in any form. The current legislative atmosphere is one that is supportive of the evolution of student judicial systems that closely mirror the criminal justice system and emphasize punishment over education (Pavela, 1992). Many critics of campus judicial affairs view campus judicial affairs as more analogous to the criminal courts than to the classroom. In order to make true progress in higher education, advocates for restorative justice must be prepared to respond effectively to these potential obstacles.

The introduction of restorative justice in student judicial programs is not without important policy issues and administrative costs. What kinds of behavior warrant or require restoration? How does the judicial officer determine the extent of the impact of the behavior in question and who is victimized? How much additional administrative time and effort will be required to take restorative measures that address impact beyond the most immediate victim(s)? What additional clerical and administrative costs will be incurred to train staff to organize, operationalize, and document such a program? While the intended outcomes of restorative justice are undeniably worthy, such policy and cost issues must be addressed.

Some commentators have also suggested the current generation of undergraduate students, often called the Millennial Generation, may be more open to restorative approaches than previous generations (Howe and Strauss, 2000; Koch, 2003; Lowery, 2001). Unlike their recent generational predecessors, the Millennial Generation college students bring with them a strong team orientation and desire for community. This suggests that these students may more readily understand the impact on the community of their actions and be willing to participate in processes, such as restorative justice, that offer opportunities to repair this harm. However, these commentators also warn that there is a potential dark side to the team orientation of these students in the form of a group mentality that suppresses individuality.

SUMMARY AND CONCLUSION

From the early history of American higher education, the role of student discipline has been central to the core educational mission of institutions. Current practice in student judicial affairs remains philosophically grounded in this educational mission, with the goal of facilitating the educational and moral development of students. But today's practice of student judicial affairs also has been shaped by court rulings over the past 40 years and by the "unfettered enthusiasm" (Footer, 1996, p. 23) for the legalistic and adversarial systems that followed. While it is essential that campuses ensure the preservation of students' rights, this excessive legalism is likely the greatest weakness of contemporary practice in student judicial affairs. Several observers (Dannells, 1997; Gehring, 2001; Pavela, 1996) have called for the development of simpler systems of student judicial affairs that still preserve student rights. This, along with the expansion of other forms of alternative dispute resolution on campus, suggests that the opportunities for the development of restorative justice are significant. These efforts will have to overcome pressures from Congress, state legislatures, and others to make campus judicial affairs more legalistic and to emphasize punishment over education. In addition, the consideration of new, alternative approaches to campus judicial affairs should and will raise important issues of policy, cost, and resource allocation. Nonetheless, restorative justice holds great promise as a valuable tool to help colleges and universities "create communities of justice and principle that seek higher levels of human possibility" (Lowery, 1998, p. 26).

References

Ardaiolo, Frank P. 1983. "What Process Is Due?" pp. 13–25 in *Student Affairs and the Law* (New Directions for Student Services No. 22), edited by Margaret J. Barr. San Francisco, CA: Jossey-Bass.

Association for Student Judicial Affairs. 1989. Constitution of the Association for Student Judicial Affairs. College Station, TX: Author.

Association for Student Judicial Affairs. 1993. Statement of Ethical Principles and Standards of Conduct. College Station, TX: Author.

Bakken, C. J. 1968. *The Legal Basis of College Student Personnel Work* (Student Personnel Monograph Series No. 2). Washington, DC: American Personnel and Guidance Association.

Baldizan, Elizabeth M. 1997. "Development, Due Process, and Reduction: Student Conduct in the 1990s," pp. 29–37 in *Beyond Law and Policy: Reaffirming the Role of Student Affairs*, edited by Diane L. Cooper and James M. Lancaster. San Francisco, CA: Jossey-Bass.

Birdseye, Charles. 1907. *Individual Training in Our Colleges*. New York: Macmillian.

Breslin, Beau. 2004. "Responding to Hate Speech: The Limitations of Speech Codes and the Promise of Restorative Practices" (this volume). Springfield, IL: Charles C. Thomas.

Dannells, Michael. 1977. "Discipline," pp. 232-278 in *College Student Personnel Services*, edited by William T. Packwood. Springfield, IL: Charles C Thomas.

Dannells, Michael. 1990. "Changes in Disciplinary Policies and Practices over 10 Years." *Journal of College Student Development* 31:408–414.

Dannells, Michael. 1991. "Changes in Student Misconduct and Institutional Response over 10 Years." *Journal of College Student Development* 32:166–170.

Dannells, Michael. 1997. *From Discipline to Development: Rethinking Student Conduct in Higher Education*. ASHE-ERIC Higher Education Report, 25(2). San Francisco, CA: Jossey-Bass.

Dannells, Michael., and John W. Lowery. In press. "Discipline and Judicial Affairs," in *Student Affairs Functions in Higher Education*, 3rd ed., edited by Fiona J. D. MacKinnon. Springfield, IL: Charles C Thomas.

Dixon v. Alabama State Board of Education, 294 F.2d 150 (5th Cir. 1961).

Esteban v. Central Missouri State College, 290 F. Supp. 622 (W.D. Mo. 1968), aff'd, 415 F.2d 1077 (8th Cir. 1969).

Footer, Nancy S. 1996. "Achieving Fundamental Fairness: The Code of Conduct," pp. 19–33 in *Critical Issues in Judicial Affairs: Current Trends in Practice* (New Directions for Student Services No. 73), edited by Wanda L. Mercer. San Francisco, CA: Jossey-Bass.

Gehring, Donald D. 2001. "The Objectives of Student Discipline and the Process That's Due: Are They Compatible?" *NASPA Journal* 38:466–481.

Hoekema, David A. 1994. *Campus Rules and Moral Community: In place of In Loco Parentis*. Lanham: MD: Rowman & Littlefield.

Howe, Neil, and William Strauss. 2000. *Millennials Rising: The Next Great Generation*. New York: Vintage Books.

Kaplin, William A., and Barbara A. Lee. 1995. *The Law of Higher Education*, 3rd ed. San Francisco, CA: Jossey-Bass.

Kaplin, William A., and Barbara A. Lee. 1997. *A Legal Guide for Student Affairs Professionals*. San Francisco, CA: Jossey-Bass.

Koch, Virginia. November 2003. *Discipline and the Millennial Student*. Presentation at the National Association of Student Personnel Administrators Region IV-East Conference, Milwaukee, WI.

Lancaster, James M., Diane L. Cooper, and Ann E. Harman. Winter 1993. "Current Practices in Student Disciplinary Administration." *NASPA Journal* 30: 108–119.

Lancaster, James M., and Diane L. Cooper. 1997. "Standing at the Intersection: Reconsidering the Balance in Administration," pp. 95–106 in *Beyond Law and Policy: Reaffirming the Role of Student Affairs* (New Directions for Student Services

No. 82), edited by Diane L. Cooper and James M. Lancaster. San Francisco, CA: Jossey-Bass.

Lowery, J. W. 1998. "Institutional Policy and Individual Responsibility: Communities of Justice and Principle," pp. 15–27 in *Beyond Law and Policy: Reaffirming the Role of Student Affairs* (New Directions for Student Services No. 82), edited by Diane L. Cooper and James M. Lancaster. San Francisco, CA: Jossey-Bass.

Lowery, J. W. (2001). "The Millennials Come to Campus: John Wesley Lowery Talks with William Strauss." *About Campus* 6(3):6–12.

Matthews, Lois K. 1915. *The Dean of Women.* Cambridge, MA: Riverside Press.

Mercer, Wanda L. 1996. "Synthesis and Additional Resources," pp. 114–117 in *Critical Issues in Judicial Affairs: Current Trends in Practice* (New Directions for Student Services No. 73), edited by Wanda L. Mercer. San Francisco, CA: Jossey-Bass.

O'Neil, Robert M. 1997. *Free Speech in the College Community.* Bloomington, IN: Indiana University Press.

O'Neil, Robert M. 2003. ". . . But Litigation Is the Wrong Response." *Chronicle of Higher Education,* August 1, B9–B10.

Pavela, Gary. 1992. "Today's College Students Need Both Freedom and Structure." *Chronicle of Higher Education,* July 19, B1–B2.

Pavela, Gary. 1996. "Judicial Affairs and the Future," pp. 107–113 in *Critical Issues in Judicial Affairs: Current Trends in Practice* (New Directions for Student Services No. 73), edited by Wanda L. Mercer. San Francisco, CA: Jossey-Bass.

Rowe, Linda P. 2003. "Framing Education with Justice: A Model for Implementing Judicial Sanctions." *Campus Safety and Student Development* 5:3–6.

Rudolph, Frederick. 1990. *The American College and University: A History.* Athens, GA: The University of Georgia Press (original work published 1962).

Silverglate, Harvey A., and Josh Gewolb. 2003. *FIRE's Guide to Due Process and Fair Procedure on Campus.* Philadelphia, PA: Foundations for Individual Rights in Education.

Silverglate, Harvey A., and Greg Lukianoff. 2003. "Speech Codes: Alive and Well at Colleges . . ." *Chronicle of Higher Education,* August 1, B7–B8.

Stoner, Edward N. II. 1998. "A Model Code for Student Discipline," pp. 3–42 in *The Administration of Student Discipline: Student, Organizational, and Community Issues,* edited by Brent. G. Paterson and William L. Kibler. Asheville, NC: College Administration Publications.

Stoner, Edward. N. II, and Kathy Cerminara. 1990. "Harnessing the 'Spirit of Insubordination:' A Model Student Disciplinary Code." *Journal of College and University Law* 17, 89–121.

Student Press Law Center. 2000. *Covering Campus Crime: A Handbook for Journalists,* 3rd ed. Arlington, VA: Student Press Law Center.

Travelstead, William W. 1987. "Introduction and Historical Context," pp. 3–16 in *Enhancing Campus Judicial Systems* (New Directions for Student Services No. 39), edited by Robert Caruso and William W. Travelstead. San Francisco, CA: Jossey-Bass.

United States v. Miami University and Ohio State University, 91 F. Supp. 2d 1132 (S.D. Oh. 2000) aff'd, 294 F.3d 797 (6th Cir. 2002).

Wilson, Jeanne M. 1996. "Processes for Resolving Student Disciplinary Matters," pp. 35–52 in *Critical Issues in Judicial Affairs: Current Trends in Practice* (New Directions for Student Services No. 73), edited by Wanda L. Mercer. San Francisco, CA: Jossey-Bass.

Zdziarski, Eugene L. 1998. "Alternative Dispute Resolution: A New Look at Resolving Campus Conflict," pp. 237–252 in *The Administration of Student Discipline: Student, Organizational, and Community Issues*, edited by Brent. G. Paterson and William L. Kibler. Asheville, NC: College Administration Publications.

Part II

RESTORATIVE PRACTICES: BOARDS, CONFERENCING, AND MEDIATION

Chapter 3

INTEGRITY BOARDS

David R. Karp

Judicial boards are widely used on college and university campuses. Many include students as members. Nevertheless, the typical judicial board differs from restorative justice integrity boards in both process and outcomes. Integrity boards are particularly concerned with a process that encourages trust, emotional expression, and community building. These go far beyond (but include) the more common concern with fair and equitable treatment that judicial boards promote. Integrity boards seek creative outcomes that strive to repair harm and reintegrate offenders and victims. Sanctions are neither simple nor drawn from a clearly delineated menu of graduated sanctions. Thus, the focus of discussion is as much about, if not mostly about, what is to be done to find a satisfying resolution.

An integrity board has the authority to negotiate a contract with the offender specifying sanctions. The mission of the board is to work with student offenders to help them understand the consequences of their behavior, to identify the harmfulness of the offense, and to identify a set of tasks that will repair the harm and reintegrate the offenders into the campus community.

The integrity board must both address the determination of guilt and arrive at a sanction. Therefore, it is a bifurcated process, in which attention initially is given to due process, as victims and/or the college presents evidence of the wrongdoing, and student defendants (called "respondents") are afforded the opportunity to claim innocence, explain mitigating circumstances, or fully accept responsibility. If the student is found responsible, then the discussion turns to a full examination of the harm caused by the offense and the discussion of a plan for redress. Because of the size of the group (often seven or eight participating), the dynamics are not conducive to intensive victim-offender healing. Thus, one of the terms in the sanctioning agreement might be a recommendation for victim-offender mediation, a restorative practice that is just beginning to be used on college campuses (see Chapter 8).

Skidmore College has maintained an integrity board for many years, but only recently has it explicitly embraced restorative principles and practices. This transition came after a close examination of Vermont's Reparative Probation Program, in which adult criminal offenders meet with a "reparative board" of citizen volunteers and negotiate a restorative justice contract that must be completed within a three-month period (Karp and Walther, 2001).

MEMBERSHIP AND TRAINING

An integrity board hearing is composed of four students, one staff member, and one or two faculty members (two in cases of academic integrity). This structure makes it distinct from other restorative practices, which typically make use of a trained facilitator or two co-facilitators. Thus, a group of board members participates in each case, representing a cross section of the community and carrying their prior experiences with hearing cases to each new case. The board members are presumed to be objective about each case since they are not direct stakeholders (neither victims nor witnesses). However, they are expected to represent the community, voicing their concern and support as appropriate. At Skidmore, we rely on a pool of members. All participate in a "willingness-to-serve" process, and must complete training. In the 2002–2003 academic year, the board heard 56 cases involving 75 student offenders. These cases primarily involved alcohol or marijuana violations, but also included a number of harassment, assault, theft, fraud, weapons, hazing, and academic integrity violations. The board currently does not hear cases involving sexual assault.

Student participation in the judicial process reinforces democratic and egalitarian values that underlie citizenship. Students learn the language of community stewardship by making real decisions about matters of local consequence. One student board member commented, "I've seen several similar tripartite committees and boards at this school where either the faculty or the administration tends to dominate the discussion, and the students tend to become minor players in the final outcome. That is not the case with IB, and I applaud that fact." Students also learn how to articulate community-level harms associated with individual misbehavior. Students have tremendous social influence and legitimacy, so offenders are more receptive to their message. They also have a keen eye for "what works" in terms of persuasive language and creative sanctions that educate the larger campus community.

Our training is conducted over the course of the Fall semester, with a weekly one-hour meeting. Readings are assigned for each meeting, and guest speakers, such as the Director of Campus Safety, the Dean of Studies, or the Volunteer Coordinator, often attend. The training offers opportunity for role-plays, discussion of philosophy, debriefing recent cases, and evaluation of practice and policy. We have created an opportunity for student members of the integrity board to receive academic credit for their participation in the training through our Law and Society Program. To receive credit for this, they must attend the training sessions, complete reflection essays for each of the readings, and write a term paper that combines research on a relevant topic of interest (e.g., college student alcohol use) and their experience as a member of the board. This training has been an essential component of our program because the restorative philosophy is new to the participants and challenges many of them to rethink their own beliefs about punishment. This dialogue takes place during the training discussions, so that in hearings board members may present a coherent philosophy during cases.

The chair of Skidmore's integrity board is always a student. His or her primary job is to facilitate a hearing, although he or she also has administrative responsibilities. Good facilitation requires training, but unlike mediation, conferencing, and circles, there is less pressure on the facilitator. We have found that all board members pay attention to process, and typically will remind a chair if something needs attention. The chair is clearly a leader, and we stress that as facilitator, the focus should be on ensuring a good process rather than taking charge of decisions. The chair uses a script that is similar to the script used in conferencing. Typically, as part of the training, chairs rewrite the script in their own words, and students' most recent rendition is included as an appendix.

In addition to board members and offenders (called respondents), several others may be invited to a hearing. First, we invite victims (called harmed parties), and they are encouraged to bring a support person. Second, we invite affected parties, such as a campus safety officer who responded to the incident. Third, a representative of the Student Affairs Office that administers the program plays the role of "judicial officer." This person is usually our Dean of Studies (for academic cases) or our Associate Dean of Student Affairs. The responsibility of the judicial officer is to present the facts of the case as they have been determined by administrative inquiry (campus safety report, interviews, etc.). The judicial officer also briefs non-member participants about the nature of the process and the role they will play.

PARTNERSHIP WITH ACADEMIC PROGRAMS

There is compelling evidence that the out-of-the-classroom experience, interactions and collaboration with peers, and institutional culture are as critical to student learning as any other facet of the college experience (Astin, 1993). Over the past decade, colleges and universities have thus developed learning communities, service learning programs, collaborative research, internships, and volunteer programs to integrate academic study with students' lives outside the classroom. The educational value of these programs is especially apparent when students see participation in them as contributing to their overall intellectual development.

At Skidmore, collaboration between the Office of Student Affairs and the Law and Society Program was born out of a belief that service learning provides an opportunity for genuine intellectual liberation and citizen development (Barber, 1991). As mentioned previously, student members of the board may receive academic credit for their participation in the board training. This service-learning experience provides students with a chance to evaluate student conduct within a larger intellectual discourse as well as contribute meaningfully to community-building measures. Through readings, discussion, role-plays, and ultimately service on the board, members of the course learn how to facilitate and maintain a campus judicial system.

The academic and cocurricular components institutionalize consistent, in-depth training of a regular pool of student volunteers and create an opportunity for students to make a relevant contribution to the campus community. The project involves students in the study of their community and promotes dialogue about community values and related problems on campus.

PARTNERSHIP WITH THE CRIMINAL JUSTICE SYSTEM

Some of our cases are pursued simultaneously by the criminal court. A problem we frequently encounter is that students appearing before the board have been instructed by their lawyers to say nothing to the board since their case is almost always still pending "downtown." Unfortunately, such behavior may be advantageous to their day in court, but serves them poorly in front of our integrity board. Cases proceed smoothly when offenders are forthcoming, expressing understanding of the harm they caused, remorse, and a willingness to make amends. "My lawyer told me not to say anything" does not advance that cause.

Ironically, we have discovered that for most minor criminal offenses, our board holds student more accountable, requiring much more of them, than does the criminal court. With this in our favor, we have established a relationship with the Saratoga County District Attorney's office in which the DA will review our findings and, hopefully, agree to let ours stand in the criminal court. Although we do not have many cases yet to illustrate this, a good example comes from a well-publicized case from 2002. The City of Saratoga

Springs sponsored an art exhibit in which painted fiberglass horses were displayed in various locations downtown. A Skidmore student stole one of the horses, causing considerable public outrage. Our board hearing included not only the student offender, but also the artist, the store owner who sponsored the artist, and the director of the arts council that organized the exhibit. The agreement included several specific sanctions, including restitution and community service among others. Several months later, the case was settled in the criminal court, and the sentence was identical to our own, the court accepting exactly what we had negotiated (McCord, 2003).

THE FIVE STEPS

Five process steps guide our restorative approach (see Table 3.1). First, participants in the judicial process seek to create an atmosphere of trust and civility, emphasizing the social ties and shared community membership of the participants. The goals are to avoid adversarial proceedings in favor of cooperative decision making, and full participation of the key stakeholders. As Stoner (1998) recommends, we avoid the use of criminal justice terminology. For example, offenders are referred to as "respondents," victims are referred to as "harmed parties," and those bringing charges are referred to as "complainants." Second, the board determines who is responsible for the harmful behavior and what codes of conduct were violated. Third, the process concentrates on identifying the harmful consequences of student

---

Table 3.1   Five Steps Toward a Successful Integrity Board Hearing

1. *Establish common ground*

   Create a space that encourages the full participation of respondents and harmed parties. Balance formality with social support and encouragement.

2. *Determine responsibility*

   Establish if the respondent is in violation. Stress objectivity when weighing the evidence.

3. *Have offender accept responsibility*

   Determine if the respondent admits any wrongdoing and evaluate his or her commitment to making things right.

4. *Identify the impact of the offense*

   Work with harmed parties and respondent to figure out what harm was done. Pay attention to personal harm (physical, emotional), material harm (lost or damaged property), and communal harm (material harm to community spaces or intangible harms, such as public fear and anger).

5. *Strategize repair and reintegration*

   Work together to identify the best way to fix the damage done. Also, identify ways that the respondent can demonstrate their commitment to the community and become more closely tied to the values and behaviors of a responsible community member.

misconduct. It assumes that no violations of policy or law are "victimless," since the violation itself raises concerns about the student's commitment to the community. At the same time, a civil discourse can afford the opportunity to reexamine policies that appear arbitrary and may need reform. Fourth, the process enables the offender to acknowledge responsibility, express remorse, and endeavor to regain the trust of the community. Fifth, the board negotiates a contract that delineates the tasks and timeline of restoration and reintegration.

REPARATIVE SANCTIONS

Typically, integrity boards attempt to respond to three types of harm: (1) emotional harm to victims; (2) property damage or loss; and (3) communal harm, such as fear of crime, demoralization, and divisiveness. For example, we use a role-play that involves a drunken student, Ted, who breaks the glass cover and pulls a fire alarm in a residence hall. Another student, Lenny, confronts Ted about the behavior and quickly becomes the recipient of a racial epithet and attempted assault. A third student in the role-play, Pauline, loses sleep, and subsequently performs poorly on an exam the following morning. This scenario illuminates the many "circles of harm." First, there is the emotional harm to victims, from Lenny's anger over the racial epithet to Pauline's frustration about her exam. Second, there is property damage; the fire alarm requires repair. Third, there is communal harm. The entire residence hall is inconvenienced by the evacuation, public resources are wasted as the fire department responds, and the community expresses mistrust about student drinking behavior and anger about racist attitudes. The quality of life for the community is diminished.

Emotional harm is partly addressed through apology, something victims want but rarely receive. Apology letters may be negotiated, but guidelines are needed to ensure their acceptability (see Table 3.2). Typically, apologies are a spontaneous and healing part of board hearings. Beyond apologies, victim-offender mediation/dialogue is often a very helpful way to alleviate ongoing conflict or distress about an incident. Boards strive to be open forums that allow for healing dialogue. Nevertheless, because of the number of participants, we see mediation as a complementary follow-up practice.

Restitution is a way to repair material harm. In many cases, students have committed a property crime, such as theft or vandalism. The board is responsible for determining the nature and extent of material harm and identifying a way for the offender to return, repair, or pay for lost or damaged property. Restitution may be completed by a lump sum payment, a payment schedule, or in-kind labor. Restitution should be distinguished from a fine, because the money is returned to the harmed party and pays for loss-

Table 3.2   Apology Guidelines

Apologies are expression of remorse and the willingness to take responsibility for a transgression. They must be sincere if they are to be taken seriously. Apologies are an important way to repair community relationships and restore trust between parties.

- All written apologies must be submitted to the integrity board for approval. Letters will then be forward to the harmed parties by the board.
- Apology letters must contain the following elements:
  - A description detailing the harm caused by the offense. This shows that the respondent understands the harmful consequences of his or her behavior.
  - An acknowledgment that the respondent was responsible for the offense. Be sure to avoid any temptation to deny, displace, or minimize responsibility.
  - An expression of remorse or regret in causing harm.
  - A statement of commitment not to repeat the offense.
- Verbal apologies should be given only after written apologies are approved. Verbal apologies should convey the same information as written apologies.

es. A fine is not explicitly linked to the harm and is designed to be a retributive deterrent rather than a means of responding to victims' needs.

Community service is used to repair harm to the community. While it can be thought of as a punitive sanction, the intention is different in a restorative process. First, it is a means of making amends for causing harm to the community. Ideally, the service will be linked to the harm, for example, by having offenders repair damage to vandalized property. Second, service is meant to be educational. It is an opportunity for offenders to learn about civic participation and the value of contributing positively to one's community. Thus, the service should be meaningful, rewarding, and even fun. Third, service is an opportunity to establish prosocial relationships with peers and authority figures who can serve as role models. The best measure of successful community service is when the offender continues to volunteer after his or her "sentence" is completed. At Skidmore, we use the following guidelines when negotiating community service (Table 3.3).

Table 3.3   Community Service Guidelines

Community service serves two important goals. First, it is a way of making amends to the community. Second, it is an opportunity to demonstrate good citizenship. Volunteering in the community is a way to be helpful to others, show that one is socially responsible, and rebuild the trust that is lost through misbehavior. Community service should be meaningful and rewarding. The board strives to find the right placement to meet these goals.

- Arranging a community service assignment is the responsibility of the respondent. Integrity board members will provide assistance, as will the volunteer coordinator.
- Respondents must submit a letter, signed by a service agency staff member, to verify that all assigned hours are completed.
- Respondents must submit a short "impact essay" (minimum 350 words), describing the nature of the service and how it serves a community need.

REINTEGRATIVE SANCTIONS

Beyond the consideration of repairing harm, the board also asks the question: "What can be done to restore trust so that we feel confident about the offender's membership in the community?" Tasks that answer this question are designed to reintegrate the offender as a member of the community in good standing. During the board meeting, participants continuously evaluate their level of trust in the offender. Many offenders, because of their sincere expressions of remorse, willingness to make amends, and stated commitment to future responsible behavior, convince the board members of their trustworthiness. Often, however, a board will seek additional reassurances.

A typical strategy is the reflective essay. The offender may be asked to write about the incident, examining his or her responsibility and how to avoid repeating the mistake. They may conduct research on the damage caused, such as tabulating the costs of vandalism to a residence hall, and provide recommendations for prevention. Another strategy is to ask the offender to join a campus group in the hopes that he or she will attain a greater stake in the community because of his or her investment in it. A board member might ask about the offender's hobbies or interests and help identify a campus group that shares it. Sometimes, offenders may be asked to seek assistance, such as by getting an alcohol abuse screening or academic tutoring. Of course, board members are not therapists, and their job is not to diagnose and treat psychological problems. The board cannot order treatment, but it may require an initial visit to someone with specialized expertise. The spirit of reintegrative sanctions is not rehabilitation. Instead, it is successful community membership. The approach assumes that offenders are operating on the margins of the campus community, and that they will become more responsible as they become more involved in both academic and cocurricular life.

Reintegration is not always possible. When the college views offenders as a threat to the safety of others or to themselves, a student will be removed from campus. Furthermore, a student who refuses to comply with our judicial process will also be removed. Table 3.4 outlines our conditions for suspension and dismissal. Our attitude toward suspension and expulsion is ambivalent. Of course, it is always a relief to be rid of a nuisance; but at the same time, we realize that our failure to reintegrate will simply mean that the problem will travel to some other community—a community likely to be less aware of the problem and less capable of addressing it.

Our routine substitute for suspension is something we call "self-suspension." For every case, we negotiate a contract and try not to impose suspension (unless the conditions outlined in Table 3.4 are met). Nevertheless, we do not provide endless chances. The contract has a timeline and the aca-

Table 3.4   Skidmore College Integrity Board Suspension and Dismissal Guidelines

The Integrity Board (IB) tries to avoid suspension whenever possible by offering students an opportunity to take responsibility for honor code violations and to make amends through prosocial activities. However, there are two conditions under which suspension or dismissal is warranted.

Condition One: Public Safety

If the IB believes a student to be a safety risk to the college community, it is best if the student is removed from campus. When evaluating risk, consider the following:

- Behavioral evidence of risk, such as documented threats
- Behavioral evidence of prior violent behavior
- Risk assessments from experts, such as Campus Safety and Student Affairs staff.
- Risk assessments from affected parties, such as victims. Note that they may not be very objective, but that IB should seek ways to help affected parties feel safe.

Condition Two: Rejection of Responsibility

The IB may suspend/dismiss a student who is unwilling or unable to take responsibility for their behavior, even if the behavior poses no risk to public safety. When evaluating a student's irresponsibility, consider the following:

- Recidivism: is this a first offense or is a pattern of violations emerging?
- Compliance: has the student successfully completed prior sanctions?
- Acknowledgment of responsibility: does the student admit responsibility or deny ("It wasn't me"), diminish ("It's no big deal"), or displace ("I was drunk") responsibility?

Suspension vs. Dismissal

Dismissal is permanent. It is a statement that the IB believes that it would be impossible for the student to become a responsible member of the community. It is equivalent to "life without parole" whereas suspension can be likened to a specific prison term. When evaluating suspension vs. dismissal, consider the following:

- Severity: is the violation so offensive to the values of the community, that the IB cannot imagine having the student associated with the College?
- Prior suspensions: has the student been suspended before?

When Suspension Is Recommended by IB

Unlike dismissal, suspension assumes that the student will return to Skidmore to complete his or her degree. The suspension period, therefore, provides the student with an opportunity to demonstrate responsible behavior. Typically, we suspend a student for one semester, believing that this is sufficient time to complete an accountability contract, and convey our disappointment with the offending behavior. Longer terms of suspension increase the likelihood that the student will not return to the College. With reintegration in mind, consider the following:

- What sanctions must be completed prior to or during the suspension period?

---

demic calendar is closely considered. Students may not register for the following semester's classes until the contract is completed. We have partnered with the registrar so that a hold is placed in the student's file until the board releases it. Thus, a student "suspends" himself or herself by failing to honor the contract and must do so to register and regain status. This is a dramatic shift in the burden of responsibility. Rather than having the board sentence the student, the student becomes the arbiter of his or her own fate.

CONCLUSION

Boards are an effective tool to engender an ethical community such as the one proposed by McCabe, Butterfield, and Treviño (see Chapter 12). It calls upon students, faculty, and staff, as well as student offenders, to reflect on the impact of student misconduct and how the situation can be resolved in a way that is both educational and reparative. The restorative philosophy underlying board practice is the same as for other restorative practices we describe in this book. When should we use one practice versus another? Table 3.5 represents my own view of the niche each fills within a campus community.

Table 3.5   Choosing Between Restorative Practices

	Integrity Boards	Victim-Offender Mediation	Conferencing	Circles
Structure	5 board members hear cases	Trained facilitator	Trained facilitator	Trained facilitator
Niche	Victimless offenses; routine processing; Active volunteer participation by various campus stakeholders, e.g., students, faculty, staff	Small number of affected parties	Moderate number of affected parties (N = 5–10)	Large number of affected parties (N>10)
Focus	Norm affirmation and negotiating restorative contract	Resolving ongoing conflict; Healing dialogue	Healing dialogue and negotiating restorative contract; Active participation of affected parties and supporters	Identifying community impacts; community healing; support circles for offender and victims
Preparation	Modest time commitment	Variable, depending on preparation needs	Moderate time commitment	Significant time commitment

Integrity boards may be best suited for routine processing of cases. They allow for ongoing participation of various campus constituents, lending the judicial process legitimacy and credibility across the campus community.

Boards can hear a wide variety of cases, particularly those without direct victims and those in which victims prefer not to participate. Because they invite but do not necessitate the participation of affected parties, case processing is more efficient. Nevertheless, participation by victims and their supporters is incredibly valuable and is often worth the extra effort to arrange it.

Facilitation models, like conferencing, differ from boards by focusing the decision-making process entirely on the stakeholders. Facilitators do not offer input about the content of sanctions, whereas board members do (except for the facilitating board chair). Boards, therefore, are more likely to have consistent sanctions because board members retain knowledge of prior agreements in similar cases. Outcomes in facilitated models are likely to vary more because they suit the particular preferences of the stakeholders in each case.

Circles are a time-consuming process, but allow for participation of a large group. Thus, for community-wide issues and highly visible cases, they may best respond to community concerns. Such practices are logistical challenges, however, and cannot be conducted routinely.

In sum, all restorative practices share a vision of conflict resolution that prioritizes dialogue between stakeholders and sanctions that seek healing and redress and avoid stigmatizing punishments and community outcasting. Having a repertoire of practices available to a community may be the best future for a judicial system, making use of one or another as the circumstances require.

References

Astin, Alexander A. 1993. *What Matters in College? Four Critical Years Revisited.* San Francisco: Jossey-Bass.

Barber, Benjamin R. 1991. "A Mandate for Liberty: Requiring Education-Based Community Service." *The Responsive Community* 1:237–245.

Karp, David R., and Lynne Walther. 2001. "Community Reparative Boards in Vermont," pp. 199–218 in *Restorative Community Justice: Repairing Harm and Transforming Communities*, edited by G. Bazemore and M. Schiff. Cincinnati, OH: Anderson.

McCord, Jason. 2003. "Saratoga Springs Horse Thief Is Sentenced to Probation: Community Service, Restitution Ordered for Spirit Horse Vandal." *The Saratogian* January 10, B7.

Stoner, Edward N. 1998. "A Model Code for Student Discipline," pp. 3–42 in Brent G. Paterson & William L. Kibler (Eds.). *The Administration of Campus Discipline: Student, Organizational, and Community Issues.* Asheville, NC: College Administration Publications, Inc.

Appendix

Skidmore College Integrity Board Chair's Script

- Turn on tape recorder
- "Welcome. This is Integrity Board Hearing # ___. Before we begin, let's introduce ourselves. I'm _____, and I'm chairing today's hearing."
- INTRODUCTIONS
- "We are here to evaluate an alleged violation of the Honor Code. The Integrity Board will work with the complainant(s) and respondent(s) to understand the situation that brought us here today, and to make a fair determination of responsibility."
- "If the Integrity Board does not find the respondent(s) in violation of the Honor Code, the case will be dismissed."
- "In the case that the Integrity Board finds the respondent(s) in violation of the Honor Code, we may assign sanctions designed to make amends to any or all parties affected by the violation. Respondents are encouraged and expected to participate in the creation of these sanctions."
- "As chair, I will try to keep the discussion organized. It is important that everyone contributes to this process, but also that we respect the person speaking. Please keep in mind that we all want this hearing to proceed in a timely manner. If anyone has any questions about how we will proceed, feel free to ask at any point during the hearing."
- "I'd like everyone to keep a few things in mind as we proceed: how this situation has affected individuals, as well as the campus community. Also, it may be pertinent to identify this violation as an isolated incident, or whether the respondent has received other sanctions from Skidmore in the past."
- "The Judicial Counsel will review the case."

- Judicial Counsel reviews case.
- Statement by **complainant/college**
- Board questions **complainant**
- Statement by *respondent*
- Board questions *respondent*
- Statements by respondent's supporters
- Final questions
- Final statements by **complainant** and *respondent*
- Deliberation (board only; turn off tape recorder)
- Determination (call parties back in, turn on tape recorder)
- "After careful discussion of the complainant and respondent's testimonies, the Integrity Board finds you in violation/not in violation of the Skidmore Honor Code, specifically conduct code(s) _____."

- "Since the Integrity Board has found you in violation of the Honor Code, now we need to have a discussion of what you can do to make things right."
- To respondent: "Are you willing to take responsibility for this violation, and to participate in the creation of restorative sanctions?"
- To complainant: "Could you tell us how the situation has affected you?"
- To respondent: "Could you tell us how the situation has affected you?"
- To everyone: "How has this affected the Skidmore community?"
- "Sanctions should aim to repair harm to individuals and the community, and completion of sanctions should show that the respondent understands the harm caused by this event."
- "If sanctions rise to the level of suspension or dismissal, the Dean of Student Affairs will review the case. Otherwise, sanctions will be assigned a specific time frame for completion. You will not be able to register for next semester's classes until sanctions are completed."
- "Now we need to create sanctions based on the nature of the violation. We all need to work together to create sanctions that will best resolve the situation."

CREATE CONTRACT

- "You will receive a letter from me in your campus mail detailing these sanctions next week."

- "You should know the grounds for appeal. A student found in violation of a policy or procedure by the Integrity Board may request a review of the case by the Board of Appeals and the Dean of Student Affairs. The request must be made in writing to the Dean of Student Affairs within five business days of the time the decision was delivered in writing (which will be included in the letter I send you detailing your sanction and any deadlines) for any of the following reasons:
  - discovery of new information
  - failure to follow stated procedures
  - belief that the sanction is unfair or too harsh given the circumstances
- "Further information about appeals can be found in the Student Handbook."
- "Thank you all for participating today, and have a great weekend."

Chapter 4

INTEGRITY BOARD CASE STUDY:
PELLET GUNSHOTS IN THE NIGHT

Don Hastings and Vané Becidyan

The setting of the case study is a small coed liberal arts college, located in upstate New York with an undergraduate population of 2,200. The incident took place at an off-campus, six-story, coed residence hall housing 160 students in single and double rooms. The hall sits in the middle of a residential neighborhood with a mixture of apartment buildings and single-family houses.

THE FACTS OF THE CASE

On a Friday afternoon, a few days into the Fall 2002 semester, two sophomore males, John and Andrew,[1] who live as roommates in a fourth floor corner room decide to split the cost and buy a high-powered pellet gun at a local store. At approximately 3:00 A.M. on Saturday, John is alone in the room with the room lights on and the stereo blasting. John (who has not been drinking) wants to get the feel of the gun's kick. He decides to try out the gun by sticking it out the open window and shooting off several rounds. John pulls the gun back into the room, turns off the music, and leaves the room to go find his friends. Unbeknownst to John, several of his rounds struck and dented the roof and hood as well as shattered the windshield of a neighbor's car that was parked in an apartment building parking lot adjacent to the residence hall. Ms. Smith is a middle-aged professional woman who recently moved to town from Texas. She is temporarily living in an apartment next to the residence hall with her husband (a private pilot who

---

1. Names and a few facts have been changed to maintain confidentiality.

is currently on assignment in Europe) and their youngest child, a 12-year-old boy, while waiting for their new house to be built. Her two oldest children are college-aged males living away from home. Ms. Smith leaves for work each day at 4:00 AM. She works at the airport for a major airline. Saturday morning, as she gets into her car (a brand new VW beetle) she feels her legs and hands being cut up from the bed of glass before she realizes her car windshield has been shattered. Frightened, upset, and angry, she goes back into her apartment to take care of her legs and to call work to let them know what happened. Due to her job's restrictive policy on attendance, she was forced to drive the car to work.

That same day, at approximately 4:00 P.M., Andrew, while waiting for John to return to their room, decides to try out the gun. He, like his roommate, sticks the gun out the open window and starts shooting off rounds. Not indiscriminately—in his mind, he is shooting at a pesky squirrel.

As shots zing through the trees and ping off the sidewalks and the sides of buildings, people start ducking for cover. One neighbor, seeing the barrel of the gun sticking out from the fourth floor window of the residence hall, yells at the student and calls the police from his cell phone. Ms. Smith, who is now at home with her 12-year-old son, taking care of her legs and the damage to her car, hears the shots. Both she and her son are terrified. Andrew pulls the gun back into the window and sits down in the room, panicked and terrified as to what will happen next. The police arrive at the scene. They take statements from witnesses, including Ms. Smith and her son. They call Campus Safety, figure out which room the shots were coming from, and find Andrew and arrest him. Andrew admits shooting the gun out the window but denies shooting Ms. Smith's car windshield. Later that same day, John returns to the hall. He hears that Andrew has been arrested and that the gun has been taken for evidence. He goes to the police station and is promptly arrested as well. Both students are charged with several violations of the New York State penal code and released on their own recognizance with orders to appear in court the following Monday morning.

Campus Safety reports the incident and the surrounding circumstances to the Associate Dean of Student Affairs in charge of the college's integrity board. The Dean decides to bring the case before the college's integrity board. The college's case will run parallel to the city's criminal court case.

THE HEARING

The hearing is held in a conference room on campus. Present around the table are the six board members. The board members include four students, one serving in the role of Chair, one faculty member, and one staff member. (One of the authors, Vané, was a senior at the time of the hearing and served as Chair, facilitating the dialogue.) Also present are the two respondents, John and Andrew, and they chose not to bring any support persons. The harmed parties, Mr. and Ms. Smith, attended and brought a support person, Ms. Jones, a friend of theirs and a local real estate agent. Finally, the second author, Don, in his capacity as Associate Dean, acted as the judicial council (JC).

The Chair opens the case, introductions are made, and the JC presents the case, reading all the charges, reports, and statements into the record. John and Andrew are charged with violating the college's honor code, in particular the college's rule against possessing a firearm. The first part of the hearing, determination of responsibility or no responsibility, moves along quickly because both John and Andrew readily accept responsibility for their actions.

To open the second portion of the hearing, Ms. Smith is first to speak. She is forthcoming about the anger she felt that morning and the fear she and her son felt later that afternoon when they heard the second round of shots ricocheting off building walls and sidewalks adjacent to the residence hall. Emotion took over when she stated that her son, having just moved to town, was afraid to leave the apartment for fear of someone shooting at him. Mr. Smith speaks next, and his anger could be clearly felt by all the parties present as he described the frantic phone call he received from his wife and how helpless he felt being 4,000 miles away from home. In addition to the emotional toll the incident levied on their family, the Smiths talked about the monetary costs. Their car insurance had a $100.00 deductible and would not cover the cost of renting a car while their car was being repaired—never mind that the car was brand new. Both spoke with vivid clarity about the "what if's." They wondered what if it was not just a car, but also her child or a neighbor's dog or another student walking along the side of the building who was shot and injured.

Ms. Jones then spoke about how she was appalled by what had happened, and she was not as understanding as the Smiths. She explained that she came to the hearing to ensure that the students received maximum punishment. She described that, as a realtor, she no longer felt that she could say nice things about living near Skidmore students. The Chair then read a lengthy letter from the Smith's landlord that included the following:

> I believe that [the respondents] should accept responsibility for [their] inappropriate actions and the damage they have done to relationships built by [the] College and the community—relationships which have worked so well over the years. . . . We will wonder, "What could happen next?" and "What if . . ." for a long time to come. When future tenants of our building ask about the impact of [college] students on the neighborhood, our honest response can no longer be 100% positive.

After hearing from the harmed parties, the board heard from John and Andrew. Both were visibly shaken after hearing the Smiths' statements. "These past two weeks have been the most difficult time in my life," stated John. Together, they related the chronology of events, starting with their decision to buy the gun and being excited about the prospect of shooting it. Both John and Andrew talked about sticking the gun out the window and feeling its power. Both students revealed that neither one of them had given any thought to any of the potential dangers or harmful situations they might create. They talked about never considering the possible consequences. It was Andrew who stated that it was only after he heard the shouts from neighbors that the gravity of his actions suddenly dawned on him. For John, it was when he was arrested and heard he had shot out a car windshield that he was shaken by his actions. But it was only after hearing from Mr. and Ms. Smith that it "hit home" just how serious and dangerous their actions were. As they looked back on the course of events, neither John nor Andrew could believe how foolish and naïve they had been.

THE CONTRACT

The final stage of the hearing includes a discussion of a restorative contract. Both respondents said that they had already taken some steps by talking with their friends about how stupid guns are and that they could talk to others about this. They also volunteered to do some community service. Although suspension was considered, Ms. Smith opposed it. At this point, she was convinced that John and Andrew understood the impact of their behavior and were remorseful. She talked about her own older sons and some of their actions and how they learned from their mistakes. Ms. Smith suggested that the respondents take a gun safety course and teach what they learned to younger children. A board member expressed concern about John's insensitivity to animals and suggested that some community service be completed at an animal shelter. Another board member suggested that the respondents write short essays on the "town/gown" relationship and the effect they have had on the college's reputation in the community. After thoughtful conversation, with all the board members and affected parties involved, it was decided that each student must complete the following: letters of apology to the Smiths and other neighbors, 100 hours of community service (a portion of which was to be completed at an animal shelter), three-page essays, completion of a gun safety course, and restitution for the damage done to the Smiths' car including any peripheral costs (i.e., car rental).

Following our case, the students faced charges in the criminal court downtown. We found it both meaningful and gratifying that the judge paid attention to the board's sanctions and demanded only that the students complete what was in the restorative contract. Subsequently, John decided to leave the college, but before his departure he had completed several of the required tasks. Andrew remained a student, successfully completed his obligations, and has not caused any further problems at the college.

VANÉ'S THOUGHTS AS THE STUDENT CHAIR

I think that everyone left this case satisfied with what happened. For me, personally, this case highlighted the importance of participation and dialogue, with both victims and respondents actively communicating and learning from each other. However, this can only work if they are willing. I have also participated in cases where the respondents were unwilling to accept responsibility or did not take the process seriously, and I left feeling like not much had been accomplished. With this case, we were confident that John and Andrew understood that what they had done was wrong and trusted that they would make amends for it. I also think the Smiths appreciated that we listened to their side of the story and were able to participate in the decision-making process.

A few months after the hearing, I spoke with Ms. Smith to see how satisfied she was with the result and she reiterated how happy she was with how the case was handled. She thought it was fair and that the process humanized the case for her and her husband. She continued to tell me that she understands that kids often learn by screwing up and that she didn't want this to ruin these boys' lives. Even her son, who is college-aged, was impressed with how the case went. He believed the outcome was better than suspension, which he suspected would have been the outcome had this occurred at his college.

DON'S THOUGHTS AS THE ADMINISTRATOR

Three years ago our traditional j-board model, which was also tripartite, would have dispatched this case in an hour's time. Our hearing lasted three hours. In that traditional model, only the board, the judicial counsel, and the respondents would have been present for this case because the harmed parties/potential complainants were not part of our college community. The college would have been the complainant. The true victims, the local community members, would not have been invited to participate. They would have been represented through the local newspaper's account of the event and/or possibly a police report. It would have been a sterile and one-sided discussion, with only information from the students being presented.

All the "right" questions would have been asked, but all the personal information, the emotion, the thoughts, and the wisdom of the harmed parties would have been missing. The respondents, our students, would not have heard or felt the anger, fear, and exasperation of the Smiths and other affected parties. The hearing would have been "fair and reasonable," and suspension of the two students would have been the probable outcome. At best, the hearing would have been efficient and we, the college, could claim that we had responded to our neighbors' outrage. At worst, the hearing would have been a missed educational opportunity and life experience for all those involved.

Although the restorative model "can be more time-consuming, awkward, at times more painful than the traditional judicial inquiry" (see Chapter 13, p. 144), it offers all affected parties the opportunity to participate. Whereas the traditional j-board is closed and restrictive, the restorative model is open and inclusive. It offers both sides the opportunity to speak and to listen. Everyone involved has a part to play and has influence in the final outcome. It was very powerful for the respondents to hear the personal accounts of the harmed parties and what they needed in order to have closure. It is equally powerful for harmed parties to hear and witness the apology and remorse of the respondents. And, instead of an outcome of mere punishment, the restorative model offers satisfaction for the harmed parties: concrete efforts to make amends and a way back into the community for the respondent. To work properly, the restorative model requires all the affected parties to buy into and participate in the process. However, if for some reason the respondent chooses not to accept responsibility to the harmed parties and community, board members have the latitude to consider this when coming to a final decision. For the administrator, who manages the judicial process, the restorative model offers the opportunity to move from an adversarial position with the respondent to a position of educator. When a student truly participates in the restorative process, considerable personal growth occurs.

Chapter 5

RESTORATIVE CONFERENCES: DEVELOPING STUDENT RESPONSIBILITY BY REPAIRING THE HARM TO VICTIMS AND RESTORING THE UNIVERSITY COMMUNITY

THOM ALLENA

Judicial affairs and other university professionals charged with the responsibility of effectively addressing student misconduct are faced with a host of challenges today. Disciplinary problems can take a variety of violation forms, including violations of campus policy and criminal codes. Yet how often do we consider the impact of this misconduct on the overall "campus culture?" How do other students, staff, and faculty generally view this behavior? Is it met with indifference and, in effect, tacit approval? This tension between campus cultural norms and campus policy is referred to as *cultural dissensus.* (Karp, Beslin, and Oles, 2002)

Traditional forms of justice and judicial affairs processes are often grounded in principles of due process yet promote a passive participation of the most impacted parties. Decision making remains hierarchical and rarely are offending students asked to consider the larger impact or harm associated with their behavior. Accountability is often defined as "taking your punishment," and little is done to attempt to reintegrate the student into the community he or she has offended. Sanctions are usually retributive and leave few footprints or other evidence of learning from the situation and, in effect, move us away from the larger academic mission associated with learning. If there are victims of these acts, their voices and concerns are usually peripheral at best to the adjudication process. In addition, the larger campus community is rarely strengthened as a result of the adjudication process.

Many university practitioners are reminded daily of the inherent limitations embedded in our traditional models of addressing contemporary student misconduct. A growing number of universities are turning to holistic practices such as restorative justice in an effort to address these growing concerns. Restorative justice is more than simply another programmatic model that administrators can implement. When restorative justice is alive and vital in a campus setting, it is often the result of a practice that has been informed by a set of restorative principles. Principles such as repairing harm to victims; holding offenders accountable to victims and communities; restoring the university community; and giving victims, offenders, and community members opportunities for fuller participation are some of cornerstones of any restorative justice program. Traditional adjudication approaches currently are and will likely remain the primary vehicles for addressing student misconduct, restorative practices offer a sometimes more effective option in responding to various types of campus offense behavior. Consequently, restorative justice is offered not as a panacea, but rather as a supplement and support to the traditional models of adjudication being employed on college campuses. Yet restorative justice does challenge several of the implicit assumptions that underlie our traditional approaches to adjudication. In the following section, several restorative principles are compared and contrasted in their relationship to existing campus decision-making models.

REFRAMING STUDENT ACCOUNTABILITY

Like most traditional justice processes, university discipline systems focus largely on the offending student. University adjudication processes by their nature are principally concerned with the laws, rules, or policies that were broken and the rights and forms of "due process" for those individuals charged with misconduct. The issues related to the victims of the misconduct and the concerns of the larger campus community are typically secondary to the guilt or innocence and subsequent sanctioning procedures. Accountability for the offending student is related to "breaking the rules" as articulated in university policies and codes of conduct. In a restorative framework, accountability moves in a direction toward the victim of the conduct (if one exists) and the community impacted by the behavior. Furthermore, while accountability for the offending student is often construed to mean punishment in a traditional disciplinary approach, in a restorative model, this same principle presents the offending student with opportunities to repair harm and regain one's place in the campus community. When an offending student is invited to give a public account of his behavior, it represents a significant step toward accepting personal responsibility, which restorative justice sees as essential to the process. For the offending student to face the people he or she has harmed is a significant departure from the model of being accountable to a university code of conduct or other policy.

REDEFINING RESPONSIBILITY AS RESTORATION

Another principle worthy of attention addresses the idea of restoration. Restorative justice views the concept of restoration as fundamental to any act of misconduct. Take the case of a student who, while intoxicated, breaks a window in his dorm room. In a restorative process, paying for the repair of the window or being involved in the actual repair is a simple solution that most readers will easily understand. Yet sitting with the people who have been affected by the incident to understand both the human and the property costs associated with the violation is a powerful way of building empathy. In taking an active role in the reparation process, offending students discover that he or she is a person of worth, that he or she has the power and responsibility to make things right and to make good choices. In addition, a willingness to "make things right" puts a human face on the offending student. Another "growing edge" for the offending student rests in his or her understanding of the potentially problematic use of alcohol and its effects on others, on his or her social relationships, and on the larger university community.

GIVING VICTIMS OF CAMPUS MISCONDUCT A CLEAR VOICE

Restorative justice recognizes that victims of crime and other campus misconduct are central to any process of adjudication. In fact, they are as essential to the process as the offending student. They need opportunities to express and validate their emotions: their anger, fear, and pain and to have their truth heard (Zehr, 1990). Frequently, victim's need for vengeance or retribution grows out of a frustration of having no arena or venue to be heard and to know that steps are being taken to restore what they have lost as a result of the wrongdoing. Restorative justice recognizes that for healing to occur, victims need to experience some form of justice; otherwise a return to some experience of personal safety becomes impossible to attain. For many victims, being able to safely confront their offenders and express how their lives have been impacted is in itself restorative. In doing so, many victims also experience the human side of offenders, a realization that is often unattainable if the violation is allowed to remain an impersonal act. Victims often want to know such things as:

1. What happened?
2. Why did it happen to me?
3. What if it happens again?
4. How will I feel safe in the future? (Zehr, 1990)

APPLYING OF RESTORATIVE CONFERENCES

In addressing student misconduct, a number of universities have recently turned to a series of restorative models that have been developed and applied within justice systems and communities across the United States and beyond. One model known as conferencing, which is discussed next, is derived from a variety of indigenous and religious cultures and disciplines. Conferencing is a restorative justice practice that is steadily gaining interest at a number of college campuses across the United States. Conferences incorporate the conflict resolution practices of a number of indigenous people, including the Maoris of New Zealand, Hawaiians, North American Indians, and Africans (Galaway and Hudson, 1996). Conferences can and do take a series of subforms: family group conferencing, community conferencing, family group decision making, real justice conferences, and community group conferencing (Allena, 2002; Kurki, 2000). Conferencing in its most generic sense has a series of parts common to all restorative processes using this framework. The conferencing process described next most closely aligns with the community group conferencing process as developed with the Longmont Community Justice Partnership (LCJP) in Longmont, Colorado, with whom the author was intimately involved in the project's early stages of development and is seminal in our understanding of restorative justice conferencing on university campuses across the United States.

STAGE ONE: CASE SELECTION AND REFERRAL

Referrals to restorative conferencing can originate from a variety of campus sources, including Judicial Affairs, Residential Life, Student Affairs, Offices of Conflict Resolution and university police departments. These cases are referred to a university restorative justice project, which often includes a conference coordinator and a team of restorative justice facilitators comprised of students, faculty. and staff who are trained in facilitating conferences. Once a case meets referral criteria as articulated by university officials, the conference coordinator (University of Colorado, University of California–Santa Barbara) approaches the offending student and his or her victim of the offense to determine if interest exists on both parties' part. Once there is an indication that both individuals do have an interest in proceeding with a restorative justice conference, the conference coordinator identifies and contacts the appropriate participants and the matter is then assigned to a facilitator and co-facilitator who will facilitate the conference. The types of cases referred for restorative justice conferences vary from university to university, but property-related crimes (vandalism, graffiti, theft, etc.) are most amenable to a restorative conferencing process. We have also applied conferencing to offenses that have involved multiple offending students (see Chapter 15 and Chapter 17). There are other relevant factors to consider in identifying an appropriate case for restorative conferencing. In addition to the parties' willingness to participate, a second factor to consider involves early acceptance of responsibility by the offending student. If a student charged with a campus offense denies responsibility (e.g.,"I did not do this!"), then it is likely that a traditional university adjudication process would be more appropriate where a presumption of innocence and the burden of proof on the university are foundational. Conferencing is most effective when an offending student is capable of taking some level of responsibility for his or her behavior. The purpose of the conference is not to prove the student guilty, but rather to develop a shared community understanding of the offending behavior, the harm it has created, and some specific ways to repair that harm. (I will articulate these outcomes in greater detail in a subsequent discussion of the restorative conference process.)

A third consideration involves whether the case involves relatively clear roles distinguishing the offender and victim. We find it important to delineate these roles in determining if a conference is the most appropriate restorative practice to employ. In cases of mixed or shared responsibility (e.g., two students fighting), we would be inclined to use a more traditional mediation approach or what is known as a peacemaking circle process. In a peacemaking circle, a "keeper" rather than a facilitator manages the process employing a "talking piece" and "rounds" where each person speaks to a common question. In contrast, conferencing is a more directed or scripted model that is described in greater detail later in this chapter.

Another important consideration involves the likelihood of revictimization of the victim in this matter. If it is determined that a conferencing process would increase the possibility of revictimization of the victim and/or his family and friends, then a conference should be most carefully considered before proceeding. The same would hold true for the offending student or any other individual where retaliation or similar consequences is a foreseeable possibility.

STAGE TWO: PRE-CONFERENCING AND PLANNING THE RESTORATIVE CONFERENCE

The success of a restorative practice lies squarely in its preparation. It has been my experience that poorly planned interventions usually result in unsuccessful conferences if and when they eventually take place. The pre-conferencing tasks are usually undertaken by a conference facilitator. In addition to interviewing the offending student and victim regarding the incident, the conference facilitator works with each of them to accomplish a variety of additional aims, namely: to educate them as to their role in the restorative conference as well as the overall flow and direction of the process; to hear the participant's "story" that will be told during the conference and to identify early ideas as to how to repair the harm related to the incident in issue. Once the offending student and his or her victim are pre-conferenced, the remaining participants are interviewed and prepared for the intervention. The size of the actual conference will vary from case to case depending on the number of people impacted by the offense. As more participants are added, the time of the conference is usually increased in direct proportion to these numbers. This is a very appropriate issue for the facilitator and/or conference coordinator to consider during the planning stages of the conference.

In the case of a critical university incident (e.g., disabled parking placard incident involving football team members at UCLA; again, see Chapter 17), there are a number of additional pre-conference planning and education tasks that are essential to the success of a restorative conference. In the referenced case of UCLA, the magnitude of the incident and the number of people and departments impacted within the university community as well as outside the campus community who would need to be involved, all created a complexity of issues that warranted a planning process which transcended a typical restorative conference to include: meeting and briefing key university officials, developing a restorative justice advisory team to advise and inform the process, and training a restorative justice facilitation team beyond that of a facilitator and co-facilitator as previously described.

STAGE THREE: THE RESTORATIVE
CONFERENCE PROCESS

The structure and shape of every restorative conference is an open circle. The circle has been used by aboriginal cultures for hundreds of years and recurs in various forms. Long before we delegated the role of resolving conflicts and wrongdoing to experts, people came together, sat in circles, and worked through their differences (Pranis, Stuart, and Wedge, 2003). In both ancient indigenous communities and modern restorative justice conferences, circles provide a place to turn conflict and misconduct among community members into opportunities for a deeper relationship. The following section provides a general description of the primary stages of the conferencing process.

Conference Opening

We begin each conference by introducing each person, their roles, our purposes for being there, and our shared process ground rules that guide the conferencing process. Values such as deep listening, speaking respectfully, trust, empathy, honesty, courage, and confidentiality all contribute to the development of an environment of safety built by the participants themselves. Even at this introductory stage we are witnessing the unfolding of a process that is more participatory and requires a greater degree of shared responsibility than most traditional adjudication approaches.

Offending Student Tells His/Her Story

In an effort to establish early responsibility for misconduct, the offending student is then asked to recount what he or she did and is asked who and how others have been harmed by the inappropriate behavior. This is an obvious departure from most judicial practices where the process begins with the reading of formal charges to which the offending student is asked to respond. In the conferencing process, it is important for victims and community members to hear students take responsibility for their behavior early in the process.

The primary forms of communication in conferences are story and dialogue, and each allows for a deeper conversation to take place. The offending student's initial story establishes a path of personal responsibility and allows for the repair of the relationship to begin. As stories of victims and other community members are later added, conference participants move toward a shared understanding of the incident and, in some conferences, a shared responsibility for the conditions that may have contributed to the offending behavior. By having the offending student reflect on the harm he or she may have caused, rather than simply the law or policy they have violated, a deeper sense of responsibility is established. This shared understanding of the harm arising from this incident will later provide the foundation for the restorative sanctioning process.

Stories of Victims and Affected Community Members

Once personal acceptance of responsibility is established, the process shifts toward those most impacted by the incident in question. At this point we hear the stories of our most impacted party, the victim. Victims are asked to describe how they have been impacted physically, emotionally, mentally, and economically. After hearing from the victim, we listen to supporters of the victim, the offending student, as well as other affected community members. Again, we are seeking to develop a shared understanding of all of the impacts and harm that have resulted from the offense. As discussed earlier, it is the collective understanding of this harm that provides the foundation for the sanctioning or agreement process.

Fashioning an Agreement

At the heart of any restorative practice, we seek answers to the questions: Who has been harmed? What is the nature of that harm? Who is responsible for the repair of that harm (Zehr, 1990)? The agreement phase of the conferencing process allows for the successful integration of these questions. In a departure from most traditional adjudications, it is the participants, rather than university officials, who are jointly responsible for developing the sanctions, which focus on three specific areas: (1) repair of harm to the victim; (2) restoration of the community; and (3) assisting the offending student to build competencies and, in effect, make better future decisions. Our shared concern about the agreement is that they are practical, achievable, and appropriate to the offending behavior.

Community justice theorists suggest that while offenders are responsible for the repair of harm emanating from a specific offense, the community has a shared responsibility to address the social, economic, and environmental issues that contribute to illicit behavior (Clear and Karp, 1999). This view suggests that justice is both an individual and a collective responsibility. An illustration of this idea was seen in an early restorative justice conference involving a vandalism incident at the University of Colorado. While the offending student in this matter was considered responsible for the financial damage caused by his personal actions, a larger community issue emerged during the conference. During the conference we learned from a university maintenance supervisor that in the past several years he had witnessed a growing distance between his staff and the overall student population. Students seemed disinterested, he related, in understanding what was involved in restoring the physical grounds of the university following a home football game. It was also apparent to this individual that he and his staff seemed to know few students by name anymore. In an effort to address this widening gap between maintenance staff and students through the agreement or sanctioning process, the offending student was required to develop a series of "breakfast focus groups" consisting of maintenance staff and students designed to increase mutual understanding of each group. Again, a core principle of any restorative practice is that crime and wrong-doing are considered to be more than a violation of policy or code; it is seen as a violation of relationship within the community (Zehr, 1990). This conference, in its efforts to restore the overall relationship between the maintenance department and students in general, clearly embodied this restorative principle.

The agreement process is built on consensus with the explicit belief that the community has the innate ability to make wise and healthy decisions, reintegrate the victim and offending student into the university community, and restore the balance lost as a result of the offending behavior. Once a written plan is established, various members of the conference assume responsibility for the oversight of specific aspects of the plan. Ultimately, the conference coordinator will be responsible for overseeing the successful completion of the overall agreement. While the agreement is being transcribed, the participants share food in a process known as "breaking bread," the celebration of the work accomplished by the community. It is often during this activity that the conference results of healing and return to community are visibly witnessed.

Closing the Conference

Once the conference agreement is drafted, it is read to the conference participants for accuracy and then signatures are gathered. Closing thoughts are added by the participants, and congratulations are offered by the facilitators. The university community's ability to resolve conflict and repair harm has been expanded, and as a result, the campus has been strengthened. In a closing activity, we often ask participants to provide feedback as to the effectiveness of the conference through a short survey. The survey provides program data that assist us in short-term process improvement and long-term program sustainability.

STAGE FOUR: CONFERENCE FOLLOW-UP

Once the conference is completed, the process enters a follow-up or monitoring phase that continues to integrate offending students, victims, and the community. While the primary responsibility for the completion of the agreement rests with the offending student, the follow-up phase requires a continued commitment on the part of the conference community. Post-conference activities usually requiring follow-up include the following: offending students frequently are asked to perform community service, financial restitution requires oversight, and letters of apology need to be carefully screened to minimize the possibility of revictimization. General monitoring of the overall plan lies with a conference coordinator. The conference coordinator can effectively problem-solve unexpected issues as they arise in the days and weeks following the conference. However, other conference participants can provide support in multiple ways: an encouraging phone call, assistance in reviewing letters, or perhaps providing a ride to a community service site.

IMPLEMENTING RESTORATIVE CONFERENCING:
A STRATEGIC APPROACH

In considering a shift toward the integration of a restorative conferencing model within an existing university system of discipline, a thoughtful strategic approach is warranted. Following are a few considerations and suggestions to consider as a university seeks to implement restorative justice.

Gain A Shared Understanding of
Restorative Justice

Restorative justice is a way of thinking that is a fundamentally different framework for understanding and responding to campus crime and wrongdoing. Moving from a an adjudication model that is focused on the offending student to a three-dimensional approach that also recognizes victims and the larger community is easier talked about than actually practiced. Restorative justice is also a way of behaving and is not simply focused on the behavior of our students. In its most credible form, restorative justice asks staff and faculty to behave in a restorative fashion as well. Again, easier said than done.

Restorative justice, by its nature, is collaborative and therefore thrives in environments where partnerships are encouraged and practiced. Partnership and collaboration are actually skills that can and must be cultivated within the university community if restorative justice is to be sustained. When first introduced to restorative conferencing, the University of Colorado involved staff from Judicial Affairs, Office of Conflict Resolution, Victim Services. and the university police department. Learning about restorative justice as a community enabled this group to build cross-departmental support and to grow as a single community in their collective understanding of these concepts.

Assess the University's Readiness for Change

In assessing the appropriateness of introducing restorative justice, it is useful to understand an organization's readiness and motivation for change. Knowing if a judicial affairs program is ripe for a positive change is an important question to answer before plunging into the "permanent whitewater" of organizational change that restorative justice will bring in its wake (Vaill, 1989). How motivated are the staff who will have to implement these new program ideas? Weisbord (1988) refers to organizational change of this nature as a "four room apartment" where stages of contentment, denial, confusion, and renewal are identified. Most change, he suggests, occurs when people are in the confusion and renewal stages. This theory appears to hold true with the introduction of restorative justice concepts. My personal experience in consulting with universities is that the decision to consider restorative justice does in fact stem from those two places: (1) a campus crisis that traditional approaches ineffectively address, or (2) there is a sincere desire on the part of staff to expand their vision of what is possible in working with disciplinary issues.

Forging University Partnerships for Restorative Justice

I noted earlier that restorative justice is best implemented in an environment of partnership and collaboration. The rich soil of cooperation provides the best opportunity for these concepts to take root and experience sustained growth. The search for restorative partners in a campus setting might take several strategic directions. Consider the following inquiry: First, for which groups or organizations would restorative justice be a philosophical "fit?" Are there victim services groups, existing mediation or ombuds offices, faith community groups, or violence prevention initiatives whose mission or purpose is consistent with the ideas and principles of restorative justice? There are numerous natural allies to any restorative start-up. The most rudimentary stakeholder mapping process will begin to reveal who these early adopters may be. It is always interesting to gather diverse groups of potential partners to discuss developing a restorative justice initiative. Involving these people and their groups in the developmental stages of the programs creates widespread investment and the best opportunity for growing and sustaining restorative justice in the university community.

Crafting Campus-Wide Credibility for Restorative Justice

Another strategy for implementing restorative justice is to consider which potential partners can give the concepts institutional support and legitimacy? Key officials from judicial affairs, student affairs and residential life, the campus police department, student governance groups, and existing legal advisory groups all are potentially strategic partners that can bring early program credibility. Often these individuals can play important advisory roles in developing a restorative program. They are usually adept at negotiating the university bureaucracy and, once "bought in," are invaluable in assisting implementation strategies that are consistent with existing university structures and policies. The University of Colorado initiative used an advisory board model that possessed a number of important stakeholders from inside the organization, including judicial affairs, ombuds office, victims' assistance, police department, residential life, and student governance groups.

Integrate Restorative Justice Within the Existing University Discipline System

Effective restorative justice programs are linked to existing university discipline programs. These programs rarely stand alone; rather they typically function in concert with other discipline tracks. When aligned with existing systems, restorative justice is offered to offending students as an alternative to judicial and student affairs approaches in specific offense categories (University of Colorado). When the University of California–Santa Barbara initiated its restorative justice program in 2002, the effort was aligned with its residential life program and referrals were generated from on-campus student housing and off-campus family housing properties. The challenge of integrating restorative programs within traditional discipline tracks often lies with the sometimes conflicting philosophies and the difficulty of knowing when and why each might be applied.

Develop a Team of Restorative Justice Facilitators

Within every university exists a deep pool of talent that can be accessed in making restorative justice a campus reality. When the University of Colorado elected to embark on the restorative justice journey, they reached out to judicial affairs, residential life and ombuds staff, police officers, victims' assistance personnel, faculty members, students, and other interested university parties who participated in a two-day conference facilitator training. Following the training, the participants formed a university facilitation team to whom cases were eventually referred from judicial affairs and residential life departments. A structure for restorative justice case referral, facilitation debriefing, and ongoing learning was established. Eventually, with the assistance of grant funding and other university resources, a conference coordinator position was created to oversee the facilitation team process and the case follow-up activities to ensure that the completed conference agreements were effectively monitored.

Small Wins

Philosophical shifts of this nature require significant time and copious amounts of patience. Restorative practices such as conferencing need to be nurtured over time. See each training event or conference as an opportunity to educate the university community. William Bridges, author of *Managing Transitions: Making the Most of Change*, reminds us that every change starts with an ending. With endings are losses as people are asked to let go of something familiar to them (Bridges, 1991). No matter how much better restorative justice may appear, it still represents a change, which in turn, suggests loss. Bearing this in mind, choose to go slower rather than faster in the first year of operation. Take fewer cases to conferences and take more time to learn from the accompanying lessons those cases will offer. Take the time to tell the university "stories" of restorative justice across the campus community. Most importantly, take the time necessary to build campus support and commitment for this new and exciting path.

References

Allena, Thom. 2002. "Sentencing Circles: The Shape of Things to Come." *Cornerstone* 24(1).

Bridges, William. (1991). *Managing Transitions: Making the Most of Change.* Lanham, MD: Perseus.

Clear, Todd, and David Karp. 1999. *The Community Justice Ideal: Preventing Crime and Achieving Justice.* Boulder, CO: Westview.

Galaway, Burt, and Joe Hudson (eds.). 1996. *Restorative Justice: International Perspectives.* Monsey, NY: Criminal Justice Press.

Karp, David, Beau Breslin, and Pat Oles. 2002. "Community Justice in a Campus Setting." *Conflict Management in Higher Education Report* 3(1). http//www.campus-adr.org/CMHER.

Kurki, Leena. 2000. "Restorative and Community Justice in the United Statessss." pp. 235–303 in Crime and Justice: *A Review of the Research*, Vol. 27, edited by Michael Tonry. Chicago: University of Chicago Press.

Pranis, Kay, Barry Stuart, and Mark Wedge. 2003. *Peacemaking Circles: From Crime to Community.* St. Paul, MN: Living Justice Press.

Vaill, Peter B. (1988). *Managing as a Performing Art.* San Francisco: Jossey-Bass.

Weisbord, Marvin R. 1988. *Productive Workplaces.* San Francisco: Jossey-Bass.

Zehr, Howard. (1990). *Changing Lenses: A New Focus on Crime and Justice.* Scottdale, PA: Herald.

Chapter 6

CONFERENCING CASE STUDY: "KENNY'S CELEBRATION"

Tom Sebok

One Saturday night, following a particularly stressful week with three exams, Kenny decided to celebrate what he thought was his good performance on the exams. He went to a party at the house of a friend in a section of town where many university students lived. Kenny drank 12 beers in two hours.

After leaving the party (about 2:00 A.M.), he walked back to his room at the Edwards Scholars House, where a few other residents were still awake. He was quite drunk. Kenny thought it would be funny to entertain his peers by doing cartwheels in the hallway. Eventually, he decided it would be even funnier to do this in a T-shirt and his bikini brief underwear. People did, indeed, think Kenny looked pretty funny doing cartwheels in this state.

Sometime before 3:00 A.M., to keep the humorous momentum moving forward, Kenny decided to take his "act" out into the street in front of the house, a four-lane street with a 35 mph speed limit. On the porch, Kenny picked up a basket of dried flowers to add to the effect. Carrying the flowers, Kenny got down in a "football stance" in the street. The first car to drive up behind him was a police car. When Kenny saw the police officer, he ran across the street toward campus. Although the officer ordered Kenny to stop, he kept running. He ran in between two academic buildings and then ran back across the four-lane street toward the Scholars House with the police officer giving chase close behind.

At the back of the house, Kenny was trying to use the keyless entry code to open the door when the police officer arrested him, put him in handcuffs, and took him to the patrol car. While sitting in the car, Kenny began talking to Tim, the supervisor of Buck, the arresting officer. Tim asked Kenny what he had been doing and Kenny replied, "I was just trying to fit in with those guys." He later repeated this same story at the jail. Trying to deflect attention away from the Scholars House, Kenny, who now readily admits he wasn't thinking too clearly at the time, thought he would lie to the police and imply that he was being hazed by members of the fraternity house that was next door to the Scholars House.

Kenny was taken to jail, where he was fingerprinted and put in a "holding cell." About 6:00 A.M. he called Harold, another member of the Scholars House, and asked Harold to come and pick him up. Harold took Kenny back to the house, where he slept until noon.

The student newspaper, *The Campus Weekly News*, routinely reviews the police blotter. A reporter picked up the story of Kenny's arrest and printed it, including a statement from the police report attributed to Kenny about trying to "fit in" with the people . . . at the Edwards Scholars House. Kenny later received a phone call from the Victim Assistance Office asking if he had been the victim of a hazing incident. He also received a letter from the Director of Student Judicial Affairs, who routinely receives information about underage students caught by city or campus police with alcohol in their possession and/or who run from police. Both of these are violations of the Student Code of Conduct.

NOTE: THE EDWARDS SCHOLARS HOUSE

The Edwards Scholars House is *not* a fraternity house, a fact about which its members are adamant. Its members come from all over the United States and have worked in the same semiskilled summer jobs in their hometowns for a number of years. They are selected based on academic criteria. Residents of this house are uniformly proud to have been selected to be an Edwards Scholar and most of them work hard to succeed academically.

FACILITATOR'S STORY

I received a phone call from Alice Goldsmith, the Director of Student Judicial Affairs, about Kenny's case. She told me that, after meeting with him, because he had assumed responsibility for his actions, she believed Kenny might be a good candidate for our Restorative Justice (RJ) program. She also said this would be his second alcohol violation. As a University of Colorado at Boulder (UCB) student, if Kenny received a third alcohol violation, he would automatically be suspended from school. On the other hand, if he successfully completed an RJ Community Group Conference, there would be no record of Kenny's having a second offense. Alice said she would give Kenny's file to our Restorative Justice Coordinator, who would make initial contacts with potential conference participants and then give me the file.

Upon receiving Kenny's file from the program coordinator, I reviewed the police report, Judicial Affairs letter, summons, and list of potential participants for a conference, several of whom the coordinator had already interviewed. In order to evaluate whether a conference was appropriate, I made arrangements to meet individually with Kenny and with a number of people who were harmed or affected by Kenny's actions. I wanted to find out if Kenny was willing to publicly take responsibility for his actions. And I wanted to assess the community impact of these events. Finally, I wanted to see if I could bring together a circle of people who cared about Kenny and/or who were affected by this situation to discuss how to repair the harm that had occurred as a result of Kenny's behavior. These individual meetings with six people took between half an hour and an hour each. In the end, I was convinced that a community group conference was an appropriate option.

THE COMMUNITY GROUP CONFERENCE

As is customary in our conferences, Nancy (the co-facilitator) and I arrived at the meeting room about half an hour early and arranged the chairs in a circle in the center of the room. We also made name tags for all participants and placed them in the seats according to a particular seating design. Kenny (the offender) sat to my immediate left with Harold (the offender support person) to his left. Mack and Bob (both harmed parties) sat to my right. Buck (the police officer and affected community member) sat to Bob's right. Nancy sat to Buck's right and across from me. Lois sat to Nancy's right and to Harold's left.

The circle began with my "facilitator monologue." I welcomed the participants and thanked them for coming. I explained that we had come together to discuss an incident involving Kenny that, in some way, affected everyone in the room. I further explained that our purpose was not to judge whether Kenny was a good or a bad person. Instead, I said, we were meeting to identify harm that occurred as a result of Kenny's behavior, to figure out how to repair it, and to come up with ideas to help Kenny make better future choices. I explained that if the group was unable to reach agreement about these things, the matter would be referred back to Judicial Affairs. I said it was my understanding that everyone present was there voluntarily and I specifically asked Kenny if he understood that his participation was voluntary. He said it was. Finally, I asked if there were any questions and there were none. I turned to Kenny.

One at a time, I asked Kenny all the questions we discussed in our pre-conference interview. When I asked him to tell us "what happened," he explained—without my prompting for details—how his evening began with his attending the party at his friend's house, consuming 12 beers in two hours. He talked about returning later to the Scholar's House, going out into the street, running from the police, and being apprehended. In response to the question, "What were you thinking at the time?" with respect to his excessive use of alcohol, Kenny focused on the desire to "cut loose" to celebrate his successful performance on an exam at the end of a particularly stressful week of school. In explaining what he was thinking about when he got back to the Scholars House, Kenny emphasized his desire to entertain and amuse his friends. He told the group about running from the police officer, even though he heard the officer's order for him to stop. Of particular importance to Kenny was the part of the story where he explained the misunderstanding resulting from his apparent hazing allegation. He carefully explained his drunken "reasoning" while talking to the police officer about what he was doing. This was very important to him because he already understood that one of the primary harms that occurred as a result of this incident was to the reputation of the Edwards Scholars House.

When asked who he affected and how he thought they were affected, Kenny named Bob, Mack, and Harold, in addition to all the scholars living in the house. He recognized that Bob was disappointed in his behavior, and that both Mack and Harold had their sleep disrupted by his being arrested. And he said he realized that all three of them, as well as a number of others on the executive board of the Scholar's House had been required to spend a lot of time discussing the incident and deciding what to do about it. He also realized that Buck, the police officer, was affected by having to chase him around campus buildings, arrest him, and take him to jail.

When asked how he felt about the incident now, Kenny replied that he was embarrassed and that he especially regretted trying to imply that he had been hazed because he knew this had hurt the house. He also said he was sorry to have disappointed Bob.

When asked, "What's happened for you since the incident?" Kenny described going to jail, having to pay fines, hire a lawyer, and face legal proceedings. He talked about being surprised to receive a call from the Office of Victim Assistance (as a result of the article in the student newspaper) and he said he explained to the person with whom he spoke that he was definitely not a victim of hazing. He also talked about conversations he had had with other members of the house and with one of his professors after the incident. Finally, he mentioned that, obviously, he was also facing sanctions by the Office of Judicial Affairs if he was unable to successfully resolve the matter through the restorative justice process in which we were engaged.

It was evident that Kenny understood what he had done and how it affected a number of people, especially his fellow scholars. What he failed to realize came out later in the circle as the other participants spoke. In the first "round," following Kenny's answers to my questions, participants were each asked to describe essentially how they were affected by what Kenny did.

(Note: This question was not "What do you think about what Kenny did?" but rather "How did what he did affect you?") Kenny did not realize how Mack had worried about the fact that the next day (technically, the same day) following Kenny's arrest, a house inspection was scheduled for which Jay, from the central office of the scholar's program in Cleveland, would be present. Kenny did not realize that Mack agonized about whether to tell Bob about the incident and, after deciding not to tell him, had serious regrets about not doing so. And he certainly did not realize that his decision not to tell Bob led to a crisis in trust in his (Mack's) relationship with Bob and to serious self-doubts on Mack's part about his own decision making and leadership.

Kenny also did not know that Harold, whom he called to get him out of jail, had nearly hung up on him that morning. Harold had not been present for Kenny's antics and arrest, and when Harold was awakened by Kenny's call at 6:00 A.M., he (Harold) assumed Kenny was calling to ask him to drive over to the house where Kenny had been partying earlier in the evening to pick him up. It wasn't until Kenny said something about "only being allowed one phone call," that Harold realized Kenny was in jail.

Kenny also did not realize what was involved for Buck, the police officer. In addition to chasing Kenny initially in his police vehicle and then on foot, this experience took hours of his time because he had to take Kenny to jail, book him, and then write a police report about the incident. In addition, Buck was voluntarily giving his time to participate in the conference.

Kenny did not know Lois prior to the conference. He had never given thought to how the near-death experience of a close friend could restimulate painful or scary memories for Lois (or anyone) by hearing about another (unrelated) student's excessive drinking. Unfortunately, Lois was the least talkative person in the conference and, although she did share how her friend's near-death experience due to alcohol abuse affected her, her comments did not seem to affect Kenny as much as I had hoped they would.

It surprised me that, although Bob and Mack had mentioned concern about Kenny's excessive drinking, neither of them said as much in the conference about that concern as they had shared with me privately. I attempted to ask them both a number of questions that I hoped would elicit this response but, for some reason, they chose not to focus on this. Ultimately, at the time, I saw my role as requiring me to give all the participants opportunities to say what they wanted to say but not requiring me to prompt them to say more than they wanted to say.

The first round of discussion in the conference helped Kenny see the ripple effect of his actions far beyond just himself and his immediate peers. Prior to initiating the second round, I asked Nancy to read from her notes about what group members had said about the effects of Kenny's behavior on them. Nancy mentioned that both Bob and Mack raised concerns about how Kenny was affecting others in the Edwards Scholars House. Mack mentioned his concern about how Kenny's behavior might be affecting the freshmen in particular. And most participants had commented on the damage to the reputation of the Edwards Scholars House due to the "hazing allegation."

Harm Kenny had done to himself due to his excessive use of alcohol (e.g., making bad decisions, acting impulsively) was not mentioned. However, group recognition of the various harms that occurred set the stage for the group (including Kenny) to address two more questions: "What could be done to repair the harm caused by Kenny's actions?" and "What could be done to help Kenny make better future choices?" I explained that our purpose in this round was to brainstorm possibilities to address these questions. I also told the group that this would be a consensus process and Kenny would need to agree as well in order to reach consensus.

Bob said he saw Kenny as a potential leader and would like to see him take more of a leadership role in the future. As the group discussed repairing harm to the reputation of the scholars, Bob remarked that he thought Kenny might be the ideal person to write a brief paper for the Dean of Students about how the Scholarship House concept might be applied to a residential academic program. Also, several members suggested that Kenny write an editorial in the student newspaper to set the record straight about the "hazing allegation."

Because much of the harm that had been identified had focused on Bob's disappointment in Kenny and the resulting damage to his trust in Mack, in the brainstorming phase, the participants offered a number of suggestions to address these concerns. This was a bit confusing for me as facilitator because, even though I knew about the damage to Bob's trust in Mack, for some reason I did not expect it to come up in the conference. I was beginning to wonder if I should encourage participants to focus on Kenny because, ultimately, he was the one for whom an agreement would be developed and monitored. As the conversation developed, Bob actually said he did not think the group should focus on his relationship with Mack because he was confident they were already on their way to repairing that harm. However, he did express concern about Kenny's decisionmaking and wanted to see the group come up with ideas to help him make better future choices.

THE AGREEMENT

After asking the group to brainstorm various possibilities they thought might address the identified harms resulting from Kenny's behavior, I asked Kenny which of those ideas he was comfortable agreeing to. He agreed to:

1. Write a letter to the editor of *The Campus Weekly News*, correcting the hazing allegation that was identified in the police blotter;
2. Meet privately with Bob to discuss Kenny's role as a leader in the Edwards Scholars House; and
3. Contact the Dean of Students and arrange a time to meet with her and discuss a possible paper topic (1–2 pages in length) of "How Edwards Scholar principles and philosophies can be translated into a residential academic program."

Prior to submitting his letter to *The Campus Weekly News*, Kenny agreed to submit it to Nora (the Restorative Justice Coordinator) for approval. And, prior to submitting his paper to the Dean of Students, he agreed to submit it to Bob for approval. In addition, while I had been concerned that Bob (and Mack) did not say very much in the conference about their concerns that there was a direct relationship between Kenny's excessive drinking and his "out of control" behavior, I was fairly confident that Bob would discuss this with Kenny privately.

I asked all participants if they were willing to allow these items to serve as Kenny's contract. They all agreed.

As Nancy wrote the contract, the participants were invited to "break bread." This ritual allowed all participants to enjoy some light food and beverages in a relaxed atmosphere. We see this as an essential component of any conference and believe it is another way in which this process can help build a sense of community for all who participate. When Nancy finished writing the contract, she circulated it among all the participants for signing.

EPILOGUE

For the past two years, Kenny has received no further sanctions from the Office of Judicial Affairs. From that standpoint, he is a restorative justice "success story." Also, he is now in his senior year and has maintained a 3.3 to 3.4 grade point average. However, in a recent conversation with Bob, I learned that, sadly, even after the conference, Kenny continued to drink excessively. According to Bob, when Kenny drinks, he sometimes "crosses a line," which makes it almost inevitable that he will cause problems for other people. According to Bob, this occurred several times after the conference and eventually led to his being asked to leave the Edwards Scholars House.

In reviewing what occurred in the conference, Bob and I agreed that our discussion focused more on the effects of the allegation that Kenny had been hazed. But, in doing so, the focus was not on the behavior that made the hazing allegation possible—the confusion caused by Kenny's excessive drinking. In this regard, this conference did not effectively "help Kenny make better future choices."

One alternative for dealing with this problem that has been used by participants in several other conferences was for the offenders to agree to being voluntarily assessed by an alcoholism expert and to agree to participate in a treatment program if it were recommended by this expert. One of the items agreed to by all participants was for Kenny to have a private meeting with Bob to ". . . discuss his role as a leader in the Edwards Scholars House." I was fairly certain that Bob would address the question of Kenny's drinking with him when they met. Indeed, Bob told me in our recent conversation that he did try to discuss this with Kenny but, unfortunately, when he did, Kenny insisted his drinking was not a problem. My own view of this is that it placed too much responsibility on Bob and allowed Kenny a relatively easy opportunity to avoid facing the possibility that he had a real problem with alcohol. I believe discussing this in the conference would have provided a better opportunity to help Kenny face this.

I really do not know why Bob and Mack opted not to address this in the conference to the extent I had expected they would. Confronting someone about a perception that he drinks too much is difficult for many people. Also, as the discussion evolved, they might have lost sight of this issue, especially as Kenny demonstrated such obvious contrition about the effects of the hazing allegation. As I second-guess my own choices as a facilitator, I can envision several things I might have done differently:

1. I might have encouraged them more in the pre-conference meetings to raise their concerns in the conference about how much Kenny was drinking and how he acted when he did;
2. I might have done more in my pre-conference meeting with Lois to encourage her to focus on the underlying issue of Kenny's excessive drinking when she spoke in the circle;
3. In the conference, I might have called for a short break and talked with Bob, Mack, and Lois privately (a very unusual move for me as facilitator); and/or
4. In the conference, before I asked the co-facilitator to review all the harmful effects of Kenny's actions, I might have said something like, "Several of you have expressed concerns about the harm Kenny's actions did to the reputation of the Edwards Scholars House and to various relationships. Does anyone have concerns related to anything else?" If this did not elicit any comments about Kenny's alcohol use, I might have asked directly, "Does anyone have a concern about Kenny's alcohol use?"

This approach would have been more directive than my usual approach. But, obviously, given the apparent reticence of group members to raise the issue, a different approach was needed if we were to have had any chance to effect change in this underlying problem. This experience, like all others in facilitating conferences, has taught me valuable lessons that I hope I will be able to use to benefit others in future conferences.

Chapter 7

CONFERENCING CASE STUDY: THE LOUNGE, LEG HAIR, AND LEARNING

ROANE AKCHURIN, JOYCE ESTER, PRICILLA MORI, AND AMY VAN METER

THE INCIDENT

While doing rounds through a residence hall early one weekend morning, a staff member approached a student lounge.[1] Upon entering the lounge, he saw that furniture was in disarray and that much of it was broken. Upon seeing the lounge in this condition, the staff member immediately contacted the professional staff on call. The staff member also proceeded to contact the university police department. By the time the on-call professional and police officer had arrived, many residents had gathered around the scene, trying to see what was going on. The on-call professional and police officer began questioning residents in order to find witnesses and/or those responsible for the vandalism of the lounge. The police officer deemed that the vandalism in the lounge amounted to at least $500 in damages, which meant that the incident would be considered felony vandalism. The person or persons found responsible would be facing not only university sanctions for vandalism but also criminal consequences.

A few days later, a resident, Steve, came forward to the police with information regarding the incident. Steve told the police that he knew who was responsible but did not want to be considered a snitch or get the residents in trouble. While talking with Steve, the police officer began to believe that he knew more about the incident than he was revealing. Steve continued to say that he was merely a witness but wanted to know what the possible outcomes were for the people responsible. He said that with this information,

---

1. This account of a restorative justice process is based on an actual case that took place at the University of California–Santa Barbara beginning in the spring of 2001. The names of the participants have been changed.

he might be able to convince those responsible to come forward and take responsibility for their actions. The police officer, believing that Steve was involved with the incident, told him it was felony vandalism and those responsible would face serious consequences. The police officer presented restorative justice as a possible option for the campus adjudication of the case. After explaining the process to Steve, the officer said that he would be willing to recommend that the felony vandalism charge be reduced to a misdemeanor charge upon completion of the restorative justice process. Steve told the police officer that he would take this information back to his friends for their decision but was very sure that they would agree with the terms set forth. The next day, Steve went to the police department and told the officer that he was the sole person responsible for the vandalism of the lounge and that he wanted to go through the restorative justice process.

Steve then went to the Housing Judicial Affairs office to admit his responsibility in the vandalism. The Judicial Affairs staff knew of Steve as he had already gone through a judicial hearing as a result of repeated policy violations. He apologized for fabricating the story of others being involved with the vandalism in the lounge. He also apologized for yet again breaking rules despite the staff's efforts to support him after his other violations. The judicial officer told Steve about the conversation that she had with his mother, who had called about the most recent incident. Steve's mother said that she was very disappointed in Steve and was very concerned about the financial implications of his actions. She said that she had recently lost her job and that the family financial situation was not as stable as it once was. She hoped that restorative justice would help her son understand the impact of his actions. Steve agreed that his actions had harmed not only the community but also his family. The Judicial Officer told Steve that the restorative justice facilitators would contact him in the next few days to begin the process.

THE INTAKE

One facilitator met with Steve to do the initial intake. She talked with him about what he could expect in the restorative justice conference. She also asked him to talk him about what had happened in the lounge. Steve told her that he wasn't thinking during the incident. He and his two friends were in the lounge of the residence hall lighting their leg hair on fire. In the course of this, he accidentally lit the arm of the couch on fire. He stomped out the fire and kicked the couch, and the leg fell off. He described his pent-up aggression and how he started to break other pieces of furniture. He told the facilitator that this had "freaked him out." When asked about the loss that had been incurred, he said he knew there was financial loss to the hall but he didn't know how much. He also thought the loss would affect some of his good friends.

The facilitator talked with Steve about people that he would want in the conference. He did not want any of his other friends involved because he didn't think they really cared about the impact of the incident. He didn't want his mother involved; he said she was scared. (The facilitator thought that he may have been trying to protect his mother from a very uncomfortable situation and challenged him a bit on that point, but he insisted that he did not want his mother to be there.) He was willing to have the police officer who was involved in the investigation participate in the conference. He was also willing to have the staff member from the judicial affairs office, whom he knew personally, participate in the conference. Steve thought it made sense to have the individual from the maintenance staff who was involved in the clean-up of the lounge take part in the conference. He also thought it would make sense to have the resident director of the hall there, but it was clear that he did not have a good relationship with that person. Steve knew a resident assistant, whom he identified as a very nice person, but he did not think the incident personally affected him. When the facilitator mentioned that a student who had gone through another restorative justice conference might be invited to this conference, he thought that would be okay.

After the facilitators conferred together in a separate meeting, the conference was made up of the following people, all of whom were acceptable to Steve:

Steve (the student involved in the incident)
Clark (a member of the judicial affairs staff)
Mike (a campus police officer)
Karl (supervisor of maintenance staff of the residence hall)
Two facilitators

One of the facilitators met or talked with each member of the conference in advance, to talk with each of them about the conference model, discussing the process and what the participant might expect.

THE CONFERENCE

At the beginning of the conference, the first facilitator welcomed everyone and invited the participants to introduce themselves. She also confirmed the approximate time frame of the session. She reviewed the purpose of the conference and led a brief discussion about ground rules for the process. The participants agreed to confidentiality and not to interrupt one another. Steve was asked to begin by telling what he was thinking at the time of the incident, what occurred, and how he believed that others were affected.

Steve reported that he was "not thinking" at the time of the incident. The evening of the incident, he and a couple of friends had been drinking. They were outside the residence hall wrestling. The resident assistant told them that they were too loud and asked them to go inside. They went into one of the residence hall lounges and started playing with a lighter, and lighting their leg hairs on fire. In the process of this, the side of one of the couches caught on fire. They laughed when they saw the flames and kicked out the fire. From there, Steve started breaking furniture in the room. He said he felt a release of pressure when he started breaking things. He left the residence hall and moved to a friend's house the next day. He went home the week after that.

When asked who he believed was affected by his actions, he said that he knew Karl, the maintenance staff supervisor, had been affected because he had to clean up the mess that Steve made. He thought Mike, the police officer, had been affected because Mike generally did not want to see incidents like these happen anywhere in the community. Steve thought that Clark, the judicial officer, had been personally hurt more than the others because he had worked with Steve through other incidents and had supported him in making better choices. Steve knew he had let Clark down.

Members of the conference then described how they had been affected by Steve's actions. Karl described how the incident affected him and his staff. Their work schedule was already very busy, and cleaning the lounge had required them to take on an additional workload. The lounge had to be closed, which impacted the students who could not study in the lounge. Karl asked Steve if he thought his actions were related to misdirected anger. Steve responded that he had a lot of bottled-up anger. At home there were outlets, such as work and surfing. At school, he enjoyed classes, but he was bored in the residence halls and felt that he had less opportunity to release his emotions.

Karl suggested that it might help to talk when issues came up. He encouraged Steve to learn from the current situation. He noted Steve's energy and hoped that Steve would focus that energy in positive ways instead of ways that were destructive to the community. Karl observed that the destruction not only was physical but also harmed Steve's relationships with staff and other residents.

Mike described how he was affected by the incident. When someone called him to report the incident, he was already busy, so it added to his already heavy workload. Mike described how Steve initially denied any involvement when Mike had asked him directly about it and how Steve called later that day and admitted his involvement. Mike felt that Steve had not been respectful of his time and energy. The total incident involved 3 to 4 hours of Mike's time, including time at the scene, documenting the incident, and sharing the report with his supervisor. Mike also knew that other students in the lounge that morning were upset by the vandalism and were extremely concerned that they would end up paying for the cost of the repairs.

Clark described how the incident affected him. He was personally disappointed in Steve because he had stood up for him on previous occasions when Steve had pushed the limits in the residence hall. Clark felt that he had already been an advocate for Steve. He described how others had already been kicked out of the residence hall for their behavior, and that they deserved it, but that he had gone to bat for Steve. Clark asked Steve how his behavior would change. He wanted to trust him but was not sure if he would be able to.

Steve said that the incident hurt his parents unbelievably. His mother thought that she was going to have to supervise him constantly and was very discouraged. Steve told the members of the conference that after this incident, his parents asked him not to drink. Although he enjoyed beer, he was currently honoring their request. Steve told the conference members that he was going to be seeing a counselor the following summer due to his use of alcohol and the way it affected how he dealt with his anger.

While Steve told the rest of the conference members that he did not feel attached to the community at large, he was willing to think creatively about ways that he could repair the harm that he had done as he understood it from those in the conference.

THE AGREEMENT

The final agreement, which was accepted by all the members of the conference, consisted of the following:

1. Complete an evaluation of the restorative justice process
2. Pay for damages (parents will pay initially and Steve will repay parents)
3. Move out and not return to the residence hall
4. Spend 100 hours on campus during the 2002–2003 school year working with Facilities Management or Housing cleaning up messes other people have created (which may include an assignment to talk with peers in residence hall having similar experiences with damage/alcohol if those in leadership identify the need)
5. Spend 8 hours working with Clark on various programming issues for students in the halls

6. Attend 30 Alcoholics Anonymous meetings during the 2002–2003 school year and have attendance verified
7. Attend 1-hour meeting in 1 year with as many conference members as available to review the impact of the restorative justice process
8. Coordinate activities of the agreement with one of the facilitators, and
9. Participate in a future restorative justice conference on campus

Steve completed his final evaluation by saying he thought the process was fair and that he appreciated the time everyone had taken out of his or her schedules for him.

THE FOLLOW-UP

Given the extent of the agreement the conference had created with Steve, one of the facilitators agreed to spend time during the following academic year working with him to make sure that he successfully completed the agreement. Before Steve left for the summer, he and the facilitator met to make sure that he got the final bill for the damages in the residence hall lounge. They agreed to meet again in the fall when Steve returned to campus.

Upon his return in the fall, Steve and the facilitator met to devise a plan of action to best accomplish the agreement. Steve told the facilitator that if he was able to complete his agreements by spring quarter (March), his parents were going to allow him to study abroad in Italy. They decided to meet once per month to check on his progress.

Steve first needed to meet with the custodial supervisor in the residence halls to set up his 100 hours of service. Because Steve was continuing to repay his parents for the damages to the lounge, he was going to request that he be paid for the time he worked. The facilitator encouraged him to negotiate this with the supervisor for whom he would be working. Steve would need to work an average of 10 hours per week to accomplish this part of the agreement by spring quarter. After Steve was hired by Housing, he arranged to have a copy of his hours e-mailed to the facilitator once per month by his supervisor.

Steve then contacted the local Alcoholics Anonymous chapter to learn where the closest and most convenient meetings were held. He found one on campus at noon, which fit both his work and school schedules and occasionally went to other meetings to fulfill his 30 meeting attendance requirement. Once a month, Steve would show the facilitator his card that was signed by the coordinator of the meeting with the dates and times of the meetings he had attended.

He met with Clark to plan what he would be doing with his 8 hours of programming. Clark worked with a men's group on campus, and one of Steve's tasks would be speaking with male freshman students about drinking.

The monthly meetings Steve and the facilitator had were an opportunity to talk about how Steve was doing and his progress on the agreement he made with the conference. He told stories of being in the residence hall and some of the difficulties he was having with the AA meetings. Some of the other discussions centered on dealing with being around some of his friends who drank excessively and the choices he was making not to drink as much. The facilitator was not sure that Steve thought he had a drinking problem but knew he was attending AA meetings and thinking seriously about it.

Steve's relationship with Clark was becoming important in his life. They had spent some time together over the summer and fall surfing and talking. Steve really looked up to Clark. He talked to the group of freshmen that Clark was working with about drinking and its consequences in his own life, encouraging them to think carefully about the choices they make.

As it got close to the end of winter quarter, Steve still had some cleaning hours to complete in the residence hall. The facilitator suggested to Steve that he ask the members of the conference if all 100 would need to be completed to consider the agreement fulfilled. Steve needed to satisfy the agreement in order for his parents to support his time in Italy. Most of the members of the conference wanted Steve to complete all 100 hours of cleaning work in the residence halls, so he worked to fulfill the agreement. The members of the conference agreed that Steve would not need to meet with the entire group again in June, as Steve would still be in Italy.

The facilitator who supported Steve through completing the agreement he made with his restorative justice conference believes that the process made a profound difference in Steve's life, especially in light of his goal of being able to study abroad in Italy. Without the restorative justice process, Steve would have limited his opportunity to study abroad because of involvement in the criminal justice system and the potential unwillingness of his parents to support him after the choices he made in the lounge that night.

Clark was killed in a car accident while Steve was in Italy. This was very difficult for Steve, who is working with people on campus to create an annual surfing contest in honor of Clark.

Chapter 8

APPLICATIONS OF MEDIATION
IN THE CAMPUS COMMUNITY

WILLIAM C. WARTERS

INTRODUCTION

For more than 20 years now, colleges and universities have been experimenting with mediation and other face-to-face third-party neutral processes for resolving student (and staff and faculty) conflicts. There has been a steady growth in formalized campus mediation programs, with the number more than doubling every five years since 1980. In this chapter, I review this trend, explore some of the underlying values that help drive it, and describe some of the current forms that campus mediation takes. In addition, I point the reader to some key resources that are making it easier for colleges and universities to add mediation to their repertoire of problem-solving techniques.

CAMPUS MEDIATION AND COMMUNITY BUILDING

The concepts of mediation and community are intimately and perhaps irrevocably connected. Auerbach (1983), in his study of informal dispute resolution methods in colonial North America, argues that informal methods of dispute resolution serve to sustain local communities and that "law begins where community ends." The most effective campus mediators get this connection between methods of conflict resolution and healthy communities. They approach colleges as unique learning communities that are inhabited by complex sets of diverse and yet interdependent actors. They understand the importance to their work of attending to the local cultures and patterns of behavior that the various campus subcultures develop over time. They are aware that the most revealing stories, the stories that help define the perceived character of the community and the spirit of the people within it, are quite often the stories told as people work their way through a conflict. Forums that invite people to tell their stories and share their perceptions in nonconfrontational ways are thus essential.

Unfortunately, since the late 1970s, published statements decrying the lack of civility and caring community on college campuses have been common. During the 1980s, concern about a lack of community on campus came to the fore of public attention, driven by an apparent increase in the number of campus conflicts over race, ethnicity, and gender. In the spring of 1988, PBS Television aired a FRONTLINE documentary entitled "Racism 101" that explored the disturbing increase in racial incidents and violence on America's college campuses. In this documentary attitudes and actions of black and white students alike revealed increasing tensions at some of the country's best universities.

Acknowledging the general lack of compassionate community on campus, in 1989 the Carnegie Foundation for the Advancement of Teaching commissioned a report on the topic to be written by Ernest Boyer. Boyer (1990) surveyed a broad range of campus leaders and subsequently developed recommendations for rebuilding the fabric of community on campus. Research conducted for the report had found that 68 percent of presidents of large research and doctoral institutions thought that race relations were a problem on their campus, with the average across all types of institutions being closer to 25 percent. Approximately 50 percent of chief student affairs officers at all the institutions surveyed thought that conflict resolution workshops were now "very important," with an additional 35 percent saying they were somewhat important. A full 77 percent thought that developing better procedures for handling complaints and grievances was between somewhat important and very important for their institutions. The Boyer report, entitled *Campus Life: In Search of Community* was released in 1990 and suggested a need to better envision, share, and strengthen a number of key elements of college and university life. As Boyer describes the ideal state,

- First, a college or university is an educationally purposeful community where faculty and students share academic goals and work together to strengthen teaching and learning on campus;
- Second, a college or university is an open community where freedom of expression is uncompromisingly protected and where civility is powerfully affirmed;
- Third, a college or university is a just community where the sacredness of the person is honored and diversity is pursued;
- Fourth, a college or university is a disciplined community where individuals accept their obligations to the group;

- Fifth, a college or university is a caring community where the well-being of each member is sensitively supported and service to others is encouraged; and
- Sixth, a college or university is a celebrative community where the heritage of the institution is remembered and where rituals affirming tradition are widely shared (Boyer, 1990, pp. 7–8)

THE EMERGENCE OF CAMPUS
MEDIATION PROGRAMS

Mediation services, which provide valuable forums for rebuilding, sustaining, and/or engendering anew feelings of community and group resiliency, began appearing in campus settings in the late 1970s and early 1980s. Many of the initial experiments with campus mediation were directly influenced by distinctly community-oriented mediation initiatives such as the San Francisco Community Boards Program. The Community Boards model relied heavily on empowering trained volunteers from the local "neighborhoods" being served to run the programs and do the outreach needed to make them relevant. A core part of the philosophy, to which I still ascribe, was that the very process of developing a grassroots-based program provided an important community-building function in and of itself.

The earliest campus mediation programs were located at places such as the University of Massachusetts–Amherst, the University of Hawaii, and Oberlin and Grinnell Colleges. Most of the initial efforts served primarily students, but over time programs emerged that served the full campus population of staff, faculty, and administrators. With help from the early experiments and the availability of a technical support manual entitled *Peaceful Persuasion* published by the Legal Studies Program at the University of Massachusetts, administrative support for campus mediation gradually expanded. By the spring of 1990, sufficient interest in campus mediation had developed to support a national conference, and in March of that year the first National Conference on Campus Mediation Programs was hosted by the Campus Mediation Center at Syracuse University. In subsequent years, national campus mediation conferences were held at the University of Waterloo in Ontario, the University of Oregon, and St. Mary's University in Texas. The annual campus mediation conference merged with the National Association for Mediation in Education (NAME) in 1994. NAME, which formerly focused on K–12 programs, expanded their mandate by establishing a Committee on Higher Education, including a regular newsletter section on higher education activities, and sponsoring a track of higher education workshops at their annual conference. The merger trend continued, and in late 1995, NAME merged with the National Institute for Dispute Resolution (NIDR) to became the Conflict Resolution Education Network (CREnet). CREnet has since joined forces with the Academy of Family Mediators (AFM) and the Society for Professionals in Dispute Resolution (SPIDR) to form the Association for Conflict Resolution (ACR). The Education Section within ACR continues to carry the torch for conflict resolution work in educational settings.

In terms of the spread of mediation programs, it was during the 1990s that mediation and conflict resolution programs began appearing more rapidly on campuses all across the country, moving from 18 specialized campus mediation programs visible in 1990 to approximately 220 by the end of 1999 (Warters, 2000). The Association of Student Judicial Affairs (ASJA), which was established in 1987 to deal with the increasing complexity of student judicial processes, passed a resolution in 1994 supporting the use of mediation as an adjunct to campus judicial processes that helped further the growth trend.

MODELS OF MEDIATION ON CAMPUS

Perhaps unavoidably, the word *mediation* itself has many different and sometimes conflicting connotations. For the purposes of this chapter I define mediation broadly as conciliatory interventions by a party (or parties) not directly involved in a problem or dispute, who works with the involved parties to facilitate the development of a shared and mutually acceptable understanding of and solution to the problem. The traditional mediator plays a neutral role, making no judgments as to the guilt or innocence, rightness or wrongness, of the parties participating in the mediation session. As we will see, the actual practice of mediation in higher education varies tremendously with regard to the degree of formality or informality, the openness of the process, the amount of time the parties spend face-to-face, the type of person(s) chosen to intervene, and the relative emphasis placed on increased understanding, problem-solving, transformation (both individual and systemic), and settlement. There are also important distinctions between regular mediation and a more restorative justice–oriented form known as Victim Offender Mediation that dispenses with neutrality with respect to who was the victim and who was the offender in the conflict. This distinction is spelled out in greater detail below.

In terms of staffing a mediation session, co-mediation (the use of two mediators to run a session) is currently the most common intervention model. Most often this involves mixed pairs of students and staff, staff and faculty, or undergraduate and graduate students serving together as mediators. Panel and single mediator models are used as well, but to a lesser extent. It appears that the additional amount of work and time involved in scheduling panels and the challenges of teaching the panel to work together as a coordinated team have been a deterrent to the broader adoption of panel models of mediation. The single mediator model, while easier to manage in some ways, is not as desirable because it does not provide for as many learning opportunities for mediators in training and because it limits a program's ability to model diversity during their sessions.

There are various "styles" of mediation that are used, based on the training the mediators have received, their backgrounds, and the types of cases handled. These differing approaches are given labels that are perhaps best understood as the endpoints on various behavioral or style continuums. For instance, a mediator's style can currently be described as being more of a bargaining vs. therapeutic style, or problem-solving vs. transformative, evaluative vs. facilitative, and settlement-oriented vs. restorative, among other terms.

The traditional mediation process is organized around a series of phases or stages that help define the flow of the session. Typically the face-to-face mediation work of a session is done all in one sitting within a span of about 2 hours. The model that I use when training new mediators is not atypical and adopts the framework presented here.

The Process of Mediation—Overview

I. **Setting the Stage**
    Mediator's Role: prepare environment, do introductions, explain
    process and ground rules, share expectations
    Participant's Role: arrive, get settled, review expectations, agree to
    ground rules, ask questions to clarify process

II. **Uninterrupted Time**
    Mediator's Role: listen to each party; manage proces
    Participant's Role: describe conflict in own terms; speak of both content and emotions in conflict

III. **Focusing the Issues**
    Mediator's Role: summarize and clarify main issues; ask for verification
    that these are the issues to be discussed
    Participant's Role: agree or modify summary of issues; agree on list of
    issues to be discussed

IV. **The Exchange**
    Mediator's Role: encourage dialogue on issues, encouraging parties to
    speak to each other; listen for points of agreement and non-mediatable issues
    Participant's Role: speak to each other about selected issues; provide
    questions and information to help dialogue

V. Generating Potential Solutions

Mediator's Role: summarize mediatable issues; facilitate brainstorming and problem solving; perhaps caucus to support movement toward agreement

Participant's Role: accept responsibility regarding conflict choices; generate potential solutions; consider interests, not just positions

VI. Agreement Building and Writing

Mediator's Role: specify points of agreement; provide a "reality check" when necessary; write down terms of agreement in plain, specific language; wrap-up

Participant's Role: negotiate in good faith; work toward a mutually agreeable solution; develop written agreements if appropriate

Various mediation models may have more or fewer stages, but in general the flow and core tasks tend to be similar. Some training models build in separate caucus sessions (private meetings) with each party as part of their core process, whereas others (like the aforementioned) only use caucuses on an "as needed" basis. Transformative mediators seek to have the parties maintain significant control over the session's flow and the topics addressed, and thus tend to avoid adhering to a particular phase or stage structure when it may limit or constrain the parties.

Campus mediation programs have not adopted a standardized service delivery model. This diversity in design is largely due to the wide range of campus environments where these programs are based, each with its own unique characteristics. Effectively functioning mediation programs exist across the full spectrum of higher education settings, in public and private institutions, at large research universities, small liberal arts colleges, community colleges, and in unionized and non-unionized environments (Warters and Hedeen, 1991; Holton and Warters, 1995). This breadth of formats means that many diverse examples of program design are now available for emulation. Programs organizational homes can be found in campus locations as varied as:

- counseling centers
- ombudsperson's offices
- student government organizations
- academic programs
- research clinics
- employee assistance programs
- human resource departments
- residential life programs
- deans of students offices
- campus judicial systems
- off-campus housing offices

- faculty committees
- student cooperatives

The types of cases handled by these programs vary widely as well. The kinds of issues handled include but are not limited to student-to-student disputes such as roommate or dating conflicts or lab partner conflicts, organizational or intergroup disputes, neighborhood conflicts, staff peer and supervisor/supervisee conflicts, sexual harassment disputes, student/staff/administration disputes, internal and interdepartmental conflicts, faculty disputes, town/gown conflicts, and student protests and occupations.

In terms of organizational structure, a variety of mediation service delivery frameworks have been developed for use in different campus environments. These basic frameworks include but are not limited to:

- peer mediation programs using cohorts of trained volunteers;
- distinct campus mediation service offices with professional staff;
- campus dispute resolution centers that include mediation as just part of a broader range of options including judicial boards, restorative services, and/or student legal services (sometimes called the multi-door courthouse model); and
- clinical models affiliated with academic or professional training programs.

While the current campus norm involves the use of co-mediators working from and supervised by a well-established institutional office of some sort (Residence Life, Judicial Affairs, Student Life, Human Resources, etc.), this is not always the case. Peer-led programs, run by autonomous groups of students or staff, also exist and have been praised for their independence and willingness to address a broad range of concerns. My first campus mediation program development effort (ca. 1985) used a panel format run by volunteers drawn from within the Family Student Housing community at UC Santa Cruz. In preparation for this, I was trained as a mediator and trainer of mediators by the Community Boards Center for Policy and Training. It is thus no surprise that the statement of core campus mediation values that I have promoted since then closely parallels those articulated by the Community Boards program. These values speak directly to the importance of members of the broader campus sharing responsibility for the resolution of conflict with the individuals involved. A statement of these values is presented here.

Core Values for Campus Mediation Programs

The structure (collaborative and boundary-crossing) and volunteerism of a campus mediation program provides program supporters with an opportunity to convey a specific set of values to the campus community. In addition to being a conflict resolution service, the center can provide an educational experience that can be quite significant both for the disputants and for center volunteers. Some of the values that can be modeled by program participants include the following:

1. **Conflicts are part of life's experiences and have positive value.** Conflict is not the exception. It is the norm and familiar to everyone. Conflicts have meaning. When this meaning is understood disputants have an opportunity to improve and change their situation.
2. **The peaceful expression of conflict within the campus community is a positive value.** Perhaps the easiest way for a campus community to assist in the resolution of conflict is to advocate for its early and peaceful expression, not waiting until it has escalated and can no longer be avoided before taking action.
3. **Combining individual and campus/community acceptance of responsibility for a conflict is a positive value.** The campus community can demonstrate its willingness to share responsibility for conflict resolution by making available to persons in conflict a team of competent and trained volunteer community mediators. However, the mediators must place the responsibility on the disputants for the actual expression and resolution of the conflict. By building a new structure like a Mediation Center on the campus, the community is maintaining a vital mechanism for the direct expression and reduction of conflicts that maintains control in the hands of the disputing parties.
4. **The voluntary resolution of conflict between disputants is a positive value.** We can model the advantages of cooperation and mutual responsibility-taking if we keep participation strictly voluntary and work toward jointly constructed agreements that address the needs of both parties.
5. **Campus diversity and tolerance for differences are positive values.** The mediation process, especially when using co-mediators or panels, can be used to model respect for diversity, and may help provide a space where tolerance for differences can be learned by disputants.

ADDRESSING CAMPUS CONCERNS THAT TRADITIONAL MEDIATION MAY NOT BE DESIGNED FOR

Campus mediation services, with more than 20 years of experimentation behind them, have begun to really take hold on many campuses and they now provide platforms for other new approaches. Campus conflict resolvers have been active in the development and implementation of a broad range of non-mediation services that are designed to help to improve the campus climate and resolve or reduce conflict and limit its destructiveness. Examples of these kinds of creative initiatives include group facilitation services, strategic planning support, negotiation and conflict skills training workshops, training in nonviolent social protest, protest monitor teams, student election monitoring, conflict coaching sessions, construction project partnering retreats, interest-based bargaining sessions, anger management programming, town hall meetings, diversity dialogues, and a variety of other creative conflict prevention activities.

While these initiatives are quite valuable, there remain whole categories of campus disputes that are not so often addressed and that deserve greater attention. The bulk of these needy situations, which as we will note subsequently are quite common, involve cases of active misbehavior and violation of campus codes of conduct, social norms, or law. In these cases, when the violation comes to light, it often becomes clear relatively quickly that one party is the wrongdoer who has made some bad choices in their behavior. Traditional mediation, with its focus on neutrality and shared responsibility is not designed for circumstances involving identified offenders who have harmed others, often innocent victims, or contravened community policies and standards. However, a useful variant of mediation can and does address some of these situations.

Victim Offender Mediation

In contrast to more "traditional" forms of mediation, Victim Offender Mediation (VOM) is explicitly designed to deal with conflicts involving identified wrongdoers. VOM as it is widely practiced has the following goals:

1. Support the healing process of victims, by providing a safe and controlled setting for them to meet and speak with the offender on a strictly voluntary basis;
2. Allow the offender to learn about the impact of the crime on the victim and to take direct responsibility for their behavior; and
3. Provide an opportunity for the victim and offender to develop a mutually acceptable plan that addresses the harm caused by the crime.

Mark Umbreit, author of the *The Handbook of Victim Offender Mediation*, explains the key differences between traditional mediation and VOM:

> Mediation is being used in an increasing number of conflict situations, such as divorce and custody, community disputes, commercial disputes, and other civil court-related conflicts. In such settings, the parties are called 'disputants,'

with an assumption being made that they both are contributing to the conflict and therefore need to compromise in order to reach a settlement....

In victim-offender mediation, the involved parties are not "disputants." One has clearly committed a criminal offense and has admitted doing so. The other has clearly been victimized. Therefore, the issue of guilt or innocence is not mediated. Nor is there an expectation that crime victims compromise and request less than what they need to address their losses.... Victim offender mediation is primarily "dialogue driven," with the emphasis upon victim healing, offender accountability, and restoration of losses. (Umbreit 1997)

A VOM mediator's position with respect to neutrality is obviously quite different from other mediators because there are clearly defined roles regarding who was wronged and who was the wrongdoer. Victim-offender programs seldom mediate with an offender unless the offender has admitted the wrongdoing at some level or has been convicted of the offense. Without an admission or a conviction, the individual remains an "accused person" or a "defendant," but not an offender. VOM mediators most often have one or more pre-meetings with each of the parties prior to the setting of a mediation session. As a result, the mediator has a great deal of information about what happened before the mediation. One reason to do this is to protect the victim from the revictimization that might arise sitting down at the table with someone who says they did not do the harmful act or is not sorry for doing it. VOM mediators are neutral toward the individuals involved and are there for both their benefits, but they are not neutral as per the wrongdoing. While VOM is being experimented with on campus, it is not the norm and is not yet widespread. However, expanded application of it or other related restorative justice variants may turn out to be quite timely given the range of current campus concerns, noted below, that involve a clearly identified offender and victim.

Responding to Present-Day Campus Concerns

Observers of campus life today note a number of growing areas of concern, including the problem of disrespectful behavior enacted by students and faculty alike. Broad-based prevention and community-building efforts have been mounted in recent years focusing specifically on maintaining campus civility, and promoting collegiality, inclusivity, respect and interethnic coexistence. While helpful as a positive influence on the campus climate, misbehavior continues. Another area of growing concern is the amount of cheating and other forms of academic misconduct occurring on campus. In addition, public concern over racist acts, hate crime, and other violent campus crime has risen, driven in part by media coverage of dramatic but relatively infrequent incidents of severe violence. As noted by Bonnie Fisher and her colleagues in Chapter 20 of this volume, contrary to the media portrayal, the categories of campus crime that are most frequent include property theft and minor assault. Fisher and colleagues also note that sexual assault and stalking represent two current campus crime areas that are especially in need of greater attention and responsiveness. Note that all of these areas of concern involve harms that tear at the fabric of campus life and the people who live and work there.

Responding to those areas where accountability and responsibility for wrongdoing remain ambiguous present perhaps the greatest challenge to restorative justice thinkers, as these situations straddle the line between traditional mediation processes (where guilt and blame are not assessed) and victim offender models that work with participants whose roles have already been defined for them by a court. Creative application of restorative justice principles and mediation techniques can support campus response to these challenges with the Boyer community principles in mind, enabling campuses to address conflict in ways that are educational, civil, just, disciplined, caring, and (perhaps to a lesser extent) celebrative. In order to be successful however, this kind of approach to peacemaking will require close coordination between the relevant sanctioning bodies, victims' advocates, and the mediation and restorative justice service teams.

A few examples of hybrid methods being used on campus may be illustrative of the creativity and challenges involved. For instance, some campus mediation programs, such as the Oberlin Campus Dialogue Center, have worked to modify their models to increase their utility in cases involving racism, prejudice, and intolerance. Often this has meant changing the focus toward increased understanding rather than a formal and final settlement, and often changing the name of their services to something other than mediation. The University of Georgia has reworked their process for addressing allegations of academic misconduct (such as cheating or plagiarism) to good effect using a process they call a Facilitated Discussion and Hearing Model. Faculty are reporting incidents of dishonesty at a rate of at least twice as many as before the change, and cases that used to take up to three months to be heard are being resolved on average in seven days. Concerns that the policy would provide lighter sanctions for dishonesty have proven incorrect as well.

Certainly more controversial has been the use of mediation techniques to address sexual harassment on campus, and mediation or "structured negotiations" to address sexual assault cases such as the process used at the University of Virginia. Weddle (1992) sets forth six conditions prescribing the use of structured negotiation of sexual misconduct cases:

1. Both parties voluntarily agree to participate and may withdraw at any time;
2. Skilled mediators participate in the process both to assist students in reaching agreement and to balance the power dynamics;

3. The discipline system stands as a next step and enforces negotiated agreements;

4. A representative of the institution must approve the settlement before a commitment is made to the college to enforce it;

5. The parties are advised that only minimal internal documentation will be created and that records will be destroyed when both have graduated; nonetheless, both are also cautioned that the college or university cannot guarantee confidentiality in the event civil proceedings or criminal charges are initiated; and

6. Both parties are urged to confer with parents/family members and with legal counsel before entering into the mediation process. (p. 291)

In the summer of 2002, Harvard University stirred the controversy around this issue when they revised their policy with regard to investigation of charges of sexual assault. Under the new policy, students who accuse classmates of rape or sexual misconduct are required to show corroborating proof of the assault—such as physical evidence or witnesses—before the school will launch a full investigation. Previously, Harvard would investigate after receiving a complaint, and seek corroborating evidence as part of that process. If no such evidence is presented, Harvard can dismiss the complaint and refer students to an outside district attorney or to a process of "confidential mediation." The announced policy change was almost immediately challenged via a Title IX civil rights complaint filed with the U.S. Education Department's Office of Civil Rights on behalf of the Harvard Student Coalition Against Sexual Violence. The Office of Civil Rights ruled on the complaint, and did not find sufficient evidence to establish that the changes to the grievance procedures, as explained by the college staff, deprive students of access to a process providing a prompt and equitable resolution of their complaints.

Obviously this campus conflict resolution work within a community framework will not be easy or clear-cut. In his piece entitled "An Agenda of Common Caring: The Call for Community in Higher Education," E. Grady Bogue (2002) argues that in fact "Designing and nurturing a sense of community in our colleges and universities is a leadership challenge of majestic complexity." His observations appear in a recent book reporting on community-building efforts developed since the 1990 Boyer Report was released. Bogue speaks directly to the connection between how we manage conflict and the quality of campus life, and to the challenges it presents to those of us who hope to make a positive difference. As Bogue (2002) notes:

The conventional wisdom is that conflict signals individual or organizational pathology, and its presence is an alarm call to seize the nearest hose and douse the fire. This narrow view, however, misses the personal and organizational growth possibilities, the clearing-away and renewal promise that may be found in conflict. And it misses the necessity for creating conflict as an instrument to combat injustice and inequity. Leaders in any enterprise—and certainly in colleges and universities—have the responsibility to prevent unnecessary and destructive conflict, to resolve conflict that threatens the welfare and promise of either individuals or organization, and to create conflict when that instrument will serve as an instrument of growth, renewal, and justice.

Not the absence of conflict but its thoughtful orchestration is what marks the presence of campus community.

MEDIATION PROGRAM DEVELOPMENT TOOLS

Thanks to funding from the Hewlett Foundation and the Fund for the Improvement of Post Secondary Education, a wide variety of practical mediation program development tools are now available online at no cost. To find these tools, point your web browser to http://www.campus-adr.org, where you will find the Conflict Management in Higher Education Resource Center hosted by Wayne State University. The site is designed to look like a college campus, with information divided up into various buildings. Available resources include:

- the Conflict Management in Higher Education Report, a once-per-semester online journal with feature articles, resource reviews and periodical abstracts of interest to campus conflict resolvers (look for it in the Newsstand Building);
- a full mediation trainer's manual donated by mediation@MIT;
- a searchable collection of mock mediation role-plays to use in training;
- a broad collection of program development tips and sample documents;
- a searchable directory of existing campus mediation programs; and
- a program evaluation toolkit focused specifically on campus mediation initiatives.

Also available is a set of guidelines drafted by a national working group that outline institutional- and program-level best practices for conflict resolution program development. Visitors will also find a range of sample policy documents (see the Staff and Admin Building) and some sophisticated research tools (see the Main Library). The site contains a lot of content, and it continues to grow as members of the user community write articles for the Report and contribute their own role-plays and sample documents to the collection.

Mediation work on campus continues to grow and expand. However, in the overall scope of higher education, less than 20 percent of all campuses appear to have mediation services in place, so there is a lot of room for growth and development. Restorative justice approaches, applying circles and other methods, involve more people in the conflict resolution process. More of the community is being brought back into the conflict and reconciliation cycle. The campus, often described as a "loosely coupled system" begins to reweave itself in more useful patterns. Working together, the dream of rebuilding community on campus begins to look quite attainable. Despite the "majestic complexity" of the task, I think we may be up to the challenge.

References

Auerbach, Jerold S. 1983. *Justice Without Law? Resolving Disputes Without Lawyers.* New York: Oxford University Press.

Avery, Michel. 1990. "Mediation of Race-Related Conflicts on Campus." *Conciliation Quarterly* 9:5–7.

Bogue, E. Grady. 2002. "An Agenda of Common Caring: The Call for Community in Higher Education," pp. 1–20 in *Creating Campus Community: In Search of Earnest Boyer's Legacy*, edited by William M. McDonald. San Francisco: Jossey-Bass.

Boyer, Ernest L. 1990. *Campus Life: In Search of Community.* Princeton, NJ: Carnegie Foundation.

Chanda, Rajib. 2001. "Mediating University Sexual Assault." *Havard Negotiation Law Review* 6:265.

Cohen, Richard. 1999. *The School Mediator's Field Guide: Prejudice, Sexual Harassment, Large Groups and Other Daily Challenges.* Watertown, MA: School Mediation Associates.

Craddock-Bell, Debbie, and Ann R. Crowther. 2002. "A Culture of Honesty Earns a Degree of Respect: Facilitating Academic Honesty at the University of Georgia." *Conflict Management in Higher Education Report* 3(2).

Fisher, Bonnie, Kristie R. Blevins, Shannon Santana, and Francis T. Cullen. 2003. "Crime on College and University Campuses: Ivory Towers or Dangerous Places?" in *Restorative Justice on Campus*, edited by David Karp and Thom Allena.

Gadlin, Howard. 1997a. "Mediating Sexual Harassment," pp. 186–201 in *Sexual Harassment on Campus: A Guide for Administrators, Faculty and Students*, edited by Bernice Sandler and Robert J. Shoop. Needham Heights, MA: Allyn & Bacon.

————. 1997b. "UCLA Conflict Mediation Program: Tools for Bridging Diversity." *CAHRO Newsletter* October/November.

Girard, K., J. Rifkin, and A. Townley. 1985. *Peaceful Persuasion: A Guide to Creating Mediation Dispute Resolution Programs for College Campuses.* Amherst, MA: The Mediation Project.

Hoover, Eric. 2003. "Harvard's Sexual-Assault Policy Does Not Violate Students' Rights, U.S. Inquiry Concludes." in *Chronicle of Higher Education.*

Marks, J. 1996. "Whatever Happened to Civility in Academe?" p. A21 in *Chronicle of Higher Education.*

National Institute of Justice. 1997. "Restorative Justice Online Notebook." Washington, DC: United States Department of Justice.

Newman-Gonchar, Rebecca. 2002. "Civility in Higher Education." Colorado State *University Journal of Student Affairs* 11.

Paine, Anne C. 2002. "A Place to Work Things Out: Oberlin College Dialogue Center Uses Cutting-Edge Technique." *Around the Square* June: Cover story.

Robert, B. R. 1983. "Investigating the Feasibility of Community Boards on a College Campus." St. Olaf College Department of Psychology.

Rule, Colin. 1994. "Collegiate Mediation Programs: A Critical Review." *The Fourth R* 50:36–37.

Ryor, A. 1978. "Who Killed Collegiality?" *Change* 11.

Sakovich, Maria. 1983. "Conciliation Programs at Colleges and Universities: Adaptation of Community Boards to Meet Campus Needs." Community Board Center for Policy and Training.

Schneider, Alison. 1998. "Insubordination and Intimidation Signal the End of Decorum in Many Classrooms," p. A12 in *The Chronicle of Higher Education*. Washington, DC.

Shonholtz, Raymond. 1984. "Neighborhood Justice Systems: Work, Structure, and Guiding Principles." *Mediation Quarterly* 5:3–30.

Sisson, V. Shamim, and Sybil R. Todd. 1995. "Using Mediation in Response to Sexual Assault on College and University Campuses." *NASPA Journal* 32:262–269.

Slaton, C., and T. Becker. 1981. "Hawaii's Community Mediation Service: The University-Based Model of Neighborhood Justice Centers." in *Annual Meeting of American Psychological Association*. Los Angeles.

Staff. 2002. "Harvard Includes Mediation in New Sexual Assault Policy." *Conflict Management in Higher Education Report* 2(4).

Thacker, Rebecca A., Mark Stein, and Samuel J. Bresler. 1994. "Resolving Sexual Harassment Disputes Through Mediation." in *Society for Human Resource Management White Paper Series*. Alexandria, VA.

Umbreit, Mark S. 1997. "Fact Sheet: Victim Offender Mediation," p. 1. St. Paul, MN: Center for Restorative Justice and Mediation.

Warters, Bill. 2002. "Extending Campus Conflict Resolution Efforts Beyond the Mediation Table." *Conflict Management in Higher Education Report* 2(3).

Warters, William. 1998. "The History of Campus Mediation Systems: Research and Practice." in *Reflective Practice in Institutionalizing Conflict Resolution in Higher Education*. Georgia State University, Atlanta, GA: Consortium on Negotiation and Conflict Resolution.

Warters, William C. 2000. *Mediation in the Campus Community: Designing and Managing Effective Programs*. San Francisco: Jossey-Bass.

Warters, William C., and Philip Moses. 1992. "Organizational Cultures of College and University Campuses and its Impact on the Function of Campus Mediation Centers." in *Seventh New York State National Conference on Dispute Resolution*. Kenesha Lake, NY: Community Dispute Resolution Centers Program of the Unified Court System of the State of New York, Albany.

Weddle, C. J. 1992. "The case for "structured negotiation" in sexual misconduct cases." *Synthesis: Law and Policy in Higher Education* 4:291-292.

Chapter 9

MEDIATION CASE STUDY: FROM BURNT BRIDGES TO GOOD NEIGHBORS— TRANSFORMING OFF CAMPUS NEIGHBOR RELATIONS THROUGH MEDIATION AND DIALOG

BRUCE DUNCAN AND BROOKE HADWEN

BACKGROUND

Mediating neighborhood relations is one way that the University of Vermont's Office of Conflict Resolution (OCR) and the Burlington Community Support Program (BCSP) have worked together since 2000. Over the years, the role of the university in the lives of its students has shifted. As with many other colleges and universities, the traditional paternal role toward students was transformed during the student radicalism of the1960s to a more "hands off" posture that became the "norm" during the past two decades.

At the same time, during the late 1990s, many of Burlington's neighborhoods with high concentrations of students began to experience a housing shortage, along with decreases in the quality of life. Within some neighborhoods, the increased concentration of undergraduate students living off campus in traditionally more family-based neighborhoods led to clashes in lifestyles; for example, work and sleep schedule differences, late night walk-by noise, alcohol-related behavior, vandalism, and public urination contributed to a deterioration of neighbor relations and proactive direct communication about neighborhood issues.

CASE INTAKE: SEPARATE REALITIES

In our approach to mediating off-campus neighborhood conflict, the OCR staff and BCSP staff first develop an understanding of the conflict through interviews with the parties involved. Second, a decision is made as to which conflict resolution strategy best fits the situation (e.g., mediation, dialog, group conferencing). After the interviews it became clear that a history of troubling events involving previous student tenants at the Burlington Avenue address was a significant factor in contributing to the present conflict. Many of the neighbors had already reached high levels of frustration with noise and parties. Diane and Bob[1] viewed the students next door as the "problem." For the students, living off campus quickly became a frustrating and confusing experience, and they found that they were starting out on poor terms with both their neighbors and the local police assigned to the neighborhood.

BURLINGTON AVENUE: THE NEIGHBOR'S EXPERIENCE

During the mid 1990s, a series of events took place at a house on Burlington Avenue that left one neighbor especially angry, disillusioned, and hostile toward Cliff, the landlord, and the university students who lived there. Historically, party noise from Cliff's property was a constant and negative experience that upset Bob and Diane, the long-term residents and homeowners who lived adjacent to Cliff's property. They soon realized that Cliff's house was a favorite rental of members of university sports teams and clubs. It was usually rented by a group of young men and was the site of numerous "off-campus parties" that impacted the neighborhood with late night noise, vandalism, and for Bob and Diane many nights of interrupted sleep.

As Diane tells the story, one night in particular was "the spark that lit the match" that burned the bridge of civility that had existed between her husband and the "guys" next door. A party was held that resulted in one of the partygoers driving his car across their front lawn and destroying some bushes in the process. When Bob decided to confront his neighbors about the actions of one of their guests, a heated conversation followed, with threats being made and a cup of urine being thrown in Bob's face by one of the students. Bob called the landlord, Cliff, and left a very angry message on his answering machine threatening to "burn the house down" if Cliff didn't do something about his tenants. Cliff's wife, upon hearing the message, misinterpreted Bob's threat as being an arson threat to his personal home. Cliff returned Bob's message with one of his own and, in short, advised him never to call or try to communicate with him again. Meanwhile the students living next door continued to hold loud parties and in general to treat Bob and Diane rudely. During that same year, Diane and Bob became divorced

---

1. All references to identifying information such as street names, neighbors, students, and landlords have been replaced with pseudonyms for purposes of confidentiality.

and Bob moved out of the neighborhood, leaving Diane alone in her dealings with the students living next door. Eventually, after more complaints from other neighbors and the police being called to the address on numerous occasions, Cliff finally had to evict his tenants.

In the fall of 2001, within a few weeks, a new group of students moved in to Cliff's property. Diane began to experience more late night noise from a party that the students had hosted. One afternoon, she also witnessed what she believed to be an act of property destruction when she saw one of Cliff's tenants using an axe to break up a wooden structure. This contributed to Diane's fear and anxiety that the new tenants would be as disruptive as the last tenants. Later it turned out to be an old loft that was being dismantled. After one party, Diane called the Burlington police and made a noise complaint that resulted in a noise ticket and fine for her neighbors, whom she had never met face-to-face. To Diane and her neighbors, it appeared that the cycle of late night noise, parties, and property destruction was about to repeat itself.

STUDENTS' EXPERIENCE

Hearing from some friends on their sports team about the availability of a great house on Burlington Avenue, Tom, Steve, Dave, Allen, and Peter all signed a lease with Cliff and moved into their first off-campus house in the fall of 2001. Almost immediately they noticed their next-door neighbors were very "cool" toward them and often avoided direct contact with the students as they came and went. What they also experienced were frequent visits from the police, sometimes even when there was no noise coming from their address, but when parties were being held at other houses in the neighborhood. After one social gathering at their house, they received a noise ticket, which was filed, they found out later, by their next-door neighbor, Diane. The students became very upset and confused, and felt that they had been treated with prejudice by their neighbor just because they were students.

As tension began to build between the students and Diane, the relationship with the landlord was also becoming strained. The city's minimum housing inspectors were putting pressure on the landlord to make improvements to the property and the new tenants were not informed of their responsibilities to work with the landlord as these improvements were made. Each party had differing expectations about what was required to happen. In many ways, the students felt prejudged and angry at their neighbor's and landlord's lack of interest in giving them a chance to show that they could be good, responsible neighbors. They wanted to work things out, but felt isolated and unsuccessful in establishing a connection with their neighbors and their landlord.

REFERRAL AND MEDIATION

Although this situation might have been appropriate for group confer-encing, there was a lack of interest on the part of other neighbors to become directly involved in what was currently an issue between Diane and her next-door neighbors. Because the impact was primarily focused within that relationship, the mediation team decided to offer to mediate a conver-sation between the two neighbors. After a change of heart, a less direct dia-logue was facilitated that resulted in a positive shift in the level of goodwill and communication between the students and their immediate neighbor.

Cliff, the landlord, was referred to the Community Support Program, a community-based conflict resolution service based in the Burlington Police Department by the city's minimum housing inspector. The inspector became aware of these neighbor issues while working with Cliff to correct some building and property code violations. Brooke Hadwen, the coordi-nator of the Community Support Program contacted Cliff, interviewed the neighbors, and suggested a meeting with his new tenants and the neighbors to help them break the cycle of disruptive noise and lack of communication about neighborhood concerns.

At first Diane was willing to participate in the mediation directly, even though the other neighbors were not interested in attending. Then soon after the referral for mediation was made, the students had another large party and, after more lost sleep, Diane changed her mind about participat-ing in the planned mediation meeting. When asked by the mediation team about her future involvement, she indicated that she would still like to see the problem-solving process move forward and asked us to communicate her interests to her new neighbors. Her primary reason for not wanting to be present at the mediation meeting was fear for her personal safety. She saw her new neighbors as large, rowdy males, who had not been very friend-ly in their passing encounters. She was also concerned about retaliation because she had called the police and that had resulted in a ticket being issued. She suggested that Cliff meet with his tenants and the mediators to represent her concerns about their behavior and the noise.

Brooke contacted the University Office of Conflict Resolution, and Bruce Duncan, a staff mediator, worked with her to schedule a meeting with the students and their landlord to discuss Diane's concerns. While this created "a shuttle diplomacy dynamic" between the mediators and the participants, it still represented forward movement and an opening for new communi-cation about the existing issues of noise and tension between the two neigh-bors. After interviewing Diane about her concerns and experiences of her new neighbor's behavior, the co-mediators interviewed the students living next door to understand what their experience had been and any concerns that they had about living in their new neighborhood. The students reported that they had noticed the "chilly" attitude that many of their new neighbors and the local police had toward them. They were interested in the history of the previous tenants and what had happened in the neighborhood prior to their arrival. We explained that "house rage" was a real dynamic in their situation, which partially explained the high level of frustration and sensitivity of their neighbors to noise and parties.

MEDIATION MEETING WITH THE LANDLORD

After our interviews with the students, the mediation team agreed it would be helpful to get the parties together and discuss ways to improve their relationship with their neighbors and their landlord. The mediation team invited Cliff and the students to sit down and talk. We began our meeting by describing Diane's experience and summarized the history of issues with Cliff's past tenants. We discussed the importance of their taking an active role in developing a positive connection with their neighbors. We talked about their rights and responsibilities as tenants in relationship to their landlord. We then summarized the student's issues with Cliff regarding the lack of timely house repairs. Finally, we identified the specific issues of noise and the lack of communication between the students and their neighbor Diane.

Cliff stated his goal of improving communication and reducing problems that resulted in calls to him from upset neighbors as well as city officials. He also committed to making more timely repairs. We then brainstormed strategies to reduce noise and improve relations. The students generated several good ideas to demonstrate goodwill, including offering to help their neighbors with snow shoveling, heavy lifting, and yard clean-up.

To help reduce noise, they decided to eliminate large gatherings in their back yard and to remind visitors to reduce noise in coming and going to their house when they held small gatherings inside. They also decided to approach Diane and their immediate neighbors with their phone numbers and an invitation to call them directly if they experienced unwanted noise coming from their house. We ended our meeting with an agreement to share their ideas with Diane and to implement some of the ideas we came up with in the near future.

GOOD IDEAS INTO ACTION

During the next few months, the students implemented many of the ideas generated in our mediation. Diane accepted the invitation to resume direct communication with her "new neighbors" and called them one night when their stereo volume was too loud. The students began reaching out to Diane and other neighbors by offering to help with heavy lifting and to collect clothes to donate to a nearby battered women's shelter. Diane also called them for help one evening when a stranger who was intoxicated came to her front porch and frightened her. With these acts of demonstrated goodwill, Diane became open to the idea of meeting with Cliff. A meeting with Cliff and other neighbors was arranged. It was the first time Diane and Cliff had ever met face-to-face and the first time they had spoken to each other in many years. They began a constructive dialogue and discussed Cliff's application to rezone and improve his property. Diane even offered to provide supporting testimony at an upcoming zoning board hearing on Cliff's behalf.

GOOD WILL: THE FOUNDATION OF
GOOD NEIGHBORHOOD RELATIONS

The old maxim "actions speak louder than words" illustrates the power of goodwill turned into action. At the heart of this dispute was a desire by all parties to have an enjoyable living experience. The erosion of goodwill over the years, created a self-fulfilling prophecy of poor outcomes for neighbors, student tenants, and the landlord.

Through the support of a joint mediation team from the university's Office of Conflict Resolution and the Burlington Community Support Program, it was possible for the students and their neighbor Diane to reestablish communication. The connection between Cliff and his tenants also improved and resulted in repairs being made to his property. The mediation meeting created a forum for discussing the current issues and the brainstorming of positive action. Actions such as offering help to their neighbors with yard work helped restore communication. Over the next few months, positive action and goodwill transformed "burnt bridges" into new and improved avenues for neighborhood communication and better relationships between students and their neighbors.

POSTSCRIPT

Several months later, at a recent conflict resolution skills training for university sports team captains, a familiar face emerged at the end of the session; it was one of the tenants from the Burlington Avenue mediation. Allen wanted us to know he continued to have a positive experience with his neighbor Diane and had moved recently to another part of the city. He said the experience helped him realize his connection with a neighborhood and the importance of establishing good communication with his neighbors from the beginning.

It is our hope that the success on Burlington Avenue will contribute to the restoration of goodwill and quality of life in Burlington's neighborhoods where university students and long-term residents live together.

Part III

CAMPUS ISSUES AND
RESTORATIVE RESPONSES

Chapter 10

THE IMPACT OF ALCOHOL
ON CAMPUS LIFE

WILLIAM DEJONG

The misuse of alcohol is the principal social problem faced by American higher education. Analyze any major challenge faced by college and university administrators—attracting and retaining high-quality students, upholding academic standards, building a strong and vibrant community, maintaining student safety, preserving the institution's fiscal integrity—and that challenge is aggravated by student alcohol use. Summing up the growing sense of crisis, a recent report by the National Institute on Alcohol Abuse and Alcoholism (NIAAA) characterized heavy drinking by college students as "widespread, dangerous, and disruptive" (NIAAA, 2002).

In response, the past decade has seen a major shift in how college and university administrators try to prevent alcohol-related problems. For many years, their faith in education led them to rely on basic awareness programs that emphasized the dangers of heavy alcohol consumption. These efforts achieved little success (Larimer and Cronce, 2002). Increasingly, administrators are realizing that educational programs by themselves cannot produce meaningful change in the context of a campus, community, and cultural environment that promotes underage and heavy drinking (DeJong and Langenbahn, 1996). With a growing sense of urgency, but also with renewed energy, administrators are now beginning to forge campus and community coalitions that seek to change that environment, applying the recent lessons of prevention science (DeJong and Langford, 2002; NIAAA, 2002).

This is the broader context in which institutions of higher education are exploring the use of restorative justice programs to discipline students found guilty of alcohol-related offenses. I begin this chapter by describing the magnitude of alcohol problems on campus. These problems are severe, but it is important to remember that the majority of American college students are not heavy drinkers. Next, I outline the prevention philosophy of *environmental management*, which puts the focus on key environmental factors associated with higher levels of student alcohol consumption. At the root of this approach is the idea of broad-based participation, with college officials, community leaders, and students working collaboratively to engineer a campus and community environment that gives expression to community norms. Restorative justice programs can be developed as an integral part of this comprehensive approach.

STUDENT ALCOHOL CONSUMPTION

Several national surveys have found that about two in five American college students can be classified as heavy drinkers, often defined as having five or more drinks in a row at least once in the past two weeks (O'Malley and Johnston, 2002). One study estimated that 6 percent of students were alcohol-dependent, according to self-reported drinking behaviors (Knight et al., 2002). Of particular concern, one survey found that the percentage of students who said they drink "to get drunk" climbed from 40 percent in 1993 to 48 percent in 2001 (Wechsler et al., 2002c).

Student drinking patterns became somewhat more polarized during the 1990s. The percentage of students who abstain from alcohol increased from 16 percent in 1993 to 19 percent in 2001, while the percentage of students who drank heavily three or more times within a two-week period increased from 20 percent to 23 percent. At the same time, the percentage of non–heavy drinking students dropped from 40 percent to 36 percent, and the percentage of students who drank heavily only one or two times dropped from 24 percent to 22 percent (Wechsler et al., 2002c).

Several factors predict which students are most likely to be heavy drinkers. One study found that heavy drinking is more common among students who attend a four-year college rather than a two-year institution. Misuse of alcohol was also found to be more frequent among students who attend a college or university in the Northeast (Presley, Meilman, and Cashin, 1996). Other studies have shown that heavy drinking and alcohol-related problems are less common at historically black colleges and universities and at women's colleges (Presley, Meilman, and Leichliter, 2002).

Men are more likely to be heavy drinkers than women. The College Alcohol Study (CAS) defined heavy drinking for men as having five or more drinks in a row at least once in the past two weeks, and as having four or more drinks for women. According to the 2001 survey, 49 percent of men and 41 percent of women could be classified as heavy drinkers (Wechsler et al., 2002c).

White students are more likely to drink heavily. According to the CAS, 50 percent of white students were heavy drinkers in 2001. Figures for other groups were as follows: Asian/Pacific Islander, 26 percent; Black/African American, 22 percent; Hispanic/Latino, 34 percent; and Native American/Other, 34 percent (Wechsler et al., 2002c).

Several studies have confirmed that fraternity and sorority members drink greater amounts of alcohol, and do so more often, than anyone else on campus (Baer, 2002). According to the CAS, among students living in Greek society houses, 86 percent of men and 80 percent of women were heavy drinkers. Fifty-seven percent of fraternity residents and 43 percent of sorority residents were frequent heavy drinkers, meaning that they drank heavily three or more times during a two-week period (Wechsler, Kuh, and Davenport, 1996). Data from the Core Institute show that fraternity and sorority leaders are at much higher risk than other members (Cashin, Presley, and Meilman, 1998).

Despite the general perception that competitive athletes are more health-conscious than other students, athletes drink at higher rates than their nonathlete peers (Baer, 2002). One national study found that 49 percent of men who did not compete in intercollegiate athletics reported heavy drinking in the two weeks prior to the survey, compared with 57 percent of the male athletes. For women students, the difference in drinking patterns was just as disparate: 40 percent of nonathlete women reported drinking heavily in the previous two weeks compared with 48 percent of female athletes (Nelson and Wechsler, 2001).

Underage drinking is a big part of the problem. The 2001 CAS found that two of three underage students reported drinking in the previous 30 days. Students under 21 tended to drink on fewer occasions than their older peers, but they drank more per occasion and had more alcohol-related problems than students of legal drinking age. Underage students also reported that alcohol is easy to obtain, usually at little or no cost (Wechsler et al., 2002b).

CONSEQUENCES OF STUDENT DRINKING

Estimates are that alcohol is implicated in over 1,400 deaths per year among college and university students aged 18 to 24 years. Nearly 80 percent of these deaths are due to motor vehicle accidents. In addition, approximately 500,000 college students in this age range suffer alcohol-related unintentional injuries (Hingson et al., 2002).

According to a CDC's National College Health Risk Behavior Survey, in 1998 over 2 million of the nation's approximately 8 million college students drove under the influence of alcohol and over 3 million rode with a drinking driver (Hingson et al., 2002). The 2001 College Alcohol Study (CAS) found that 30 percent of students who drank said they had driven after drinking during the previous 30 days (Wechsler et al., 2002c).

Regarding sexual behavior, approximately 400,000 students each year have unprotected sex due to their use of alcohol, while more than 100,000 students are too intoxicated to know whether they consented to sexual intercourse (Hingson et al., 2002).

Research also shows that poor academic performance is highly correlated with higher levels of alcohol consumption. One national survey reported that students with an "A" average consumed an average of 3.4 drinks per week, while "B" average students consumed 4.5 drinks, "C" average students 6.1 drinks, and "D" or "F" students 9.8 drinks (Presley et al., 1996).

About 25 percent of college students report academic problems caused by alcohol use, such as earning lower grades, doing poorly on exams or papers, missing class, and falling behind in their studies (Perkins, 2002). College administrators report that large numbers of students drop out each year, many of them because drinking had interfered with their studies, a problem that has both personal and institutional ramifications (Perkins, 2002).

SECONDARY EFFECTS OF ALCOHOL USE

Heavy drinkers negatively affect their own health and safety, but also impact the physical, mental, and emotional well-being of their peers, including those who abstain or are light or moderate drinkers. The negative consequences suffered by other students are referred to as "secondary effects."

More than half of abstainers and non–heavy drinkers living in residence halls, fraternities, or sororities report that they have experienced two or more secondary effects due to another student's drinking during the academic year (Wechsler et al., 2002c). These secondary effects range in nature from small annoyances that interfere with studying to criminal behavior and serious acts of violence. Fully 60 percent of the survey respondents had their study or sleep interrupted; 48 percent had to take care of an alcohol-impaired student; 29 percent were insulted or humiliated; 19 percent had a serious argument or quarrel; 15 percent had property damaged; and 9 percent were pushed, hit, or assaulted.

Twenty percent of the survey respondents said they had experienced an unwanted sexual advance due to someone else's drinking. Among female respondents, 1 percent said they were victims of sexual assault or acquaintance rape (Wechsler et al., 2002c). In a survey of students who had been victims of some type of sexual aggression while attending college, the women reported that 68 percent of their male assailants had been drinking prior to the attack (Frintner and Rubinson, 1993). By one estimate, more than 70,000 students each year are victims of alcohol-related sexual assault or acquaintance rape (Hingson et al., 2002).

More than 600,000 students are assaulted each year by another student who had been drinking (Hingson et al., 2002). Other studies have estimated that between 50 percent and 80 percent of violence on campus is alcohol-related (Roark, 1993). One study found that 71 percent of violent acts directed toward residence hall advisors was alcohol-related (Palmer, 1996).

COMMUNITY CONSEQUENCES OF STUDENT DRINKING

Residents living near college and university campuses also experience negative consequences due to college student drinking. Research shows that those living within one mile of a campus are much more likely to report alcohol-related noise and disturbances, vandalism, public drunkenness, litter, and vomit or urination on their property than are people living more than one mile from campus (Wechsler et al., 2002a).

Neighborhoods closer to campus have a much higher density of alcohol outlets than neighborhoods farther from campus (Wechsler et al., 2002a). Fully 92 percent of people living within one mile of campus report the presence of a nearby alcohol outlet, compared to 75 percent of those living more than one mile from campus. These outlets are especially abundant near campuses with higher levels of heavy drinking on campus.

OTHER DRUG USE

There is a clear relationship between drinking and other substance use. According to the 1993 CAS, abstainers were the least likely to have used other drugs during the past year, while heavy drinkers were the most likely to have used other drugs (Wechsler et al., 1995). It is noteworthy that illicit drugs create far fewer problems on campus than alcohol, which is by far the most frequently used drug by college students.

The Monitoring the Future (MTF) study (Johnston, O'Malley, and Bachman, 2002), which is based on a survey of 1,350 college and university students, reported that 36 percent of students used marijuana on at least one occasion during 2001. Reported usage for other substances was far less frequent, with ecstasy at 9 percent, hallucinogens at 8 percent, amphetamines at 7 percent, and tranquilizers at 5 percent. Fewer than 5 percent used cocaine, barbiturates, inhalants, methamphetamine, or heroin.

The MTF study noted a significant rise in the annual use of the club drug ecstasy among college students, from less than 3 percent in 1991 to 9 percent in 2001 (Johnston et al., 2002). Other club drugs of concern, especially for their use in predatory sexual assaults, are gamma hydroxybutyrate (GHB), rohypnol, and ketamine. The news media have recently reported the use of "wet" or "fry," which are tobacco or marijuana cigarettes dipped in formaldehyde and PCP.

THE ENVIRONMENTAL MANAGEMENT APPROACH TO PREVENTION

A prevention approach known as *environmental management*, introduced by the U.S. Department of Education's Higher Education Center for Alcohol and Other Drug Prevention (HEC), is the foundation for a broad set of policies and programs to reduce alcohol problems among college students (DeJong et al., 1998; DeJong and Langford, 2002). This approach rests on the principle that the decisions young people make about alcohol use are shaped by their environment, a complex of physical, social, economic, and legal factors that affect alcohol's appeal and availability (Toomey and Wagenaar, 2002). Accordingly, the most effective and resource-efficient way of reducing substance use problems is to change that environment from one that encourages to one that discourages high-risk and underage drinking.

The HEC has identified five general types of environmental management strategies for effective prevention, each focused on a problematic aspect of typical college and university environments:

1. Offer and promote social, recreational, extracurricular, and public service options that do not include alcohol and other drugs;
2. Restrict marketing and promotion of alcoholic beverages both on and off campus;
3. Create a social, academic, and residential environment that supports health-promoting norms;
4. Limit alcohol availability both on and off campus; and
5. Develop and enforce campus policies and local, state, and federal laws.

Table 10.1 shows that all five of these categories involve a wide range of possible program and policy options.

The HEC urges campus officials to put in place an infrastructure for developing prevention programs and policies (Presidents Leadership Group, 1997). On campus, there must be a permanent task force that represents several important constituencies, including students, and that reports directly to the president. To facilitate prevention work in the surrounding community, there should be a campus/community coalition.

**Table 10.1   Strategic Objectives and Tactics
Focused on Environmental Change**

Note: Tactics can be classified according to the level of research evidence for their effectiveness, as suggested by the NIAAA Task Force on College Drinking:

Tier 1: evidence of effectiveness among college students

Tier 2: evidence of success with general populations

Tier 3: evidence of promise

Tier 4: evidence of ineffectiveness

The Task Force did not list any environmental change tactics under Tiers 1 or 4. Tactics listed under Tier 2 are identified below. The remaining tactics can be classified under Tier 3, although the Task Force did not explicitly list all of them.

Alcohol-Free Options

Problem: Many students, especially at residential colleges, have few adult responsibilities and a great deal of unstructured free time, and there are too few social and recreational options.

Strategic Objective: Offer and promote social, recreational, extracurricular, and public service options that do not include alcohol and other drugs.

Tactics (examples):

- Create new alcohol-free events
- Promote alcohol-free events and activities
- Create and publicize student service learning or volunteer activities
- Require community service work as part of the academic curriculum
- Open a student center, gym, or other alcohol-free settings
- Expand hours for student center, gym, or other alcohol-free settings
- Promote consumption of nonalcoholic beverages and food at events
- Provide greater financial support to student clubs and organizations that are substance-free

Normative Environment

Problem: Many people accept drinking and other drug use as a "normal" part of the college experience.

Strategic Objective: Create a social, academic, and residential environment that supports health-promoting norms.

Tactics (examples):

- Change college admissions procedures
- Increase academic standards
- Modify the academic schedule (e.g., increase the number of Friday classes)
- Offer a greater number of substance-free residence halls
- Increase faculty-student contact
- Employ older, salaried resident assistants
- Create a social norms marketing campaign to correct student misperceptions of drinking norms

(continued on next page)

**Table 10.1   Strategic Objectives and
Tactics Focused on Environmental Change** (continued)

Alcohol Availability

Problem: Alcohol is abundantly available to students and is inexpensive.

Strategic Objective: Limit alcohol availability both on- and off-campus.

Tactics (examples):

- Ban or restrict use of alcohol on campus
- Prohibit alcohol use in public places
- Prohibit delivery or use of kegs or other common containers on campus
- Prohibit tailgate parties
- Control or eliminate alcohol sales at sports events
- Disseminate guidelines for off-campus parties
- Install a responsible beverage service (RBS) program (Tier 2)
- Require use of registered and trained alcohol servers
- Provide training programs for both servers and managers
- Limit container size and number of servings per alcohol sales
- Restrict sales of pitchers
- Cut off sales to patrons who might otherwise become intoxicated
- Eliminate last-call announcements
- Limit number and concentration of alcohol outlets near campus (Tier 2)
- Increase costs of alcohol sales licenses
- Limit days or hours of alcohol sales
- Eliminate home delivery of alcohol purchases
- Require keg registration
- Increase state alcohol taxes (Tier 2)

Marketing and Promotion of Alcohol

Problem: Bars, restaurants, and liquor stores use aggressive promotions to target underage and other college drinkers.

Strategic Objective: Restrict marketing and promotion of alcoholic beverages both on- and off-campus.

Tactics (examples):

ON CAMPUS

- Ban or restrict alcohol advertising
- Ban or restrict alcohol industry sponsorship of on-campus events
- Limit content of party or event announcements

OFF CAMPUS

- Ban or limit alcohol advertising in the vicinity of schools
- Ban alcohol promotions with special appeal to underage drinkers
- Ban alcohol promotions that show drinking in high-risk contexts
- Require pro-health messages to counterbalance alcohol advertising
- Institute cooperative agreement to institute minimum pricing (Tier 2)
- Institute cooperative agreement to ban or restrict low-price drink specials (Tier 2)

(continued on next page)

**Table 10.1   Strategic Objectives and
Tactics Focused on Environmental Change** (continued)

Policy Development and Enforcement

Problem: Campus policies and local, state, and federal laws are not enforced consistently.

Strategic Objective: Develop and enforce campus policies and local, state, and federal laws.

Tactics (examples):

ON CAMPUS

- Revise campus alcohol and other drug (AOD) policy
- Disseminate campus AOD policies and publicize their enforcement
- Require on-campus functions to be registered
- Increase ID checks at on-campus functions
- Use decoy operations at campus pubs and on-campus functions
- Increase patrols near on-campus parties
- Increase disciplinary sanctions for violation of campus AOD policies
- Increase criminal prosecution of students for alcohol-related offenses
- Notify parents of rules violations

OFF CAMPUS

- Enforce minimum legal drinking age laws (Tier 2)
- Increase ID checks at off-campus bars and liquor stores
- Use decoy operations at retail alcohol outlets
- Enforce seller penalties for sale of liquor to minors
- Enforce penalties for possessing fake ID
- Increase patrols near off-campus parties
- Establish new DUI laws (Tier 2)
- Set legal per se limit for adult drivers at .08% BAC
- Set legal limit for drivers under age 21 at .02% BAC or lower
- Establish administrative license revocation for alcohol-impaired driving
- Increase enforcement of DUI laws (Tier 2)
- Use targeted patrols (Tier 2)
- Use sobriety checkpoints (Tier 2)
- Impose driver's license penalties for minors violating alcohol laws
- Change driver's licensing procedures and formats
- Pass ordinances to restrict open house assemblies and noise level
- Educate sellers/servers about potential legal liability

Community participation must be broad, including neighborhood residents, the business community, public health agencies, health care providers, faith-based institutions, and alcohol and other drug treatment organizations. Finally, action at the state level, including the development and operation of multiple campus/community coalitions and the development of state-level policy, can be fostered through a statewide association of academic prevention leaders (Deucher et al., 2003).

Consistent with the HEC's approach, a small but growing number of colleges are implementing population-based interventions focused on environmental change, some with apparent success. For example, led by the Albany, New York, mayor's office and officials from the University of Albany, State University of New York (SUNY), a city Committee on University and Community Relations worked with the Empire State Restaurant and Tavern Association to persuade owners of bars and restaurants in off-campus student neighborhoods to subscribe to a voluntary set of marketing and advertising guidelines. The owners agreed:

- To include a statement asking patrons to be respectful of neighborhood residents and to behave responsibly and in a civil manner when leaving the establishment;
- To eliminate low-price drink promotions, which encourage high rates of alcohol consumption;
- To emphasize the legal necessity of being 21 years of age or older, with a valid form of identification, to obtain alcohol;
- To avoid language or illustrations that promote irresponsible alcohol consumption; and
- To promote nonalcoholic beverages and food specials at the same level as alcoholic beverage specials.

Establishments that agree to the advertising code are allowed to display a Cooperating Tavern logo in their ads. The committee monitors publications to ensure compliance and works with tavern owners to revise ads that do not comply. Since the program's inception, hotline complaints about students' off-campus conduct have dropped dramatically (Gebhardt, Kaphingst, and DeJong, 2000).

Case study reports from Lehigh University (Smeaton et al., 2003), the University of Arizona (Johannessen et al., 2001), the University of Delaware (Bishop, 2000), and the University of Rhode Island (Cohen and Rogers, 1997) also suggest that environmental change strategies can help reduce alcohol-related problems among college students. In Ohio, a statewide initiative has resulted in the formation of over 30 new campus/community coalitions to pursue a similar environmental change agenda (Deucher et al., 2003). With support from the HEC, statewide initiatives based on the Ohio model are moving forward in Illinois, Maine, North Carolina, Pennsylvania, Washington, and many other states.

STATE OF THE ART IN CAMPUS-BASED PREVENTION

The state of the art in campus-based prevention is defined by *A Call to Action: Changing the Culture of Drinking at U.S. Colleges*, a report issued by the

National Institute on Alcohol Abuse and Alcoholism (NIAAA) in April 2002. The NIAAA Task Force on College Drinking—composed of college presidents, researchers, and students—conducted an extensive review of the research literature in order to provide the most current science-based information on college drinking.

The Task Force's report strongly reinforces the Higher Education Center's viewpoint that college and university administrators should take an active role in monitoring and reshaping the environmental factors that affect student drinking. *A Call to Action* organizes current programs and policies into four tiers according to the quality of research evidence that is presently available.

Tier 1: Evidence of Effectiveness Among College Students

Tier 1 strategies have two or more research studies that prove their effectiveness. Programs in this category are educational and intervention programs that target students who are alcohol-dependent or problem drinkers. A program called BASICS (Brief Alcohol Screening and Intervention for College Students), for example, uses two brief motivational interview sessions to give students feedback about their drinking and an opportunity to craft a plan for reducing their alcohol consumption (Baer et al., 1992; 2001).

The ultimate challenge is how to establish the Tier 1 intervention programs on a scale big enough to affect the behavior of large numbers of students, not just a small number of research participants. Using trained professionals to conduct one-on-one or small group sessions, as was done in the research studies, would be prohibitively expensive. One alternative might be to use peer educators. Another alternative might be a web site–based screening tool with computerized feedback and guided development of an individualized drinking reduction plan. Research is presently under way to determine the feasibility and effectiveness of these and other low-cost options.

Meanwhile, limited application of these programs using one-on-one or small group procedures is clearly warranted for students who belong to high-risk social groups (e.g., fraternities and sororities, athletics teams), are being disciplined for violating the school's alcohol policies, or have identified themselves as alcohol-dependent or problem drinkers.

Tier 2: Evidence of Success with General Populations

Several environmental change strategies for reducing alcohol-related problems have not yet been tested with college students but have been successfully used with general populations and therefore merit serious consideration.

Increased Enforcement of Minimum Legal Drinking Age

Raising the minimum legal drinking age has proved very effective, resulting in substantial decreases in alcohol consumption and alcohol-related motor vehicle accidents. This is the case even though enforcement of the "age 21" laws has been spotty. Studies do show that increased enforcement can substantially reduce sales to minors (Wagenaar and Toomey, 2002). By extension, college and community officials should seriously consider applying a variety of measures to prevent underage drinking, including cracking down on fake IDs, eliminating home delivery of alcohol, registering kegs, and so forth.

Implementation and Enforcement of Other Laws to Reduce Alcohol-Impaired Driving

As noted, the best available estimate is that nearly 80 percent of alcohol-related fatalities among college students are the result of automobile accidents (Hingson et al., 2002). In response, campus and community officials should call for state laws that will lower the legal per se limit for adult drivers to .08 percent blood alcohol concentration (BAC), set legal BAC limits for drivers under age 21 at .02 percent BAC or lower, and permit administrative license revocation after DUI arrests (DeJong and Hingson, 1998). Greater enforcement, including the use of sobriety checkpoints and targeted patrols, is also recommended.

Restrictions on Alcohol Retail Outlet Density

The density of alcohol licenses or outlets is related to alcohol consumption and alcohol-related problems, including violence, other crime, and health problems (Toomey and Wagenaar, 2002). One influential study found that both underage and older college students reported higher levels of alcohol consumption when there were larger numbers of alcohol outlets within one mile of campus (Chaloupka and Wechsler, 1996). Additional research is needed to test whether zoning and licensing regulations can be used to help reduce alcohol-related problems, but the strong correlation between outlet density and alcohol problems suggests that this approach does have merit.

Increased Prices and Excise Taxes on Alcoholic Beverages

The effect of price on alcohol consumption is well documented. Studies have shown that when the price of alcohol goes up, many alcohol-related problems, including fatal motor vehicle accidents, go down. Price variations especially affect young people, even those who are already heavy drinkers (Toomey and Wagenaar, 2002). Price rises can be brought about through increases in alcohol excise taxes. Another tactic is to work out cooperative agreements with local merchants to institute minimum pricing or to limit low-price drink specials (Gebhardt et al., 2000).

Responsible Beverage Service (RBS) Policies

RBS involves several policies to reduce alcohol sales to minors and intoxicated patrons at bars and restaurants, among them checking for proof-of-age identification, serving alcohol in smaller standard sizes, limiting the number of servings per alcohol sale, restricting sales of pitchers, promoting alcohol-free drinks and food, eliminating last-call announcements, and cutting off sales to patrons who might otherwise become intoxicated. Studies suggest that such policies—reinforced by training for both managers and staff and by compliance monitoring—can reduce inappropriate alcohol sales significantly (Saltz, 1987).

Tier 3: Evidence of Promise

The NIAAA Task Force's report identified additional program and policy ideas that make sense intuitively or seem theoretically sound but so far lack strong empirical support. These are listed in Table 10.1, along with additional promising ideas inspired by the Higher Education Center's environmental management approach. Clearly, any tactics that might serve to increase alcohol-free options, change the normative environment, reduce alcohol availability, alter alcohol marketing and promotion, or increase consistent enforcement deserve to be tried and evaluated.

Tier 4: Evidence of Ineffectiveness

The programs listed in this final category have consistently been found to be ineffective when used in isolation. Whether they might make an important contribution as part of a more comprehensive prevention program has not yet been demonstrated. Basic awareness and education programs, although a major part of prevention work on most college campuses, belong to this tier. Typical among these efforts are orientation sessions for new students; alcohol awareness weeks and other special events; and curriculum infusion, through which instructors introduce alcohol-related facts and issues into their regular academic courses. While college administrators have an obligation to make sure that students know the facts, such educational programs do not by themselves generally lead to widespread or consistent behavior change.

IMPLICATIONS OF THE NIAAA REPORT

The NIAAA Task Force's report underscores the value of a comprehensive prevention approach. There are two key elements. First, there is a need to target individual students identified as problem, at-risk, or alcohol-dependent drinkers. Required here are strategies to engage these students in appropriate screening and intervention services. Second, there is a need to target the general student population by addressing factors in the environment, both on campus and in the surrounding community, that encourage underage and dangerous drinking.

For prevention planners concerned about underage and high-risk drinking, the NIAAA Task Force's list of effective and promising approaches should serve as the departure point for crafting a comprehensive prevention program. The legal system will increasingly expect institutions of higher education to be grounded in this body of work when designing, implementing, and evaluating their prevention programs and policies (Lake, 2003).

CAMPUS/COMMUNITY COALITIONS

Community coalitions involving civic, religious, and governmental officials are now widely recognized as a key to successful prevention of alcohol and other drug problems (Bonnie and O'Connell, 2003; Hingson and Howland, 2003). Higher education officials can take the lead in forming such coalitions in their communities and moving them toward an environmental approach to prevention that focuses on policy change (Presidents Leadership Group, 1997). As noted previously, newly formed campus/community coalitions have been inspired by several community-based interventions to reduce alcohol-related problems among youth and the general adult population. Both the NIAAA Task Force's report and a newly issued report on underage drinking by the Institute of Medicine (Bonnie and O'Connell, 2003) also endorsed campus/community coalitions as the primary vehicle for pursuing this prevention agenda.

For many years, community-based prevention coalitions have made changes in state, local, and institutional policy a priority. Part of what is happening today is that campus officials are beginning to think about a similar set of prevention strategies. Where a community prevention coalition already exists, college officials should be invited to join. Where no coalition is in place, higher education officials, especially college and university presidents, can take the lead with community partners to form the coalition and move it toward an environmental management approach to prevention (DeJong and Epstein, 2000).

The planning group charged with organizing a campus and community coalition should seek broad participation of campus and community leaders. Possible choices for coalition membership include the following: (1) *campus leaders:* senior administrators, faculty and staff, students, campus police chief; (2) *business representatives:* liquor store owners, bar and restaurant owners, apartment owners; (3) *local government leaders:* elected officials, public health director, community development and zoning officials; (4) *local law enforcement officials:* municipal police chief, alcohol beverage control (ABC) officials; (5) *prevention and treatment experts:* alcohol and other drug treatment directors, community-based prevention leaders (e.g., MADD representative), community-based traffic safety leaders; and (6) *other community leaders:* neighborhood coalition leaders, faith-based organization leaders, local news media representatives.

One or more senior administrators should serve on the initial planning committee and then on the larger campus and community coalition. These administrators should strive to provide visible, consistent, and strong leadership as the coalition does its work. Later, when the coalition begins to implement its strategic plan, senior administrators will be in a unique position to ensure that the new policies and programs are understood and embraced throughout the academic institution and fully supported. Faculty and staff also have an important role to play. Their participation is vital, not only as members of the coalition, but also in giving life and substance to the new policies and programs during their day-to-day interactions with students (Ryan and DeJong, 1998).

Student participation is equally imperative. The more that students are involved with developing and implementing the prevention intervention, the more credible its policies and programs become in the eyes of other students. Failure to have visible student participation risks creating a "we vs. they" division that can undermine support for a new program. More generally, student involvement can help make the point that enforcement of school policies and state and local laws is not based on a moral condemnation of alcohol use, but on the negative consequences it can cause, not only for the drinkers themselves, but also for the broader community.

Community participation in the coalition must be broad, including neighborhood residents, the business community, public health agencies, health care providers, faith-based institutions, and alcohol and other drug treatment organizations. Depending on their point of view, community leaders may see students as valuable and welcomed customers of their businesses or as a nuisance, given to throwing loud parties on weekends, or even as a destructive menace. These potentially conflicting viewpoints can be reconciled when all segments of the community work together and eventually agree on the need to take action.

RESTORATIVE JUSTICE PROGRAMS

Restorative justice programs offer a way for offenders to provide restitution to the people they have harmed. Such programs seem especially appropriate for alcohol-related offenses when offenders have violated the norms of the community by creating a disturbance or damaging property. The victims have an opportunity to express their anger or hurt and to express what they think offenders should do to repair the harm they have caused. In turn, offenders have an opportunity to express remorse, right the wrong they have done, and begin the process of reconciliation with those they have harmed and the broader community. With many programs, no permanent record of the offense is kept after an offender successfully completes the program ("Restorative Justice," 2002).

Exactly how offenders repair harm to the community can be negotiated. One option is to have offenders be assigned to community service work that will support prevention programs and policies on campus. The list of strategic objectives and tactics in Table 10.1 suggests several alternatives. Examples include the following: (1) staffing alcohol-free social events on campus; (2) doing office work for a student service learning or community service program; (3) distributing materials for a social norms marketing campaign to correct student misperceptions of drinking norms; (4) monitoring and removing party or event announcements that violate campus regulations; (5) picking up litter after weekend parties; and 6) providing research assistance to program evaluators. With imagination, many ideas can be developed for alternative punishments that would serve both the offenders and the larger campus community.

A restorative justice program is potentially an important component of environmental management. As noted, weak or inconsistent enforcement is one of the factors that can create an alcohol culture on campus, and, generally, inadequate enforcement is more likely when the only sanctions that can be applied are relatively severe. Students will often decide not to register complaints or testify against other students. Campus police will occasionally fail to write up students for what they deem to be minor offenses. Campus judicial boards will sometimes decline to apply sanctions that might have long-term impact on an offender's future. Therefore, by expanding the range of available sanctions that can be applied, especially sanctions that are potentially healing, a restorative justice program might help bring about swifter and more consistent enforcement of the school's policies.

At a deeper level, a restorative justice program might serve to remind campus officials, faculty, and students that the school's prevention programs and policies are designed to give expression to the broader community's norms of civility, caring, and mutual respect. As noted, a new or revised prevention program should be developed by a broad-based coalition of campus- and community-based constituencies, including students. Ideally, then, the full community will participate in developing, implementing, and revising a program of environmental management, and the full community will participate in its enforcement. When this is the case, student offenders are more likely to see themselves as responding, not to an impersonal authority, but to the community to which they belong ("Restorative Justice," 2002).

References

Baer, John S. 2002. "Student Factors: Understanding Individual Variation in College Drinking." *Journal of Studies on Alcohol* Supplement 14:40–53.

Baer, John S., Daniel R. Kivlahan, Arthur W. Blume, Patrick McKnight, and G. Alan Marlatt. 2001. "Brief Intervention for Heavy Drinking College Students: Four-Year Follow-Up and Natural History." *American Journal of Public Health* 91:1310–1316.

Baer, John S., G. Alan Marlatt, Daniel R. Kivlahan, Kim Fromme, Mary E. Larimer, and Ellen Williams. 1992. "An Experimental Test of Three Methods of Alcohol Risk Reduction with Young Adults." *Journal of Consulting and Clinical Psychology* 60:974–979.

Bishop, John B. 2000. "An Environmental Approach to Combat Binge Drinking on College Campuses." *Journal of College Student Psychotherapy* 15:15–30.

Bonnie, Richard J., and Mary Ellen O'Connell (Eds). 2003. *Reducing Underage Drinking: A Collective Responsibility.* Washington, DC: National Academies Press.

Cashin, John R., Cheryl A. Presley, and Philip W. Meilman. 1998. "Alcohol Use in the Greek System: Follow the Leader?" *Journal of Studies on Alcohol* 59:63–70.

Chaloupka, Frank J., and Henry Wechsler. 1996. "Binge Drinking in College: The Impact of Price, Availability, and Alcohol Control Policies." *Contemporary Economic Policy* 14:112–124.

Cohen Fran, and David Rogers. 1997. "Effects of Alcohol Policy Change." *Journal of Alcohol and Drug Education* 42:69–82.

DeJong, William. 2001. "Finding Common Ground for Effective Campus-Based Prevention." *Psychology of Addictions* 15:292–296.

DeJong, William, and Joel C. Epstein. 2000. *Working in Partnership with Local Colleges and Universities.* Alexandria, VA: Community Anti-Drug Coalitions of America.

DeJong, William, and Ralph Hingson. 1998. "Strategies to Reduce Driving Under the Influence of Alcohol." *Annual Review of Public Health* 19:359–378.

DeJong, William, and Linda M. Langford LM. 2002. "A Typology for Campus-Based Alcohol Prevention: Moving Toward Environmental Management Strategies." *Journal of Studies on Alcohol* Supplement 14:140–147.

DeJong William, and Stacia Langenbahn. 1996. *Setting and Improving Policies for Reducing Alcohol and Other Drug Problems on Campus: A Guide for Administrators.* Washington, DC: U.S. Department of Education, Higher Education Center for Alcohol and Other Drug Prevention.

DeJong, William, Cheryl Vince-Whitman, Tom Colthurst, Maggie Cretella, Michael Gilbreath, Michael Rosati, and Karen Zweig. 1998. *Environmental Management: A Comprehensive Strategy for Reducing Alcohol and Other Drug Use on College*

Campuses. Washington, DC: U.S. Department of Education, Higher Education Center for Alcohol and Other Drug Prevention.

Deucher, Roseanne M., Constance Block, Patricia N. Harmon, Robert Swisher, Candace Peters, and William DeJong. 2003. "A Statewide Initiative to Prevent High-Risk Drinking on Ohio Campuses: An Environmental Management Case Study." *Journal of Drug Education and Awareness,* in press.

Frintner, Mary P., and Laurna Rubinson. 1993. "Acquaintance Rape: The Influence of Alcohol, Fraternity Membership, and Sports Team Membership." *Journal of Sex Education and Therapy* 19:272–284.

Gebhardt, Thomas L., Kimberly Kaphingst, and William DeJong. 2000. "A Campus-Community Coalition to Control Alcohol-Related Problems Off Campus." *Journal of American College Health* 28:211–215.

Hingson, Ralph W., Timothy Heeren, Ronda C. Zakocs, Andrea Kopstein, and Henry Wechsler. 2002. "Magnitude of Alcohol-Related Mortality and Morbidity Among U.S. College Students Ages 18–24." *Journal of Studies on Alcohol* 63:136–144.

Hingson, Ralph W., and Jonathan Howland. 2002. "Comprehensive Community Interventions to Promote Health: Implications for College-Age Drinking Problems." *Journal of Studies on Alcohol* Supplement 14:226–240.

Johannessen, Koreen, Peggy Glider, Carolyn Collins, Harry Hueston, and William DeJong. 2001. "Preventing Alcohol-Related Problems at the University of Arizona's Homecoming: An Environmental Management Case Study." *American Journal of Drug and Alcohol Abuse* 27:587–597.

Johnston, Lloyd D., Patrick M. O'Malley, and Jerald G. Bachman. 2002. *Monitoring the Future National Survey Results on Drug Use, 1975–2001. Vol. II: College Students and Adults Ages 19–40* (NIH Publication No. 02-5107). Bethesda, MD: National Institute on Drug Abuse.

Knight, John R., Henry Wechsler, Meichun Kuo, Mark Seibring, Elissa R. Weitzman, and Marc Schuckit. 2002. "Alcohol Abuse and Dependence Among U.S. College Students." *Journal of Studies on Alcohol* 63:263–270.

Lake, Peter. 2003. "Law as Prevention." *Prevention File* 18(2):5–7.

Larimer, Mary E., and Jessica M. Cronce. 2002. "Identification, Prevention, and Treatment: A Review of Individual-Focused Strategies to Reduce Problematic Alcohol Consumption by College Students." *Journal of Studies on Alcohol* Supplement 14:148–163.

National Institute on Alcohol Abuse and Alcoholism (NIAAA), Task Force of the National Advisory Council on Alcohol Abuse and Alcoholism. 2002. *A Call to Action: Changing the Culture of Drinking at U.S. Colleges.* Washington, DC: National Institutes of Health.

Nelson, Toben F., and Henry Wechsler. 2001. "Alcohol and College Athletes." *Medicine and Science in Sports and Exercise* 33:43–47.

O'Malley, Patrick M., and Lloyd D. Johnston. 2002. "Epidemiology of Alcohol and Other Drug Use Among American College Students." *Journal of Studies on Alcohol* Supplement 14:23–39.

Palmer, Carolyn J. 1996. "Violence and Other Forms of Victimization in Residence Halls: Perspectives of Resident Assistants." *Journal of College Student Development* 37:268–278.

Perkins, H. Wesley. 2002. "Surveying the Damage: A Review of Research on Consequences of Alcohol Misuse sin College Populations." *Journal of Studies on Alcohol* Supplement 14:91–100.

Presidents Leadership Group. 1997. *Be Vocal, Be Visible, Be Visionary: Recommendations for College and University Presidents on Alcohol and Other Drug Prevention.* Newton, MA: Higher Education Center for Alcohol and Other Drug Prevention.

Presley, Cheryl A., Philip W. Meilman, and Jeffrey R. Cashin. *Alcohol and Drugs on American College Campuses: Use, Consequences, and Perceptions of the Campus Environment IV, 1992–94.* Carbondale, IL: Core Institute, Southern Illinois University.

Presley, Cheryl A., Philip W. Meilman, and Jami S. Leichliter. 2002. "College Factors That Influence Drinking." *Journal of Studies on Alcohol* Supplement 14:82–90.

Restorative Justice on the New Frontier." 2002. *Prevention File* 17(2):7–9.

Roark, M. L. 1993. "Conceptualizing Campus Violence: Definitions, Underlying Factors, and Effects." *Journal of College Student Psychotherapy* 8:1–27.

Ryan, Barbara. E., and William DeJong. 1998. *Making the Link: Faculty and Prevention.* Washington, DC: U.S. Department of Education, Higher Education Center for Alcohol and Other Drug Prevention.

Saltz, Robert F. 1987. "The Roles of Bars and Restaurants in Preventing Alcohol-Impaired Driving: An Evaluation of Server Intervention. *Evaluation in Health Professions* 10:5–27.

Smeaton, John W., Madalyn B. Eadline, Brenda Egolf, and William DeJong. 2003. "Lehigh University's Project IMPACT: An Environmental Management Case Study." *Journal of Drug Education and Awareness* 1:59–75.

Toomey, Traci L., and Alexander C. Wagenaar. 2002. "Environmental Policies to Reduce College Drinking: Options and Research Findings." *Journal of Studies on Alcohol* Supplement 14:193–205.

Wagenaar, Alexander C., and Traci L. Toomey. 2002. "Effects of Minimum Drinking Age Laws: Review and Analyses of the Literature from 1960 to 2000." *Journal of Studies on Alcohol* Supplement 14:206–225.

Wechsler, Henry, George W. Dowdall, Andrea Davenport, and William DeJong. 1995. *Binge Drinking on Campus: Results of a National Study.* Washington, DC: U.S. Department of Education, Higher Education Center for Alcohol and Other Drug Prevention.

Wechsler, Henry, George Kuh, and Andrea E. Davenport. 1996. "Fraternities, Sororities and Binge Drinking: Results from a National Study of American Colleges." *National Association of Student Personnel Administrators* 33:260–279.

Wechsler, Henry, Jae E. Lee, John Hall, Alex C. Wagenaar, and Hang Lee. 2002a. "Secondhand Effects of Student Alcohol Use Reported by Neighbors of Colleges: The Role of Alcohol Outlets." *Social Sciences and Medicine* 55:425–435.

Wechsler, Henry, Jae E. Lee, Toben F. Nelson, and Meichun Kuo. 2002b "Underage College Students' Drinking Behavior, Access to Alcohol, and the Influence of Deterrence Policies: Findings from the Harvard School of Public Health College Alcohol Study." *Journal of American College Health* 50:223–236.

Wechsler, Henry, Jae E. Lee, Meichun Kuo, Mark Seibring, Toben F. Nelson, and Hang Lee. 2002c. "Trends in College Binge Drinking During a Period of Increased Prevention Efforts: Findings from 4 Harvard School of Public Health College Alcohol Study Surveys, 1993-2001." *Journal of American College Health* 50:203–217.

Chapter 11

CONFERENCING CASE STUDY: COMMUNITY ACCOUNTABILITY CONFERENCING WITH A RECALCITRANT JONATHAN

ROBERT L. MIKUS

Jonathan was a student who seemed to find trouble easily, although he believed it was trouble that ultimately found him. He was a reclusive young man, interacting with only a few close friends. These friends figured significantly in his history of making poor decisions and acting inappropriately. He was a man of few words, often answering questions with his standard "I don't know" or "Whatever. . . ." His nonverbals were just as revealing. One often thought that the subtle smirk on his face reflected his sense of personal gratification achieved by witnessing the frustration exhibited by authority figures engaged with him. As his college career progressed, it became clear that Jonathan's name would frequently cross the Judicial Officer's desk.

Violations of the Student Code of Conduct quickly added up for Jonathan. Incidents of underage consumption of alcohol, parking in unauthorized spaces, possession of an excessive quantity of alcohol, destruction of college property, possession of marijuana, and failure to comply with the directives of a college official were all dealt with in stride. His incidents were not limited to campus, having twice been cited by the local police department for alcohol-related incidents.

Along with rendering a decision of responsibility for these policy violations came a variety of judicial sanctions. The routine formal warnings, letters of apology, and suspension of parking privileges did not deter this young man from his habitual inappropriate behavior. The fines and bills for restitution of damages likewise were not effective. Community service and even more creative educational sanctions proved fruitless. Jonathan readily admitted that the Alcohol Education Class was a waste of his time and the formal Alcohol Assessment and Evaluation was unnecessary. "I have no problem with alcohol," he stated. The college had exhausted the normal judicial sanction options and strived to identify a new sanction for this young man, one that might provide an opportunity for meaningful introspection and enlightenment.

Toward spring semester's end of his junior year, Jonathan once again found himself in the office of the college Judicial Officer. A search of his residence hall room yielded a small quantity of marijuana, which Jonathan advised belonged to his girlfriend. Having accepted disciplinary probation status from a previous incident, Jonathan knew this latest incident would surely result in immediate suspension from the college. To his surprise, an alternative was offered. The Judicial Officer raised the idea of engaging in a Community Accountability Conference (CAC), a restorative justice practice. Jonathan reluctantly agreed to participate.

The Drug and Alcohol Addictions Specialist introduced the restorative justice philosophy to the Director of Residence Life. Having witnessed first-hand the value of the process, the Director of Residence Life became a trained REALJustice Family Group Conferencing facilitator and eventually secured grant funding to implement a campus CAC program.

To illustrate the commitment to the CAC program, the Chief Academic Officer willingly obliged when asked to facilitate the conference. He had been trained in REALJustice Family Group Conferencing as part of the grant-funded program. In attendance at the conference was Residence Life staff, Campus Security staff, the Judicial Officer, the Dean of Students, and the Drug and Alcohol Addictions Specialist. Jonathan asked his girlfriend to participate as his support person, and his mother traveled 2.5 hours to support her son.

Jonathan began the conference acknowledging his responsibility in this latest incident. "I should have been stronger," he stated, "and not allowed myself to be in that situation." He further expressed remorse to all the conference participants for the numerous other infractions. One by one the college staff began to express their disappointment, resentment and frustration. The Residence Life staff was frustrated, believing that Jonathan willingly engaged in inappropriate behavior without regard for other floor residents. Campus Security staff clearly thought Jonathan had overstayed his welcome at the college. They invested too much time and energy in this young man, time and energy quite likely better spent with other students in need. The Judicial Officer and Dean of Students reiterated the institution's expectations as well as their own. Studying at this institution is a privilege. Members of the community are expected to behave toward one another with civility. Personal integrity is expected of the community. Jonathan clearly had yet to embrace these expectations.

Jonathan listened as participants shared their feelings, rarely offering anything but an occasional nod of his head. The dialogue was polite, courteous, and nonthreatening to this point. Once Jonathan's mother began to express her feelings, his demeanor changed completely. Perhaps it changed because she expressed appreciation to the college staff that supported her son thus far for remaining patient and committed to addressing his needs despite his apparent lack of concern. Perhaps it was the tears that streamed down her face showing both her love of her son and her disappointment in his behavior, eliciting in Jonathan an awareness of his mother's exasperation, that she had reached the end of her rope. From this point forward, Jonathan listened more intently and responded with candor and emotion even though at times he knew his words would not endear him to his fellow conference participants.

During the contractual phase of the conference, it became clear that each participant had specific needs to be addressed. The key issues revolved around alcohol and drug treatment, sobriety, Jonathan's housing environment, and his responsibility to the college community. The most intense dialogue involved the recommendation that Jonathan engage in intensive inpatient alcohol treatment. He was fervently opposed to inpatient treatment. The subsequent discussion enabled the conference participants to understand Jonathan's fear of being "institutionalized" with heavy drug addicts and his concern about securing summer employment so he could earn money to pay his tuition. The conference participants agreed to allow the Drug and Alcohol Addictions Specialist to determine which outpatient treatment program would be appropriate. This, essentially, was the only sticking point in achieving a CAC agreement. Other points of the conference agreement included:

- Jonathan would remain sober until his graduation from the institution.
- Jonathan would perform community service in the form of speaking with local community groups (adolescents and young adults) and rehabilitation clients about his alcohol use.
- Jonathan would move off campus into the local community only if he successfully completed his treatment program (including any recommendations made during treatment). In addition, Jonathan would give careful consideration to his choice of roommate, realizing that his parents must be involved in this deliberation.
- Jonathan would have regular contact with the Drug and Alcohol Addictions Specialist.
- Jonathan's disciplinary probation would remain in effect throughout the remainder of his college career.
- Jonathan understands that failure to comply with this agreement will result in suspension from the college.

While most participants of the CAC believed the process was valuable, there remained some skepticism that Jonathan would uphold his end of the contract. He returned to the institution following completion of an alcohol treatment program during the summer. Jonathan also secured off-campus housing for the remainder of his college career. No new violations of the Student Code of Conduct occurred during the remainder of his career. Jonathan persisted through to graduation. Days before commencement he visited with the Judicial Officer, thanking him for his patience when dealing with his numerous and varied judicial infractions. Jonathan acknowledged that the CAC was a much more difficult process for him than he expected, and without having endured that emotionally charged conference, he would not have been able to appreciate all that the college staff endured while working with him.

Chapter 12

ACADEMIC INTEGRITY:
HOW WIDESPREAD IS CHEATING
AND PLAGIARISM?

Donald L. McCabe, Kenneth D. Butterfield, and Linda Klebe Treviño

INTRODUCTION

Research has demonstrated that cheating on college campuses is a widespread and growing problem (see, e.g., Crown and Spiller, 1998). This chapter reviews the recent literature on academic integrity, focusing on the prevalence and growth of college cheating and the ways in which college administrators, faculty, and students are responding. It also examines these issues in light of new data from a survey of over 18,000 students and 2,600 faculty conducted at 23 U.S. colleges and universities in the 2002–2003 academic year.

THE PREVALENCE OF COLLEGE CHEATING

The topic of student cheating at U.S. colleges and universities has been receiving increasing research attention. The vast majority of evidence suggests that cheating, which includes behaviors such as plagiarism, cheating on tests and exams, and "collaborative cheating" (i.e., when students collaborate on written assignments for which the instructor has explicitly asked for individual work), is a common problem. Data from a survey of 18,000 students and 2,600 faculty at 23 U.S. colleges and universities in the 2002–2003 academic year show that not only do a significant number of college students in the United States cheat, but also they are willing to admit to these transgressions (see Table 12.1). However, a majority of students would argue that at least some behaviors many faculty consider to be cheating (e.g., group collaboration on what faculty has assigned as individual work) are not serious.

Table 12.1 Self-Admitted Cheating—Summary Statistics (%)
2002–2003 Survey of U.S. Colleges and Universities

Behavior	Undergraduate Students[a]	Graduate Students[b]
Copied on test or exam	15%	4%
Used unauthorized crib notes	9%	3%
Helped other cheat on test or exam	10%	3%
Copied few sentences from Internet w/o citation	38%	22%
Copied few sentences from written source without citation	40%	25%
Submitted paper from term paper mill	4%	2%
Plagiarized (all or large section of paper)	9%	5%
Unpermitted collaboration on assignment	39%	20%

[a]n = 16,117. [b]n = 2,117.

Trends in College Cheating

In 1963, William Bowers conducted the first large-scale, multicampus study of academic integrity. Bowers (1964) surveyed more than 5,000 students at a diverse sample of 99 college campuses and found that at least half of those sampled had engaged in some form of academic dishonesty. This landmark study provided a baseline for later research, which has suggested that many cheating behaviors are on the rise. For example, as detailed in Table 12.2, in 1993 McCabe and Treviño (1996) surveyed students at nine large public universities from Bowers's original sample and found significant increases in the rate of self-reported cheating on tests and exams over this 30-year period and generally more modest changes in cheating on written work.

Table 12.2 Self-Admitted Cheating—1963 vs. 1993

Behavior	1963[a]	1993[b]
Copied on test or exam	26%	52%
Used unauthorized crib notes	16%	27%
Helped other cheat on test or exam	23%	37%
Copied few sentences from written source without citation	49%	54%
Plagiarized (all or large section of paper)	30%	26%
Unpermitted collaboration on assignment	11%	49%

[a]n = 455. [b]n = 1,793.

Table 12.3 shows similar data for undergraduate students from two projects that were designed to study the relationship between self-reported student cheating and academic honor codes. The first project (McCabe and

Treviño 1997) involved more than 6,000 students at 31 academic institutions and was conducted in the 1995–1996 academic year. Fourteen of these schools had traditional academic honor codes. The second study (McCabe, Treviño, and Butterfield, 2002) surveyed 2,232 students on 21 campuses. This study included nine schools with traditional academic honor codes, nine with no code, and three that had recently implemented a modified honor code. Traditional honor codes typically include unproctored exams, the use of some form of honor pledge, and a strong student role in the judicial process that addresses allegations of cheating. Many traditional codes include a provision placing some level of obligation on students to report any violations of the honor code they may observe. While modified codes rely on significant student involvement in the judicial process and emphasize the promotion of integrity among students rather than the detection and punishment of dishonesty, unproctored exams and the use of an honor pledge are often left to the instructor's option and reporting requirements generally are not mandated. In both cases, however, the underlying thrust of the honor code is to address the issue of student cheating through the development of strong community standards and the significant involvement of students in the formation and implementation of these standards. As shown in Table 12.3, research suggests that such codes have generally been more successful than non-code approaches in promoting student integrity.

Table 12.3   Self-Admitted Cheating—The Influence of Honor Codes

| Behavior | 1995–1996 | | 1999–2000 | | |
	Code[a]	No Code[b]	Code[c]	Modified Code[d]	No Code[e]
Copied on test or exam	20%	32%	15%	24%	32%
Used unauthorized crib notes	11%	17%	9%	13%	19%
Helped others cheat on test or exam	11%	23%	10%	19%	26%
Copied few sentences from Internet w/o citation	—	—	10%	12%	16%
Copied few sentences from written source without citation	32%	43%	36%	42%	45%
Submitted paper from term paper mill	—	—	3%	6%	7%
Plagiarized (all or large section of paper)	10%	20%	14%	19%	19%
Unpermitted collaboration on assignment	27%	49%	40%	43%	49%

[a]n = 2,303. [b]n = 1,970. [c]n = 1,080. [d]n = 376. [e]n = 776.

Many of the findings reviewed in Tables 12.1 through 12.3 are discussed in greater detail later in this chapter, but several important findings and their implications deserve attention here. First, a large number of college students in the United States engage in various forms of academic dishonesty. Second, honor codes, both traditional and modified, reduce student cheating. Third, cheating on large campuses, with corresponding large class sizes, appears to be particularly high (compare Table 12.2 with Tables 12.1 and 12.3). As we will argue later, this may relate to the lack of a well-developed and effectively communicated community ethic on the topic of cheating on many larger campuses. Fourth, the past few decades have seen a significant rise in the level of cheating on tests and exams (see Table 12.2). While the data on various forms of cheating on written assignments do not reflect the same trend, this may be due to a change in how students define cheating . And while one could conclude, when comparing Table 12.1 with Tables 12.2 and 12.3, that cheating has been declining more recently, this conclusion may be premature. Unlike our previous surveys, most of the data in Table 12.1 were gathered in an online survey. While assurances were given students that their responses would remain anonymous, it appears that this assurance did not have the desired effect, leading to less forthright responses. For example, one school administered the survey in both written and online forms and the self-reported level of cheating was significantly higher for those responding on the written survey. In addition, four of the 23 schools participating in this project used the written survey approach exclusively, and they also reported a significantly higher level of cheating than their peers at the 19 campuses where students completed an online survey. The one exception evident in comparing the 1999–2000 survey results in Table 12.2 with the 2002–2003 results in Table 12.1 is the sharp increase in Internet "cut and paste" plagiarism. This underscores the final major implication of our data—the impact of technology on student cheating.

Recent Developments in Cheating

Advances in communications and computer technologies have raised new issues related to academic dishonesty on many campuses. For example, in a recent case, 12 students at the University of Maryland allegedly used cell phones to cheat on a test (Argetsinger, 2003). The instructors, suspicious of previous cheating in their course, posted erroneous answers to the final exam outside the classroom where the exam was being taken before all students had completed the exam. Several students leaving the exam early discovered this posting and, believing that these were the correct answers, contacted friends still taking the exam via their cell phones and read them the posted answers. Because some cell phones are equipped with web browsers, cheaters can alternatively look up answers on the web without needing an accomplice. These issues underscore the findings of a recent survey of high school students, which indicated that the Internet is continuing to create new opportunities for plagiarism and other forms of technology-based cheating (McCabe, 2001–2002). Our recent survey suggests these problems are now an issue on our college campuses as well. For example, as shown in Table 12.3, while only 12 percent of the undergraduates responding to our 1999–2000 survey reported copying a few sentences from sources on the Internet without citation, as shown in Table 12.1, this had grown to 38 percent by 2003–2003.

HOW COLLEGE CAMPUSES ARE RESPONDING

Given that cheating appears to be on the rise, how are faculty, students, and administrators responding to this trend? We focus here on two common approaches: the deterrence approach and the ethical community-building approach.

The Deterrence Approach

One way that faculty and administrators can respond to college cheating is via a deterrence approach. The "deterrence" approach is based on the power discrepancy between faculty/administrators and the student body and focuses on exercising authority and imposing rules and sanctions. This approach assumes that students are compliant, that they generally will do what they are told, and that they are rational in the sense of pursuing their self-interest. According to this approach, administrators and faculty can reduce cheating by convincing students that if they cheat, they will be caught and punished. Empirical research has shown that faculty and administrators can deter cheating behavior through a variety of actions, including increasing the perceived certainty that cheaters will be caught and punished (e.g., by publicizing cases in which students are caught and punished), increasing understanding of the school's policies regarding appropriate and inappropriate behavior, and increasing the perceived severity of penalties (McCabe and Treviño; 1993, McCabe et al., 2002).

A deterrence method normally associated with traditional academic honor codes, involves requiring students to report their peers. Peer reporting pertains to "lateral control attempts that occur when an in-group member discloses a peer's wrongdoing to higher authorities outside the group" (Treviño and Victor, 1991). Peer reporting requirements deter cheating behavior by increasing surveillance and by increasing the perception that cheaters are likely to be detected and punished (McCabe, Treviño, and Butterfield, 2001b).

Our qualitative research offers additional student perspectives on deterrence methods (McCabe, Treviño, and Butterfield, 1999). Student comments suggest that individual faculty members can pursue many deterrence-based strategies to deter cheating in the classroom. These include clearly communicating expectations and consequences, establishing class-specific policies regarding appropriate and inappropriate conduct and encouraging students to abide by those policies, reducing cheating pressure by not grading on a strict curve, providing harsh penalties, removing the opportunity to cheat (e.g., by monitoring tests and ensuring that there is ample space between test-takers), assigning interesting and nontrivial assignments, and replacing incompetent or apathetic teaching assistants.

The Ethical Community-Building Approach

A more "aspirational" response to cheating behavior involves efforts to create an "ethical community," or a "culture of integrity and responsibility" on campus (e.g., McCabe, Treviño, and Butterfield, 2001a; Treviño and McCabe, 1994; McCabe and Treviño, 1993). In contrast to the deterrence approach, which focuses on reducing cheating behavior, theorists have argued that cheating can be addressed more effectively by attempting to build a culture of integrity (e.g., Treviño and McCabe, 1994). The ethical community-building approach differs in its assumption about the nature of college students. This approach assumes that students are social beings who will adhere to cultural values and norms. This approach focuses on moral education, the creation of normative pressures, and the promotion and development of commitment to prosocial values and norms (e.g., mutual trust, respect, supportiveness). An ethical community is one that includes clear communication of rules and standards, moral socialization of community members, and mutual respect between students and faculty (McCabe et al., 2001a). One of the more important elements of an ethical community is involving both students and faculty in an ongoing dialogue about academic integrity. Some schools do little more than tell their students where to find the school's policy on academic integrity. Schools that are attempting to foster an ethical community use orientation sessions, initiation ceremonies, or both to convey to their students the importance of academic integrity and what is expected of them as new members of the community. These actions also serve to establish role responsibilities (e.g., McCabe et al., 2001b). When an institution defines ethical behavior as part of the student's role, ethical behavior is more likely to become the norm.

When incorporated in an ethical community, approaches such as peer reporting of misconduct can be viewed through an "organizational justice" (rather than a deterrence) lens (Treviño and McCabe, 1994). Students learn that being part of an ethical community requires that the rules be upheld and they participate actively in the enforcement process. In fact, students who subscribe to the ethical community approach will say that they value being part of a community where fairness and trust prevail, and that the community is better off without members who would violate its norms.

Building an ethical community involves creating a "hidden curriculum" in which students not only receive formal ethics training, but also actively discuss ethical issues and develop moral reasoning capacity through discussion of hypothetical and real ethical dilemmas. Schools that implement a hidden curriculum may involve students in discussions about the ethical issues that arise in the day-to-day operations of an educational institution. In such an environment, messages about ethics and values are implicitly sent to and received by students throughout their college experience, both in and out of the classroom (e.g., Treviño and McCabe, 1994).

Empirical evidence supports the notion that efforts to build an ethical community can be effective in reducing cheating behavior on college campuses. One form of community building involves ensuring that students have suitable peer role models. Evidence strongly suggests that peer behavior is one of the most significant influences on student cheating behavior—more influential than deterrence-based factors such as the perceived certainty of being reported and the perceived severity of penalties (McCabe et al., 2002; McCabe and Treviño, 1993, 1997). Academic dishonesty is, to a large degree, learned from observing the behavior of peers; if students see their peers cheating, they will be more likely to cheat. Peer behavior also provides normative support for cheating—when peers are seen cheating, cheating may come to be viewed as an acceptable way of getting ahead (McCabe and Treviño, 1993). However, if students see their peers engaging in prosocial behaviors such as behaving with honesty and integrity, designing academic integrity policies, making pledges regarding personal integrity, and educating other students about the importance of academic integrity, then cheating will be less likely (McCabe et al., 2002; McCabe and Treviño, 1993). Thus, peer perceptions concerning academic dishonesty can be an important influence as students make individual decisions about cheating in the classroom.

Previous research also supports the use of other community-building techniques, including establishing a dialogue regarding academic integrity between faculty and students, clearly communicating expectations and responsibilities to students, training students to be role models of good behavior, increasing student and faculty understanding and acceptance of academic integrity policies, demonstrating that academic integrity is a clear institutional priority, and involving students in attempts to change the institution's cheating culture (e.g., McCabe et al., 2002; McCabe and Treviño, 2002, 1993).

Our qualitative work provides additional insights into how faculty can promote a culture of integrity from the students' perspective (McCabe et al., 1999). Student comments suggest that faculty can better manage cheating in the classroom by encouraging dialogue with students regarding the faculty member's academic integrity expectations. Some students discussed the idea of establishing a classroom honor code, one that places appropriate responsibilities and obligations on the student, not just the faculty member, to prevent cheating. Several students also commented on the importance of faculty being supportive. They reasoned that being supportive promotes respect, which students will reciprocate by not cheating. Other ideas included focusing on learning (not on grades) and encouraging the development of good character.

Many of these student suggestions are mirrored by research from the faculty or administrative perspective. For example, McCabe and Pavela (1997) offered 10 principles of academic integrity that faculty can pursue to reduce cheating. These principles include affirming the importance of academic integrity, fostering a love of learning, treating students as an end in themselves, fostering an environment of trust in the classroom, and encouraging student responsibility for academic integrity. Other principles include clarifying expectations for students, developing fair and relevant forms of assessment, reducing opportunities to cheat, challenging academic dishonesty when it occurs, and helping to define and support campus-wide academic integrity standards.

Honor Codes

Traditional honor codes represent a hybrid approach—one that contains elements of the deterrence approach, but is highly consistent with the ethical community-building approach. As documented in Table 12.3, research has demonstrated that academic dishonesty is significantly lower in honor code environments (McCabe, Trevino, and Butterfield, 1999, 1996; Treviño, Butterfield, and McCabe, 1998; McCabe and Treviño, 1993; Bowers, 1964). Honor codes reduce cheating behavior by (1) defining the expectations placed on students with regard to academic dishonesty; (2) placing a significant share of the responsibility for maintaining academic honesty on students rather than on faculty and/or administrators, and many students respond to this responsibility by not cheating; and (3) giving students privileges such as unproctored exams and the incentive to maintain such privileges may lead to lower levels of academic dishonesty (McCabe and Treviño 1993).

As suggested previously, honor codes do more than deter cheating—various elements of an academic honor code are also useful in building an ethical community. These elements include extending certain privileges to students, such as unproctored exams, self-scheduled exams, and participation in the judicial system. Strong honor codes not only give students the primary role in the resolution of suspected transgressions of the community's standards but also set up an expectation that community members will share responsibility for holding each other accountable to established community norms and policies (Treviño and McCabe, 1994). Honor code environments also generally allow students to play a participative role in dispute resolution, including the adjudication of cheating cases. Allowing students to participate in such processes "is potentially a powerful intervention for addressing both the ethical and citizenship education of college undergraduates" (Ignelzi, 1990).

Our qualitative work suggests that honor code students generally feel the same pressures to cheat as do non-code students (McCabe et al., 1999). The difference is that honor code students are less likely to act on those pressures or to use them to rationalize or justify cheating behavior. Honor code students tend to feel that they are part of a special community—one that places a great deal of trust in them, and in return, they must accept various responsibilities in order to maintain this trust and the various privileges associated with it (e.g., unproctored exams).

Honor codes also help to develop ethical community norms via their impact on faculty. When it comes to dealing with cheating, faculty are on the front lines and their institutions depend on their cooperation. They can choose to disregard their institutions' policies and deal with cheating on their own (as many do), or they can reinforce and support the institutional policy. Our research suggests that faculty who have experienced an honor code, either as a faculty member or as a student, generally have more positive attitudes about honor codes than faculty who lack such experience (McCabe, Butterfield, and Treviño, 2003). Our results also suggest that faculty who have experience with an honor code are more willing to share cheating-related responsibilities with students. These faculty may be more motivated to support changes to campus academic integrity policies that incorporate the basic philosophy of an honor code—especially greater student involvement in the judicial process. As we argued in that study, administrators who are considering moving toward an honor code system might turn to such faculty for assistance in leading a move toward such a system.

Whether an institution adopts a formal honor code or not, at least some of the basic elements of an honor code can make an important contribution to promoting academic integrity at any school. As argued by McCabe and Treviño (2002, p. 41), "faculty and administrators can work with students to create a campus culture where trust is higher, cheating is lower, and students learn to behave more ethically. Honor codes, both traditional and modified, seem to be effective. But we also know of several non-code colleges that have reduced academic dishonesty among students. Although they lack a formal code . . . they communicate the campus's commitment to academic integrity and make it an active topic of discussion among students and faculty to help them understand that every member of the campus community is responsible for promoting it."

Recent Developments in College Responses

There have been a number of recent developments in how college campuses are responding to cheating behavior. As noted earlier, one such development is the use of "modified honor codes." McCabe and Pavela (2000, p. 34) argue, "[c]onventional wisdom suggests it is more difficult to develop and nurture a strong sense of campus community at large universities—an important foundation on which an honor code tradition can be built." At such universities, modified honor codes represent a viable alternative, one that can bring at least some of the benefits of traditional codes (e.g., reducing cheating) to campuses where implementing a traditional honor code may not be a realistic option (McCabe, Treviño, and Butterfield, 2002). As suggested by McCabe et al. (2002, pp. 362–363), there is no single definition of what constitutes a modified honor code, but they generally focus on two strategies: "First, the institution, through any number of mechanisms (e.g., integrity rallies, presidential involvement, integrity seminars, etc.), clearly communicates to its students that academic integrity is a major institutional priority. Second, students are given a significant role both in the judicial or hearing body on campus and in developing programs to inform other students about the purposes of the code, its major components, enforcement strategies, and so on. This often includes programming to convince students that academic integrity is something to be valued. . . . [S]everal modified codes allow the possibility of unproctored exams or the use of a pledge at an instructor's option. The single most important thing modified codes may do, however, is focus a campus's attention on the issue of academic dishonesty and clearly communicate to students that integrity is an institutional priority." According to McCabe and Pavela (2000), significant student involvement may be the most important factor in developing and implementing a successful modified honor code.

Colleges with both traditional and modified honor codes are also using "signing-in ceremonies" and "pep rallies" to develop greater student commitment to their codes. At Vanderbilt, after entering students complete a mandatory orientation regarding the campus honor code, each student is asked to sign a parchment to indicate personal commitment to the code. The signed parchments for each class are prominently displayed in the university's student center as a constant public reminder of their commitment to the code. Similarly, at the University of Maryland, pep rallies have been used to garner commitment and support for, and to focus attention on, their new modified honor code. These rallies involved high-level officials, including the university's president and the state's governor, to demonstrate the university's level of commitment to academic integrity.

CONCLUSION

In this chapter, we have reviewed research on academic dishonesty. The data suggest that cheating is widespread among college students and that some types of cheating are growing (e.g., test cheating) while other types of cheating are relatively stable over time (e.g., cheating on written work). Some forms of cheating are growing rapidly, particularly those involving technology (e.g., Internet-based plagiarism). Colleges are responding to student cheating in multiple ways. Some are working to develop an ethical community of honor and trust. Others use deterrence-based approaches, based more on rules and punishment for noncompliance. Honor codes, both traditional and modified, combine elements of both approaches and have been found to be successful in reducing cheating in multiple studies.

References

Anonymous. "Berkeley: Liars Need Not Apply". March 14, 2003. cnn.com/education.

Argetsinger, Amy. January 25, 2003. "U-MD. Says Students Use Phones to Cheat: Text Messaging Delivers Test Answers". www.washingtonpost.com, p. B01.

Bowers, William. 1964. *Student Dishonesty and Its Control in College.* New York: Bureau of Applied Social Research, Columbia University.

Crown, Deborah and Shane Spiller. 1998. "Learning from the Literature on College Cheating: A Review of the Empirical Research". *Journal of Business Ethics* 17:683–700.

Ignelzi, Michael. 1990. "Ethical Education in a College Environment: The Just Community Approach." *NASPA Journal* 27:192–198.

McCabe, Donald. 2001–2002. "Cheating: Why Students Do It and How We Can Help Them Stop." *American Educator* Winter:38–43.

McCabe, Donald, and Gary Pavela. 1997. "The Principled Pursuit of Academic Integrity." *AAHE Bulletin* 50(4):11–12.

McCabe, Donald, and Gary Pavela. 2000. "Some Good News About Academic Integrity." *Change* 33(5):32–38.

McCabe, Donald, and Linda Treviño. 2002. "Honesty and Honor Codes." *Academe* 88:37–41.

McCabe, Donald, and Linda Treviño. 1997. "Individual and Contextual Influences on Academic Dishonesty: A Multi-Campus Investigation." *Research in Higher Education* 38:379–396.

McCabe, Donald, and Linda Treviño. 1996. "What We Know About Cheating in College: Longitudinal Trends and Recent Developments." *Change* 28:28–33.

McCabe, Donald and Linda Treviño. 1993. "Academic Dishonesty: Honor Codes and Other Contextual Influences." *Journal of Higher Education* 64:522–538.

McCabe, Donald, Kenneth Butterfield, and Linda Treviño. 2003. "Faculty and Academic Integrity: The Influence of Current Honor Codes and Past Honor Code Experiences." *Research in Higher Education* 44:367–385.

McCabe, Donald, Linda Treviño, and Kenneth Butterfield. 2002. "Honor Codes and Other Contextual Influences on Academic Integrity: A Replication and Extension to Modified Honor Code Settings." *Research in Higher Education* 43:357–378.

McCabe, Donald, Linda Treviño, and Kenneth Butterfield. 2001a. "Cheating in Academic Institutions: A Decade of Research." *Ethics and Behavior* 11:219–232.

McCabe, Donald, Linda Treviño, and Kenneth Butterfield. 2001b. "Dishonesty in Academic Environments: The Influence of Peer Reporting Requirements." *Journal of Higher Education* 72:29–45.

McCabe, Donald, Linda Treviño, and Kenneth Butterfield. 1999. "Academic Integrity in Honor Code and Non-Honor Code Environments: A Qualitative Investigation." *Journal of Higher Education* 70:211–234.

McCabe, Donald, Linda Treviño, and Kenneth Butterfield. 1996. "The Influence of Collegiate and Corporate Codes of Conduct on Ethics-Related Behavior in the Workplace." *Business Ethics Quarterly* 4:461–476.

Treviño, Linda, and Donald McCabe. 1994. "Meta-Learning About Business Ethics: Building Honorable Business School Communities." *Journal of Business Ethics* 13:405–416.

Treviño, Linda, and Bart Victor. 1991. "Peer Reporting of Unethical Behavior: A Social Context Perspective." *Academy of Management Journal* 35:38–64.

Chapter 13

INTEGRITY BOARD CASE STUDY: SONIA'S PLAGIARISM

Jon Ramsey

Sonia was not her actual name, and a few other details of the case have been changed to maintain the confidentiality we generally observe for integrity proceedings in an educational setting. One wonders, at the same time, how the privacy of the actors in an integrity case can be protected within the close-knit community of a small college such as ours, or perhaps even in a larger university. Keeping the issues contained among the hearing participants is not, moreover, exactly what a restorative system of justice is about. When the restorative model is applied to academic matters that have traditionally been the private domain of individual faculty dealing directly with their students, our understanding of both the judicial and the educational communities stretches toward a less privatized sense of mission and protocols. The case involving Sonia necessarily explores some of the traditional assumptions about lines of authority in a college, about individual and community responsibilities, and about the efficacy of excluding offenders from or reintegrating them into the learning community.

In the typical college judicial system, Sonia's offenses, her plagiarizing a paper in a sociology course and another paper in an English course during the last week of the same semester (and as an experienced senior student), would have resulted in a grade penalty in each course. This process would conform to the "deterrence approach" that Don McCabe and his colleagues describes in Chapter 12 of this volume. If the faculty had not reported the honor code violations to a member of the administration—and clearly many do not, regardless of faculty handbook agreements and despite the imperatives of equal justice—the issue would have ended with the student's embarrassment and contrition and the faculty members' conflicted feelings about the student's betrayal of trust and about the teachers' substitution of police work for pedagogy. If the honor code problems had been reported

136

to an administrative office, a hearing board would quickly have found Sonia guilty, would have expressed profound disappointment with her dishonesty, and would likely have suspended or dismissed her from the college. That is a relatively economical, straightforward process, and not without its virtues. The repeat offender is excluded from a community whose most important values she has subverted. She is temporarily or permanently ostracized and is presumed to learn from this penalty, and the consequence she suffers confirms and strengthens the community's allegiance to academic integrity.

Sonia experienced a different process and outcome. Since her double violation of the honor code was reported at a time when we could not assemble the students, faculty, and staff who handle most Integrity Board (IB) cases, we moved to an Administrative Hearing Board (AHB), in this particular case a panel of two faculty members and one member of student affairs. All three participants had helped bring our restorative justice system into being and were thus thoroughly familiar with the values and processes of this approach to justice. The same could have been claimed for an IB panel: The students on our IB have been formally trained in the philosophy of restorative justice (and in alternative models), and the faculty and staff members of the jury pool have been provided with less formal training.

The judicial counsel (JC) for the hearing opened with a review of the charges against Sonia (two "major offenses" of plagiarism, according to our definitions) and the supporting documents. He then led the faculty members who had reported the problems through a series of questions regarding course expectations, the nature and quality of Sonia's overall work in the course, and how the faculty members discovered and would characterize the integrity infractions. Sonia, aided by a support person from the faculty, provided an opening statement in which she readily acknowledged that she had lifted major portions of her work from web sites. Sonia also expressed regret and apologized to the two faculty whose trust she had disappointed: "As a person who prides herself on being honest and moral, admitting this mistake has been one of the hardest things I have done in my life thus far. I think what scares me the most is that there was a part of me that allowed me to make such a mistake. The regret and embarrassment I feel cannot be described."

The section of Sonia's statement quoted here suggests how far she had come in recognizing the seriousness of her actions. Her statement also carries hints of what emerged more clearly as the board members conducted a conversation with her. She had a very hard time seeing her "mistake" as an intentional dishonesty (we use similar euphemisms, I suppose, when we replace the older language of crime and punishment with "errors of judgment" divorced from volition, of "problems" without perpetrators). She spoke of herself in a dissociative way, as though an alien "part of me," an aspect of self hitherto unknown and now exorcised, had done the deed. She was also hard pressed to explain just how the web site materials had migrated into her two papers (since she could not regard herself as being purposefully dishonest) or how she might guard against dishonest labors in the future—impossible to imagine, of course, when self-reflection is somewhat divorced from doing. One wonders how the distancing effect of students' using remote, instantly accessible, often anonymous Internet resources without obvious boundaries within a vast electronic soup might contribute to this displacement from volition and discrimination. Sonia was yet another participant in the ever-growing misuse of virtual sources documented in McCabe and his colleagues' most recent research (Chapter 12).

It is worth mentioning that we hear versions of Sonia's dissociative psychology in many hearing boards. One wants to reread Camus' *The Stranger* in hope of finding clues to human events that "just happen." The inquiry conducted by the panel with Sonia and the two faculty explored her state of mind and intent more effectively than would have been true in the more behavior-oriented questioning of our traditional approach. The panel asked Sonia to examine closely her responsibility and motives, in addition to the actual process of her research and writing. Panelists also asked the faculty to describe the impact of the plagiarism on their trust of students and their future pedagogical strategies, how they felt about Sonia's actions, and what they thought the outcome of the hearing should be.

As the conversation proceeded, Sonia gradually was able to articulate a bit more clearly why and how she had committed the plagiarisms, and certainly she was impressed by the stress to which she had subjected teachers whom she admired. The central insight that emerged was Sonia's belief that she had good ideas for her papers but that "my writing just doesn't sound the way a college paper should be." Issues of self-confidence and self esteem—especially the student's perception that all the other students speak and write in a more sophisticated way—is not uncommon in college plagiarism cases. The concern was exacerbated, it appeared, by Sonia's working-class, ESL, ethnic minority background. Teachers may know that self-perceptions of this sort cut across socioeconomic categories, that many a student from a comparatively privileged background is just as lacking in self-confidence and in analytical and writing skills, but to Sonia the other students seemed confident, in the know. She never presented her feelings as an excuse, but the hearing was useful in drawing this important self-understanding into the open where it might be challenged and, over time, ameliorated.

There is no doubt that restorative justice conversations can be more time-consuming, awkward, at times more painful than the traditional judicial inquiry, which centers on evidence, behavior, and consequences. It also is easy for the restorative discussion to lapse into pop psychology, to probe too deeply into areas of psychic privacy, and to tempt the respondent to shape his or her answers according to the panelists' desires. It is our experience, however, that the benefits of these riskier discussions are more likely to clarify:

- the anger felt by victims of the offense;
- the respondent's understanding of how he or she has disappointed other community members;
- the respondent's and panelists' understanding of the forces that prompted the offense;
- how the respondent might learn and grow intellectually and personally from the transgression; and
- the steps through which the respondent might make amends and reconnect with the learning community.

I would also suggest that the restorative process, while not specifically referenced in Chapter 12 in this volume, could contribute to the "ethical community-building approach" that McCabe et al.'s research support. As he remarks, peer behavior has a strong impact on building a "culture of integrity and responsibility" (Chapter 12, p. 135). Peer behavior, both good and bad, as this case study demonstrates, is exhibited in the majority of our hearing processes, and many of the sanctions imposed require the offending student to show his or her enhanced understanding and integrity to the larger community of students. That second piece is entirely lost when the culprit is simply sent away, as happens in the strict "deterrence" model.

The restorative process is harder when the respondent cannot admit any sense of wrongdoing, even when the evidence points clearly in that direction. In some academic cases, where the documents tell an obvious tale, respondent denials are mind-boggling. Panelists do, however, take denials into account as they consider whether reintegration with the community is possible or desirable for the offender. Panelists must be careful not to force faked confessions and contrition. Still, moving a conversation of this type toward consensus is difficult when the core assessment of guilt or innocence remains in dispute.

Since Sonia had acknowledged her responsibility for the two plagiarisms even before the hearing began, the discussion moved smoothly from reasons and impact toward consequences and next steps. This is also an awkward part of the process, in that victims, perpetrators, and panelists all participate in deciding what should happen next, whereas the traditional process empowers the jury to decide, in private, all the issues. Inevitably the discussants will harbor different views on the severity of the academic offense, the degree to which the academic community should tolerate subversion of its core values, the extent of the respondent's improved understanding and commitment, and what restorative steps, if any, are justified by the case, would promote the respondent's growth, satisfy the offended community, and possibly further the education of both respondent and community.

We were on the cusp of our May commencement ceremonies, and Sonia had actually completed all degree requirements (the two faculty members had turned in poor but passing grades). The first question was whether Sonia could process with her class. The group decided that she could do so but with the asterisk applied to students who have remaining degree requirements. Before commencement she also needed to write letters of apology to the faculty in whose courses she had cheated. Two remaining steps were more complicated: Sonia agreed to resubmit the two papers by an August deadline, papers rewritten to show that she had mastered the appropriate use of sources; she was also required to design and present a program on plagiarism to the college community during the subsequent (fall) semester. The stipulations seemed to complement the grade penalties with apologies, evidence of intellectual growth, and an educational service to the community.

Sonia completed the apologies and rewrote the papers on time, but one of the faculty found her resubmitted paper (on a new topic) unacceptable. There was no evidence of cheating in the paper, but the intellectual content was not very strong and the accuracy and consistency of the citations were faulty. The faculty member washed his hands of any further involvement but allowed that others could draw their own conclusions. Even more problematic, a series of failed communications and delays, largely on Sonia's part, dragged out the preparation of her integrity presentation well into the spring semester. We actually withdrew her from the college and withheld her degree until the time when she might complete all the stipulations.

We had not anticipated just what we would do, and who would carry the authority, if Sonia failed to meet one or more stipulations by the deadlines or to present work of acceptable quality. Nor had we been clear among ourselves about the "quality" criteria we would use for the resubmitted papers or for the presentation. Were the stipulations too multilayered in the first place? Was Sonia up to the tasks we had set for her? What would we do if a faculty member who was key to the restorative outcome could not approve his part of the process? How often, if at all, would we draw a new line in the sand with respect to deadlines? How tough were we willing to be with a student who had in fact completed all requirements for the bachelor's degree but who had not met the integrity expectations?

Unresolved questions and unanticipated delays occupied an extraordinary amount of faculty and staff time before the case finally concluded; even Sonia's support person, whose ongoing role was to guide her in preparing the presentation, was fed up with her and irritated by others who, in his view, prolonged the agony and hesitated to let Sonia suffer the consequences of her inaction after the hearing. These are eventualities that every school undertaking a restorative process should anticipate. In theory, a student who does not complete stipulations is "self-suspended" as a member of the community; that being said, does the respondent's partial or complete failure lead to a decisive conclusion or only to further restorative options?

About a year after the original hearing, Sonia's case did resolve productively, and most of us involved thought that the results for both Sonia and the college community repaid our investment. It was clear from Sonia's presentation on integrity that she had progressed well beyond the level of understanding she had displayed during the hearing. She had prepared PowerPoint materials that, with some refinement, would prove useful to future presentations to our students—thus, as McCabe et al. (Chapter 12) suggest, her restorative sanctions would help educate "other students about the importance of academic integrity" (Chapter 12, p. 136). Her appreciation for the rigors of intellectual inquiry was sharpened. Her remorse over what she had done was, if anything, too intense and self-flagellating, but at least she had avoided our easy ability to construct a self-serving rationale. Her audience, composed largely of those who had participated in her hearing and its aftermath, were gratified as educators to witness her growth and to award her college degree.

Sonia's case, which occurred at an early point in our experience with restorative justice as applied to academic infractions, satisfied the punitive, retributive impulses of the traditional judicial system and, in keeping with that model, also vindicated the community's allegiance to the honor code. The philosophy and process we used with Sonia, however, also accomplished more for Sonia, her faculty, and her peers. Our hopes as educators played a larger part in the outcome, our wounded expectations were healed through Sonia's apologies and growth as a person, and we helped one student emerge from disgrace to rejoin and instruct her peers. The process was more challenging to our beliefs, patience, and private authority than in the traditional mode, and we enhanced our own levels of understanding as we compelled Sonia to learn and change.

Chapter 14

FRATERNITY AND SORORITY CULTURE: A GUIDE TO IMPLEMENTING RESTORATIVE PROCESSES IN THE GREEK COMMUNITY

CHRISTINA BAKER-ZWERENZ, MATTHEW LOPEZ-PHILLIPS, NORA ROGERS, AND LAURA STROHMINGER

ARREST WARRANT ISSUED IN FATAL FRATERNITY BRAWL
(Associated Press January 30, 2002)

FAMILY SUES FRATERNITY OVER HAZING DEATH
(Associated Press November 19, 2002)

ACROSS U.S., HAZING LIVES DESPITE LAWS
(Chicago Tribune May 26, 2003)

GREEK ROW PARTIES DEGENERATE INTO RUCKUS INVOLVING HUNDREDS
(Associated Press September 29, 2003)

AT LEAST 10 UNRECOGNIZED FRAT/SORORITY GROUPS AT UNIVERSITY
(Associated Press October 24, 2003)

INTRODUCTION

The task of writing an all-inclusive chapter of the Greek experience is impossible. Therefore, as three alumni of Greek organizations and as four student affairs professionals, we utilize our combined knowledge, to paint with broad strokes, generalizations about the Greek experience, drawing from both our personal and professional experiences. As authors, we have been members, leaders, and advisors of local and national fraternities and sororities and have been involved in Order of Omega, the national Greek honor society. Further, our professional experiences have included advising entire Greek systems, including Inter Fraternity (IFC) and Panhellenic Councils, at major research institutions.

In this chapter, we explore the Greek experience and how it relates to restorative processes. We discuss the variety of internal restorative processes already being used by local and national organizations, the foundational values of Greek organizations, the issues facing fraternities and sororities, things to know when working with Greek chapters, and how all of this relates to using restorative processes with members of the Greek system.

National Umbrella Organizations

The principles, values, and reasons Greek organizations are established are accessible on many national web pages for individual chapters and national governing boards. The national governing organizations serve as umbrella councils for their member organizations. These groups include the National Panhellenic Conference (NPC), 26 inter/national sororities as members; the North American Interfraternity Council (NIC), 66 inter/national fraternities as members; the National Pan-Hellenic Council, Inc. (NPHC), nine predominantly Black Greek-letter organizations as members; and the National Association of Latino Fraternal Organizations, Inc. (NALFO), 24 Latino Greek letter organizations. These groups exist to support and promote the mutually agreed upon values of their member organization. It is important to understand the policies these governing groups create for their organization members as these policies have a day-to-day impact on how local chapters operate on their individual campuses. For example, the National Panhellenic Conference has what they call the Unanimous Agreements. These are policies that all 26 member organizations have agreed all of their member chapters will follow. When working with restorative processes, it is important to understand and know the guidelines already established by the national umbrella organization.

WHAT THE GREEK COMMUNITY BRINGS TO THE INSTITUTION AND THE INDIVIDUAL STUDENTS DURING THE COLLEGIATE EXPERIENCE

From the headlines listed at the opening of the chapter, it could appear that fraternities and sororities do not provide much benefit to the students who belong to them or the institutions who host them. Why do they still exist on college campuses if they cause so many problems? They do because there are many benefits associated with membership in a fraternity or soror-

ity, both to the students and to the university. Astin (1985, p.157) said that
". . . the greater a student's involvement in college, the greater the learning
and development." Greek-letter organizations provide tremendous opportunities for student involvement on a college campus from leadership and
officer positions within the chapter, to organization of campus-wide philan-
thropies and social events. Student involvement has also been partially
linked to a student's persistence to graduation (Tinto, 1987).

After the Collegiate Experience

The skills and connections made while an undergraduate member of a
fraternity or sorority are also linked to many benefits for the students and
university after graduation. The bonding of member to member and
member to institution that occurs through the fraternity experience
results in such positive outcomes as increased self-confidence and
assertiveness, satisfaction with college, and educational attainment (Astin,
1975; Carney, 1980; Iffert, 1957; Johnson, 1972; McKaig, 1993; Pascarella
and Terenzini, 1991). In 1996, leaders of the National Panhellenic
Conference and the North-American Interfraternity Conference conducted a research study to determine the long-term impact of Greek affiliation
in college. In this study, they found that Greek affiliation significantly
impacted career placement, volunteerism, and student satisfaction with
their collegiate experience. "With some exceptions . . . the weight of evidence suggests that there may be a small positive and statistically significant correlation between involvement and subsequent earnings."
(Pascarella and Terenzini, 1991, p. 520)

National statistics compiled by the NIC provide an opportunity to look at
the accomplishments of members of fraternities and sororities. Given that
Greeks make up only 3 percent of the U.S. population, the following statistics are quite impressive: 48 percent of all U.S. presidents have been Greek;
42 percent of U.S. senators are Greek; 30 percent of U.S. congressmen/
women are Greek; 40 percent of all U.S. Supreme Court justices have been
Greek; 30 percent of Fortune 500 executives are Greek; 10 percent of all listed in "Who's Who" are Greek (www.nicindy.org/publicrelations.html,
December 1, 2003). These high percentages of leaders with Greek background should be a sign to campus administrators that skills learned in a
Greek community can propel students to great leadership opportunities in
the larger community.

As you can see, there are many great benefits for both the student and
the institution through membership in Greek-letter organizations.
Unfortunately, all too often these many positives are overshadowed by inappropriate behavior and poor choices made by members of the individual
chapters on a campus.

CURRENT ISSUES OF GREEK MISCONDUCT

Before exploring the most current issues in Greek misconduct, it is important to note that Greek misconduct can be separated into three categories. First, there are incidents that involve individuals who happen to be affiliated with a Greek-letter organization. Second, there are incidents that we consider chapter incidents. This type of misconduct either includes a large number of members from the same fraternity or may be a chapter-wide decision to violate policy. The third type of misconduct within the Greek system is a pattern of individual behavior by members of a Greek organization that calls into question the culture within the chapter and the values of the chapter. These three types of misconduct can be handled in a variety of ways, ranging from internal Greek processes, through the university judicial system, or through an investigation by the National Greek Organization. Additionally, these processes may be combined to provide accountability both on and off campus.

The issues that students and administrators are facing regarding misconduct nationally are quite extensive. Most higher education institutions struggle with alcohol and drug use, assault, harassment, sexual assaults, bias-motivated incidents, body image disorder, self-mutilation, and mental health concerns. The amount of research on students involved in Greek organizations and their involvement on these issues is very limited. It is also important to delineate the difference between incidents that involve individuals who happen to be members of Greek organizations versus chapter decisions that violate policy. In our experience, the issues that Greeks deal with are typically the issues that all students are experiencing. Greek life is one microcosm of student culture. In our experience, we have found that Greek students are not much different from the rest of society, or the student populations as a whole. However, they tend to receive more scrutiny as they are more identifiable due to their affiliation. The two issues that we focus on in this chapter are alcohol and hazing.

Alcohol

Alcohol use and abuse-related misconduct are issues that all campuses deal with. "The whole thing needs to be put into the context of alcohol abuse being the number one problem on college campuses nationwide. Whether they've got Greek letters on the T-shirt or live in a dorm or apartment, alcohol is America's number one college problem" (Hinnefeld, 1992, p. A8).

In our professional experiences, we have found that alcohol-related misconduct occurs at the same rate as it does in the larger university community. However, a number of studies have shown excessive drinking in Greek organizations. This difference may be explained by the ease with which Greek organizations can be identified and studied.

A recent study by the Harvard School of Public Health on alcohol nationwide revealed that 86 percent of men who live in fraternity houses identified themselves as binge drinkers; fraternity house residents drink three times as much as all college students, 15 drinks per week as opposed to 5 drinks per week; and 56 percent of fraternity members compared to 26 percent of all college men are more likely to become involved in arguments or fighting as a result of drinking. Other studies have shown that the heaviest, most frequent, and most problematic drinking in college is done by fraternity members (Faulkner, Alcorn, and Gavin, 1989; Globetti, Stem, Marasco, and Haworth-Hoeppner, 1988; Goodwin, 1990; Hendren, 1988; Kraft, 1985; Mills, Phaffenberger, and McCarty, 1981; Miser, 1981; Tampke, 1990.) These statistics reveal a problem that needs to be addressed on our campuses.

We have identified three areas where campus administrators can tackle these issues. Alcohol use and abuse tends to happen during Greek social events and inside unsupervised housing, typically of second-year students. By recognizing where alcohol abuse and use happens, action plans can be created. Further, more research needs to be done on the connections between alcohol use and abuse, Greek peer pressure, Greek cultural norms, and individual Greek behavior.

Hazing

While there is much general research on alcohol and drug issues on college campuses, less research has addressed the complex issue of hazing. It is an issue that perplexes administrators. A deep look at hazing, secrecy, and Greek culture is required. Hazing has been defined by the Fraternity Executives Association (FEA, 2003) as:

> . . . any action taken or situation created, intentionally, whether on or off fraternity premises, to produce mental or physical discomfort, embarrassment, harassment or ridicule. Such activities and situations includes paddling in any form; creation of excessive fatigue; physical and psychological shocks; quests, treasure hunts, scavenger hunts, road trips or any other such activities carried on outside the confines of the house; wearing, publicly, apparel which is conspicuous and not normally in good taste; engaging in public stunts and buffoonery; morally degrading or humiliating games and activities, late work sessions which interfere with scholastic activities and any other activities which are not consistent with fraternal law, ritual or policy or the regulations and policies of the educational institution.

Hazing occurs at a variety of levels and ways; mental, physical, organized, informal, to entire pledge classes as a whole, and to individuals. Although hazing occurs within athletics, club sports, military units, and other campus-related groups, the Greek system receives the majority of scrutiny by the public at the college level.

Rather than list examples of hazing, we believe it is helpful to understand student perspectives on hazing. The following paragraphs describe some typical responses we hear from students when discussing hazing.

First, it is common for Greek members to justify hazing as a necessary and important rite of passage into the organization. Through the hazing process, new Greek members form close bonds, problem solve, and prove their loyalty. Many students see no good alternative to this intensive bonding and resocialization process. One undergraduate new member educator, or pledge trainer, had this to say;

> Obviously anytime you want to indoctrinate anyone, you restrict their food, restrict their sleep, get them run down and then really emotionally play with them. . . How else would I get a group of guys to assimilate them into the house? There really is no other way to , in ten weeks, take 27 guys, a group of strangers, . . . cocky, good athletes, intelligent, . . . and make them into INSs [fictitious fraternity name]. This is the way it had to be done. Arnold and Kuh, 1992, p. 76

Second, when confronted about hazing and asked why it needs to be continued, members often answer that it is the way to earn membership. Since hazing practices are seen as tradition in their chapter, it is justified.

Student members are not the only ones who believe in maintaining hazing traditions. As a result of public scrutiny, some national organizations have completely rewritten their membership development programs to eliminate pledge programs and hazing. However, some alumni advisors will not allow the students to follow the new program, as it would create a fraternity experience different from their own. Additionally, parents who were members of Greek organizations can also reinforce hazing, sometimes by lying during hazing investigations. Many parents encourage hazing, as it provides their child what they believe to be the "full fraternity experience."

At this point, it is important to acknowledge all of the work that is being done to prevent, reduce, and eliminate hazing from the Greek system. National organizations, universities, IFC/Panhellenic councils, and such organizations as stophazing.org have outreach programs that educate people on the dangers of hazing and the need for organizational change. These programs also extend to parents and suggest ways they can report hazing. Today, most universities and national organizations take alleged reports of hazing very seriously.

As we identified a number of areas where student affairs professionals can tackle issues with alcohol use and abuse, we provide similar thoughts here. First, the acts of hazing can be replaced with less dangerous activities. There are often alternative activities that students could use in place of traditional hazing exercises that would reach the same outcomes of unity, problem solving, and learning of a chapter history. Second, when asked how a particular hazing activity is essential to their new member program, Greeks often cannot connect the hazing activity to the values of the organization. As professionals, we can encourage Greeks to eliminate traditional hazing rituals with activities that better reflect values such as the pursuit of knowledge, loyalty, leadership, and service to others. Finally, as we discuss in the next pages, hazing is a difficult practice to investigate, and thus difficult to change. However, by recognizing the restorative processes already in place in the Greek system and by adapting university restorative processes, inroads can be made one step at a time.

CURRENT MODELS OF ACCOUNTABILITY BEING USED

Greek organizations have developed their own university subcultures that have established values and standards of behavior. Greek norms, values, and standards may be in addition to, or separate from, those of the larger institution. Because Greeks have such a well-defined set of standards, based in chapter-specific and larger Greek culture, fraternities and sororities have developed various ways of holding themselves accountable. Some of these practices are restorative in nature. The goal of their internal processes of addressing behavior is to bring the members back into the community defined as the brotherhood or sisterhood, not necessarily to exclude or remove them from the organization. Often these processes are so integrated into their values and concept of brotherhood and sisterhood that they do not recognize them as a restorative measures or formal processes of holding people accountable, as they would a hearing with the Office of Judicial Affairs or a peer review board. Greek members have an understanding of the values of their organization and established individual relationships with the members of their organization. As such, when faced with a community standards violation, Greek students usually can articulate the impact their behavior has had on fellow Greeks and on their Greek organization as a whole. This provides a natural environment for a restorative process to take place.

The types of restorative methods that are used within the Greek system are many—formal and informal, open and closed. Next we have listed examples of restorative justice processes we have experienced and/or witnessed in Greek systems.

- *Informal Individual Justice.* Individual Greeks organizations hold themselves accountable and confront situations as they arise; some chapters have a culture where individual confrontation of unacceptable behavior is encouraged and expected. This may be done on a one-on-one basis, usually including apologies. Sometimes the president or other officer of the organization takes a leadership role in addressing the behavior. However, any individual member can address individual acts perpetrated by a brother or sister. In some cases, an informal, (unsupervised and untrained) mediation may also take place between the offender, the harmed party, and the president. Generally, individual examples of restorative justice are informal.

- *Individual Accountability.* This is a practice where an individual member will be asked to stand in front of the entire membership while her ot his behavior is addressed. During such an episode, the president or executive board and sometimes the general membership addresses the problematic behavior of an individual. Usually, an informal agreement of how to repair the harm is created by the entire house membership with the individual. Accountability events are generally closed to non-members.

- *Formal Internal Standards or Judicial Boards.* Some Greeks have a formal judicial board. This formal judicial process is usually established by the national organization and includes fundamental due process. Other Greek organizations may not have a formal judicial board, but may require individuals to meet with the executive board about their misconduct. Members of judicial boards vary by Greek organization and institution and may include appointed or elected members. Boards may be comprised of representatives from the general membership, executive board members, or alumni. Alumni advisors are often part of these judicial processes. Outcomes of these hearings may be open or closed to the entire membership.

- *National investigations.* National organizations may investigate allegations of campus misconduct. These investigations, also called membership reviews, may be triggered by reports or requests from university administrators, police reports, alumni advisors, or anonymous reports received at the national office. The investigation may include interviews with some or all of the members of that Greek chapter. During these meetings, national representatives often ask each individual member to discuss her or his involvement with, and future membership in, the Greek organization. Investigation teams can be comprised of alumni volunteers and/or members of the national office staff. Outcomes range from educational sanctions, community service, probation, to removal of national recognition of the chapter. These investigations are generally closed, although the outcomes are open to the membership and typically to the university administrator responsible for Greeks.

- *National IFC/Panhellenic Judicial Policies.* There is some variation in how national Greek organizations view misconduct. The National Interfraternity Council (NIC) does not have an established judicial procedure for its collegiate chapters to follow. Conversely, the National Panhellenic Council, Inc. (NPC) has developed a very detailed outline for judicial procedures that is based on agreements between all of its member organizations. NPC procedure must be followed by the local collegiate Panhellenic council when trying to resolve an alleged violation of policies.
- *Greek and Campus Administration Collaboration.* On many campuses, the responsibility for direct oversight of the Greek system is the university judicial office. Judicial officers investigate incidents, determine the judicial restorative process to be used, and issue sanctions if appropriate. Usually, this is done in conjunction with the IFC/Panhellenic council. Collaboration is sometimes necessary to determine if the misconduct is a chapter-wide issue or the behavior of an individual member. If it is determined that this is a chapter issue, and the chapter is willing to accept responsibility for their behavior, an informal resolution is sometimes reached rather than having a full hearing with the Greek Judicial Board.

Greek students are often confused by the multiple community perspectives on misconduct. For a single incident, an individual may be dealing with their president, their advisors, their chapter, their national organization, the university, and the courts. It is difficult to have an educational and developmental conversation about the impact on community when the Greek student feels that the community is not working together, or acknowledging that the behavior is being addressed. As we discuss in the next section, a number of issues arise when university judicial officers participate in the adjudication of Greek behavior.

ISSUES IN WORKING WITH GREEKS
IN RESTORATIVE PROCESSES

Although a variety of restorative processes are used within the Greek system, restorative processes that involve campus judicial officers are fraught with problems. Judicial facilitators and administrators are often stumped when restorative processes involving Greek students are not successful. Although university-led restorative processes seem like a natural fit, there are many issues related to Greek culture, organizations, and leadership that make restorative processes difficult. In this section, we explore six obstacles to using university-led restorative processes with individual Greek students and with local chapters.

Greek Culture

As with any form of cross-cultural communication, judicial officers must have some understanding of Greek life before they can enter into meaningful conversations with students. Lundberg (1990) lists six characteristics to which those who are working with fraternities and sororities must be sensitive: (1) a common frame of reference for interpreting behavior; (2) socially learned rules that govern group life; (3) a shared way of viewing and talking about the unique aspects of the groups identity; (4) a social structure that is aware of its history and is fairly stable; (5) visible symbols of group values and aspirations manifested in behavior and language; and (6) a tacit set of guiding beliefs and assumptions (Arnold and Kuh, 1992, p. 10). Without a basic understanding of Greek subcultures, judicial officers cannot expect complete success with a restorative measure. Kuh and Whitt (1988) note, "it is also likely that, as with other organizations that develop strong cohesive, integrated cultures over time, a fraternity's culture is difficult to intentionally change" (Arnold and Kuh, 1992, p. 10). Issues related to the Greek subculture, namely, norms, rituals, and values are pervasive and are described in more detail in the coming pages.

Greek Leadership

For a university restorative process to be successful, it is essential that campus judicial officers work effectively with Greek chapter leaders. Greek leadership is generally comprised of young, inexperienced students who receive little or no training in preparing for their position. Officers usually hold their positions for one year. Often, this short tenure is due to the overwhelming number of responsibilities assigned to Greek leadership. As outgoing officers, many leaders perpetuate the lack of training and preparation for their successor.

Developmentally, leaders are so close to their peers that it is sometimes difficult for them to hold each other accountable. They struggle with being a friend versus being an authority figure and leader. Some leaders choose to be extremely rules-oriented, while others choose to act as the lenient "friend." Either way, leaders lose respect and struggle to hold peers responsible. Unless Greek leadership is strong and accountable, university restorative processes will be challenged.

Advisors

A unique aspect of Greek organizations, and the third issue we discuss, relates to advising. Volunteer alumni advisors are involved in every aspect of the Greek experience and are the backbone of the national organizations.

Local alumni advisors serve as the local connection between the national office and the chapter.

The experience and roles of alumni advisors vary widely from chapter to chapter. In general, advisors are selected from a pool of local alumni who are willing to volunteer their time. Advisors can spend as much as 20 to 30 hours a week at times working on chapter issues. They are also in a position of liability and are on the front lines for crisis management. Their role in relationship with the student organization varies from highly involved to minimally involved. However, in general, advisors are highly involved in university-based adjudication.

Judicial officers who work with Greek advisors should understand that many advisors receive little training unless they have previously worked for their national organization in a consultant position. Since the position is strictly voluntary, many advisors have not been prepared for the level of commitment that is involved in being an advisor. Further, few advisors have a background in student development theory nor have they had experience or training in advising college students.

The bottom line is that the Greek advisors feel accountable to their national organization. Although most advisors want what is best for their chapter, they often see themselves in opposition to the university. Although our goals for Greek students tend to be the same, the approaches and language used by national Greek organizations and the university can seem contradictory. Advisors are often placed in the awkward position of bridging the gap between their national organization and the university judicial office. Lack of advisor training and poor communication between parties causes a rift in the restorative process.

Secrecy

A fourth issue, and a great source of frustration for many administrators, is the secrecy involved in Greek organizations. Historically, Greek organizations created secret rituals to make each individual organization unique. Over time, secrecy of the ritual has evolved into secrecy related to many aspects of Greek life. Greek leaders, members, advisors, and national representatives can perpetuate secrecy. Students sometimes feel that they are betraying their brotherhood or sisterhood if they cannot maintain secrecy about their chapter in general and acts of misconduct in particular. Fellow members of a house are trained to support their brothers or sisters regardless of personal feelings. This loyalty makes it difficult for any Greek to acknowledge that one of the members was involved in an act of wrongdoing. Advisors and national organizations sometimes perpetuate this secrecy due to fear of liability issues or fear of university recognition being removed.

Secrecy proves to be a major roadblock to success in university-led restorative processes with Greeks. Conduct officers lose any chance to use restorative and educational practices when the story is scripted or when the truth is not being told by students and advisors. Restorative justice works only when all participants participate in an open and honest way.

Sense of Community

Community is a central component to restorative justice processes. It is apparent that Greek students feel a sense of community within their house. Sometimes, Greeks feel a sense of community among the fraternities and sororities on their campus. However, restorative justice officers may struggle in their task of having Greek students recognize that they are a member of the larger university community.

A Greek organization creates an environment in which strong community bonds, in the form of sisterhood and brotherhood, are formed. To obtain a Greek identity individuals are expected to place group identity above their individual needs. This "group" identity can be problematic when individual behavior is addressed in a restorative setting. Thus, there is the potential for virtually no genuine accountability for individual actions.

A strong of community identity is only possible if students feel a sense of commitment not only to their brothers and sisters, but also to their chapter. Dedication to their chapter reputation may also contribute to secrecy around misconduct. The notoriety of a house name and reputation poses a number of problems. Groups may be willing to go to any lengths to save face, regardless of whether they truly realize that the misconduct has caused harm.

In contrast to the strong sense of community that Greeks feel with their house or campus community, commitment to a university community is weak and often absent. When Greeks are involved in misconduct, they are often unable to recognize how the behavior has impacted a larger university community. During a restorative process, Greeks are asked "who is impacted by their behavior." Too often, Greek students are unable to identify any affected community beyond their individual Greek community.

Lack of Trust Between Greeks and University

The final issue that we believe is most challenging to successful restorative measures is perceived intrusion from the university community. As previously mentioned, Greek students often feel a lack of a sense of community with the larger university community. As a representative of the larger university community, university restorative justice facilitators are viewed as intruders in house business. This creates quite a problem when trying to work with Greeks using restorative process. To rely on restorative justice facilitators who are not members of the house community would be strictly taboo. The university is often seen as the "them" in the us versus them scenario. Without trust, a restorative community group circle is certain to fail. University administrators have to gain trust and develop relationships with Greek leaders, advisors, and individuals if we would like to see university-led restorative measures succeed with consistency.

CONCLUSION

The principles and values upon which Greek organizations are established (i.e., loyalty, trust, confidentiality), although intent on establishing model individuals, are the very ideals that pose major challenges to restorative justice practitioners when attempting to resolve disputes involving Greek affiliates. Whether a restorative conferencing model has been chosen to deal with an interfraternity issue, between fraternities, or between a fraternity and the community, it is important to fully comprehend the scope of the issue before beginning the conferencing process. There are internal processes that make it difficult to fully get to the core of the conflict. Loyalty among members can create a situation in which members are obliged not to admit to wrongdoing and express accountability. Greeks may not fully trust the restorative process and often feel victimized themselves against the threat of further or external investigation. Secrecy also presents a major challenge because it prevents individuals within a group from fully coming to terms with the problem and honestly working toward resolution.

Facilitators to the restorative justice process are trained to be able to identify possible barriers to a successful conference outcome. Their job is fully prepare all participants prior to the conference, being wary of anything that could sabotage the process. This is an extremely challenging aspect of the facilitator's task, regardless of the circle's circumstances. When dealing with Greek organizations in particular, this task becomes compounded by long-standing internal characteristics that preexist the restorative process. The purpose of this brief synopsis of the system of Greeks is not to lead one to believe that it is impossible to successfully resolve a Greek issue in a restorative manner. Rather, our objective is to lay the foundation upon which Greek organizations are founded in order for facilitators to be aware of obstacles to the restorative process, their origin, and how to constructively handle them.

References

Arnold, J. C., and G. D. Kuh. (1992). *Brotherhood and the Bottle: A Cultural Analysis of the Role of Alcohol in Fraternities.* Bloomington: Indiana University.

Astin, A. W. (1985). *Achieving Educational Excellence: A Critical Assessment of Priorities and Practices in Higher Education.* San Francisco: Jossey-Bass.

Fraternity Executives Association. 2003. *Statement of Position on Hazing and Pre-Initiation Activities.* http://www.fea-inc.org/hazing.htm.

Hinnefeld, S. (Feb. 19, 1992) "IU Fraternity, 26 students face disciplinary charges." *The Herald Times* (Bloomigton, IN), pp. A1, A8.

Lundburg, C. C. (1990). "Surfacing Organizational Culture." *Journal of Managerial Psychology* 5 (4):19–26.

Chapter 15

CONFERENCING CASE STUDY: HAZING MISCONDUCT MEETS RESTORATIVE JUSTICE—BREAKING NEW REPARATIVE GROUND IN UNIVERSITIES

THOM ALLENA AND NORA ROGERS

The following chapter chronicles a sorority hazing incident that took place in a large public university. In addition to physical and emotional injuries suffered by two sorority pledges, the incident resulted in a significant amount of local and regional media attention that eventually had widespread consequences for the sorority and the overall university community. This chapter details the efforts employed by the university to address the harmful effects of this incident through the use of a restorative justice intervention. In an effort to preserve the anonymity of the individuals involved and the confidential aspects of the restorative process used to address this misconduct, any names (except for the facilitators) that appear are fictitious. The account is presented to provide the reader with an example of restorative justice, which was applied to a complex act of campus misconduct involving 30 offending students. For the purposes of this chapter, the authors reference the concept of "hazing" as articulated by the Fraternity Executives Association (2003):

> ... Any action taken or situation created, intentionally, whether on or off fraternity premises, to produce mental or physical discomfort, embarrassment, harassment or ridicule... and any other activities which are not consistent with fraternal law, ritual or policy or the regulations and policies of the educational institution.

THE SORORITY "TUCK-IN" EVENT AND
THE STORM THAT FOLLOWED IT

It is widely understood that the ritual of hazing is commonplace within Greek life at many large universities. These events are often created to induct a new pledge into a sorority or fraternity house and frequently involve the use of alcohol and at times can have unintended and hurtful outcomes. One such event that was a tradition for a sorority at a large university was termed a "tuck-in" ceremony, initiated under the premise that the older, sophomore sorority sisters would bond with the new freshman pledges by taking them out for an evening of activities, then safely returning each girl to her residence hall bedroom at the night's conclusion. Although its intentions were seemingly harmless, this event resulted in major physical and emotional pain and embarrassment for the university, the sorority, and, most of all, one of the pledges who, for the purposes of this case study, we will call Amy.

Because the evening was to conclude with each new girl being "tucked-in" bed, the pledges were instructed to arrive wearing their pajamas. The older sorority sophomores then blindfolded the pledges and offered each of them a baby bottle full of alcohol, which was to be consumed that evening. It is important to note that the pledges were aged 17 and 18, while the older sisters were only 19 and 20. Each pledge was given a pillowcase to wear over her head so that they would be unaware of where they were being driven that evening. The older sisters drove the pledges around town, arriving at various fraternities where the pledges were instructed to consume more alcohol, as well as perform various humiliating acts, such as eating bananas fed to them by fraternity men while on their knees. Very late into the evening, the pledges, highly intoxicated, departed from the final fraternity house to be driven home and put to bed by their sorority sisters-to-be. One such pledge, Amy, was so inebriated that she fell on some concrete stairs outside of the fraternity house, severely damaging her teeth and face. However, she was so intoxicated that she barely noticed the blood on her face and mouth. None of the older sisters, whose care the pledges were in, bothered to notice either, and Amy was dropped at the doorstep of her residential hall, hardly returned safely to bed as the event had initially intended. There, Amy passed out on the floor of her residential hall lobby, where her roommate discovered her. Her roommate was so alarmed at discovering Amy that she immediately contacted an emergency services unit who transported her to the emergency room of the local hospital, where she was treated for near alcohol poisoning and severe dental damage. While at the hospital, Amy's trauma was compounded by comments made by an emergency room staff member who inferred that because she was a drunk sorority member, she got what she deserved. Once the hospital emergency room officials had learned the nature of Amy's injuries, they contacted the city police department. Eventually, one of the sorority women who had admitted to purchasing the alcohol was cited in municipal court.

One of the residential assistants onduty at Amy's dorm also witnessed her in her injured state. She proceeded to call the university police and filed a report of the incident. Several days later, the university police report of the incident arrived at the university's Office of Judicial Affairs. When the Director of Judicial Affairs read the report, she realized that over 30 women were facing charges of provision of alcohol to minors as well as hazing charges, both major violations of the university's student code of conduct. The director considered whether this particular case would be appropriate to be handled through the restorative justice program, which would serve as a diversion to the regular judicial process. If successful, the charges faced by each woman would be dropped. In considering a restorative approach, the Director of the Judicial Affairs Office made preliminary contact with sorority officers and adult advisors to explain the process.

The university restorative justice program had never addressed a case of this magnitude before and the working group wondered whether this case was more appropriate for a peacemaking circle, rather than the traditional community group conference model that the program had always used. The model that would eventually be used to address this incident would be a hybrid of the conferencing model already in use at the university and would incorporate "Open Space," an organizational development approach used to find common ground with large groups and organizations (Owen, 1992). University officials also decided that restorative justice facilitators external to the university who were also familiar with large group restorative interventions would be contacted to assist with the design and the facilitation of the restorative intervention. Thom Allena of Innovations in Justice, Taos, New Mexico, and Beverly Title of Teaching Peace, Longmont, Colorado, both experienced facilitators who had also been part of the initial university facilitator training, were invited to facilitate the restorative justice intervention. Assisting them were university staff who were skilled in restorative justice processes on campus that comprised a restorative justice working group. The restorative process development was also supported by the director of judicial affairs and several sorority officers and advisors who assisted with providing communication with the sorority members. Our sorority liaisons also played a key role in identifying other participants with sorority affiliations in terms of alumni advisors and officers who could speak to other ramifications of this incident beyond the parameters of the campus. The inclusion of these stakeholders was essential to the planning of this intervention.

PRE-CONFERENCING ACTIVITIES: POTHOLES IN THE ROAD

The facilitators met with Amy and a university victim's advocate to describe the process we would be using, assist her in understanding her role, and hear her story of the incident. With regard to pre-conferencing with the offending sorority members, because of the considerable size of this group (30 members), we elected to divide this group into two groups of 15. The Office of Judicial Affairs had previously determined that there were two general levels of participation or culpability associated with this incident. The first and most culpable group involved the women who participated in the planning of the "tuck-in," as well as in its execution. The second group of women, deemed less culpable, had simply been involved in the planning of the incident. Both groups were separately convened on campus prior to the actual restorative practice. Our time constraints, coupled with our desire for the offending women to learn about the restorative practice, led us to depart from our traditional approach to pre-conferencing procedure where participants are individually interviewed. The pre-conferencing process, while less than ideal given the size of both groups, did give us considerable insight into the "stories" we would hear in the circle as well the issues and concerns of the women involved. During the pre-conference sessions, we also attempted to convey to the offending students the structure and flow of the restorative conference.

The pre-conferencing activities with these students did take some interesting turns when they began to express some of their own concerns about what had occurred since the incident had taken place. First, we encountered what we have come to term the "multiple jeopardy" phenomenon, a not uncommon set of circumstances when campus offenses have overlapping jurisdictional authorities. In this matter, the involved sorority members were facing sanctions from their national sorority chapter, their local chapter, as well as the university judicial affairs process. In addition, one woman had been cited in municipal court for her role in the incident. In our pre-conferencing sessions, we learned that the extensive media coverage coupled with the issue of the multiple adjudication venues had left several of these women with the experience of feeling victimized by the events that unfolded following the actual offense.

Compounding these circumstances was the fact that several months had passed from the time of the incident to this point and many of the women involved in the incident had fashioned a "common story" that proved difficult at times for several of them to get beyond. Inviting them to consider alternative interpretations beyond the established story would prove challenging. We encountered an insular subculture of the sorority where its members were deeply committed to their own reality and dismissing anyone or anything that did not support it. Despite this discovery, we elected to move ahead with the restorative justice approach with the expectation that the restorative practice itself could assist the offending women in developing a larger "shared understanding" of the incident, beyond that of their own experience.

Another pre-conferencing consideration involved the emotional safety of our harmed party, Amy. Asking her to face 30 of her "big sisters" who had been involved in the offense required an unusually large act of courage on her part. Even with the inclusion of victim advocates and others who would play a supportive role for Amy, we were presented with concerns as to how to achieve a balanced process as all restorative practices strive to achieve. A second harmed party, a pledge who had suffered a violent allergic reaction during the incident as a result of the banana feeding, had declined to participate.

THE RESTORATIVE JUSTICE CIRCLE:
AN EXERCISE IN TRUST AND PATIENCE

Our group of 42 gathered on two consecutive evenings in a meeting room of a campus residential life building to explore a harmful incident using a process that, while based on restorative principles, was still experimental in its design. The circle itself was structured as two concentric circles. In our inner circle were our harmed party, her supporters, the most culpable of our offending student group, and other "affected community" members. Our outer circle consisted of those women who were identified as having participated only in the planning of the hazing activity. At designated points in the process, we would reverse the seating positions of our two groups of sorority members. Our reason for this seating design was to provide a sense of balance between our offenders' group and the harmed party, her supporters, and our affected community members.

Following our opening introductions and the establishment of our process ground rules, we first heard from our offending sorority members in order to establish some degree of responsibility for our offending parties. The focus of these stories was placed on the individual behavior of each of the offending women with the express purpose of providing a vehicle for understanding how the individual actions had contributed to the collective or group dynamic, where accountability had become diffuse and abstract. Each spoke to their personal involvement and what they could have done to prevent the incident. The stories we heard reflected varying degrees of acceptance of responsibility. As anticipated, some of the statements of culpability were more forthcoming than others. From the facilitators' viewpoint, this created a process dilemma in terms of how deep to probe with several of the individual stories. We remained cognizant of the logistical concerns with regard to the time constraints we were facing coupled with the need to create speaking opportunities for several more individuals beyond our group of offending students. Included in the admissions were several women who acknowledged contributing to an alcohol fund with which to purchase the alcohol used in the hazing; one woman who admitted to actually purchasing the alcohol; several women who admitted driving the vehicles from location to location that evening; and a number of women who accepted responsibility for ignoring Amy once the repercussions of the incident came to light. While there was some acceptance of responsibility, some of the statements at this stage appeared minimizing and self-serving. Statements such as, "Nobody made her [Amy] drink that much" were, in some sense, revictimizing to Amy.

Once all of our most culpable offending women had spoken, we invited our secondary offenders into the center circle to exchange seats with the sisters who had just spoken. Their admissions consisted principally of their involvement in the planning of the event.

After all of the offending sorority women had spoken, we turned to Amy, who spoke emotionally about the incident and the impact it had had on her. In her view, the very sisters in whom she had placed her personal safety failed to protect her. She expressed uncertainty as to whether she actually fell that evening or was pushed by someone. Feelings of a loss of trust and betrayal permeated her story. While the tuck-in ritual itself had had severe physical and emotional consequences for her, perhaps equally as harmful were the events that unfolded following the hazing incident. Amy spoke of feeling ostracized by sorority members in the weeks and months that followed. She spoke of the conflict of wanting to belong and yet the need to speak her truth about a troubling and abusive situation.

One of our facilitators then read letters written by Amy's mother and sister, neither of whom were able to attend the event. These were emotionally impactful letters. We were hearing the residual impact on family members many miles away from campus, deeply affected nevertheless. We also listened to a letter from Amy's roommate at the university, who spoke critically of the sorority women who had simply abandoned Amy in the lobby of the residence hall in an inebriated and injured state. While the letters did provide some additional context for the conference, they also added to our logistical dilemma as a number of the offending women felt a strong need to respond in their own behalf. The facilitators believed that too much "debating" among participants about their perceptions would diminish the respectful tone of the conference and our climate of listening to understand would be lost.

We then turned our attention to the affected community members in attendance. From sorority alumni and advisors we learned of the impact of their sorority having been the subject of intense media scrutiny and criticism. This incident had resulted in a series of embarrassing repercussions for these individuals. One university staff member who was also a former Greek member spoke passionately of the spirit of the Greek history and ideals that had been violated by this incident. Another sorority advisor spoke of the many phone calls she had received from family members and acquaintances in the area who learned of the incident through the extensive media coverage the matter had received. Most of these callers were deeply offended by what they heard, and several wondered if the sorority should not be shut down altogether. The group also heard from a university official who administered a foundation-funded university program that focused on student binge drinking and the widespread effects of this current campus phenomenon.

Once we had heard from everyone, one of our facilitators provided a summary of the collective harm from all of the participants. Beyond the value of the summary, this step provides the foundation for fashioning the restorative sanctions or agreements for each of the offending women. Some of the specific harm and costs associated with the incident included:

- Physical damage to Amy's mouth and teeth;
- Emotional damage and stress suffered by Amy;
- Emergency room costs;
- Amy's mother's anguish about her daughter's safety at a time when her husband was seriously ill;
- Amy's loss of trust in her "big sisters," who were supposed to protect her;
- Negative academic consequences for Amy and other sorority members;
- Amy's subsequent feeling of being an "outcast" in the sorority;
- Amy's concern of being seen as a "troublemaker" with the sorority;
- The reputation of the sorority suffered as result of negative media coverage;
- The reputation of the overall university had been deeply affected; and
- Parents of sorority members were very concerned about how their children were being portrayed in the media.

Upon hearing these impacts, it was time to move on to the agreement stage, where specific ideas for repairing these and other harmful effects was our focus. As in most restorative conferences, we first turned to Amy to learn what she saw as being appropriate sanctions in terms of repairing harm to her. Eventually, the entire group generated a list of potentially restorative ideas that were posted on flip chart pages throughout the room. Some of these reparative options included:

- Write a sincere letter to Amy recognizing and apologizing for "the situation that I participated in that caused harm to you;"

- Participate in a fireside event at the sorority and explain your exact role and involvement the night of the tuck-in;
- Speak at a sorority event about the restorative justice circle and the lessons learned;
- Form a committee to help Amy reacclimate to the sorority house;
- Create and implement a forum to discuss the breach in communication that recently occurred among sorority members;
- Participate in creating a fun, non-hazing, non-alcohol event as an alternative to the tuck-in;
- Write a sincere letter to your parents recognizing and apologizing for your participation in tuck-in and the specific harmful effects this had on your parents.
- Provide a list of three concrete ways in which you encouraged new sorority members to welcome Amy;
- Write a sincere letter of apology to the house director and to the nine advisors apologizing for your participation in tuck-in;
- Create a new sophomore ritual that focuses on the meaning of this recent event, why this was contrary to the ideals of the sorority, what happened to everyone involved, and why it is important for members to live up to the sorority ideals; and
- Write a sincere letter of apology to Amy's parents and sister recognizing and apologizing for your participation in the tuck-in.

Once these ideas had been developed and screened for their reparative content, we applied our Open Space component. We invited our offending students to select three items that they were willing to take responsibility for and then asked each of them to sign their names on the flip chart page containing the corresponding restorative item. The actual agreement for each individual woman would be developed after the circle process. Following the conference, the daunting task of sorting out and finalizing the agreements fell to the university restorative justice coordinator, who, unfortunately, was unable to be part of the restorative justice circle. With the assistance of university staff present during the process, the restorative justice coordinator finalized 30 agreements. In the ensuing weeks and months, all 30 of the sorority members successfully completed their agreements. One unfortunate footnote to report was that Amy withdrew from the university later in the spring semester.

LESSONS LEARNED: OUR BEST (AND SOMETIMES MOST HUMBLING) TEACHERS

This case yielded some important lessons for the facilitators and the university staff who were involved in the process. Many aspects of this intervention were clearly successful. Amy had been given an opportunity to have a voice in the process and presumably facilitate some aspects of her healing. The sorority members involved heard the fuller ramifications of their actions and were part of a process that created opportunities for them to repair the harm they had caused. Numerous restorative actions were taken by the sorority members to redress many of the individuals and organizations impacted by this event. The sorority policy involving initiation was critically assessed. The university concerns about the detrimental effects of alcohol use on campus gained the public stage.

While it is sometimes difficult to critically assess cases that are less than fully successful, some evaluation of each restorative intervention has value. This case proved to be no exception. In assessing what aspects of the process were problematic and in need of improvement, in hindsight, several areas were apparent. First, there were clearly insufficient periods of time allotted for both the planning process and the conference itself. The planning process itself did not effectively address the buy-in needed from the necessary university and sorority stakeholders. While the pre-conferencing process was conducted in groups, it did not allow for the full personal acceptance of responsibility by the offending sorority members. The emotional safety of Amy had been compromised by the less than full acceptance of responsibility by her sisters. The issue of multiple sanctioning bodies compounded by the extensive negative media coverage contributed to a sense of victimization on the part of the offending sorority members. Second, integrating restorative justice within the culture of a Greek organization proved challenging. Third, the development and management of the agreements after the conference could have benefited from a more thoughtfully planned approach. Each of these issues is addressed subsequently.

The lessons presented in the immediate case study are not presented to discourage the use of large-scale restorative interventions in the future. Instead, they are presented as a way of assisting the reader (and certainly ourselves) in expanding our understanding and application of restorative justice in large-scale, complex campus incidents. We continue to hold firm to the belief that one of the key inherent values of restorative justice is to assist our students in understanding the impact of their individual behavior within the context of a group or community. Below are some of most important lessons learned from this experience?

1. The Necessity of a Thorough Conference Planning Process

In complex cases where multiple offending students or victims exist, sufficient time and space must be allocated. Cases of this nature also require significant education prior to the actual restorative event. In this instance, the actual incident had occurred four months earlier and significant time had passed before the decision was made to use a restorative justice approach to adjudication. Once the decision was made to proceed, there was a push to get the matter addressed as quickly as possible. While we support the idea of adjudicating these incidents in a reasonable period of time, in hindsight, this matter required significantly more time to effectively prepare participants and university stakeholders for the conference. More onsite planning would also have enabled us to better understand and address some of the existing concerns and reservations among university stakeholders. Again, knowing what we now know, we would have directly involved many of these stakeholders in the planning process of the circle process and addressed their concerns in an open forum *before* moving forward. Bringing together university and key sorority administrators to speak directly to each other would have built stronger support for the process. One of our primary responsibilities as facilitators in the planning process is to build institutional support for the process. Giving sufficient time and resources to the institutional planning process is one of those tasks that is critical to the eventual overall success of the restorative justice process. As outside facilitators, we would have been better served insisting on getting the time and resources to effectively develop support for the process at the outset.

2. The Importance of Having Key University Stakeholders Involved

It is critical, we learned, to have as many of the university and sorority administrators brought in to the restorative approach before proceeding. Again, this requires time and opportunities for key stakeholders to have input at important decision-making stages that lead to institutional support for and understanding of the restorative process. For example, bringing together a cross-functional group of decision makers (e.g., judicial affairs, sorority advisors, victim advocates, restorative justice working group members) to collectively assess whether restorative justice was an appropriate adjudication model to this matter would have added an important layer of support for the process. In cases of this magnitude, a more formal assessment process may be warranted in which, again, key stakeholders are directly involved. Once the decision has been made to proceed with a restorative justice approach, the development of a university advisory team to guide the development of the overall process would likely prove beneficial in sustaining and expanding support for the initiative as needed.

3. Provide Adequate Time for Pre-Conferencing Activities

Pre-conferencing interviewing activities are crucial to the success of any restorative conference. Consequently, adequate time must be afforded this stage of the planning process. As noted earlier, our time constraints left us with few options other than to use a group pre-conferencing approach with our involved sorority members. As a result, we felt compelled to work as efficiently as possible. While this approach allowed for the offending sorority members to develop a shared understanding of what restorative justice was and what intervention model we would use, this approach also limited the facilitators' ability to individually connect with each woman and build trust in the process at that level. This individual approach to pre-conferencing, we have found, presents opportunities for offending students to deepen his or her sense of personal responsibility for their inappropriate behavior, a cornerstone for the restorative justice process.

4. Pay Close Attention to Emotional Safety
Issues of Harmed Parties

It is natural for any harmed party to feel ambivalent about facing his or her perpetrator. This situation is only exacerbated when multiple offenders are involved and those individuals are in a position of trust. One area we pay particular attention to is concerns about revictimizing the harmed party. It is crucial that the harmed party have sufficient emotional support before, during, and after the intervention. Furthermore, perhaps the best defense against emotional revictimization is when an offending student understands the harm he or she has inflicted on this individual and is able to develop a personal sense of remorse for that behavior. Without this key emotional recognition, revictimization remains a likelihood.

5. To the Extent Possible, Address Sanctioning
Issues of Multiple Jurisdictions

As noted earlier, incidents such as the one described here are subject to multiple venues of sanctions. It is sometimes useful to seek to consolidate the sanctioning processes for several reasons. First, sanctions are often overlapping and repetitive, thus minimizing their intended effectiveness. Second, offending students can sometimes begin to adopt the emotional position of becoming a "victim" after being punished in multiple sanctioning venues. Third, there is an issue of proportionality and fairness to consider. One needs to ask at what point a student has paid for his or her transgression and where does excessive sanctioning become simply "piling on."

6. Be Mindful of the Cultural Issues of Greek Organizations

To plan for and facilitate a successful restorative process involving any Greek organization, it is essential to consider the internal culture in which these societies exist (see Chapter 14). Concepts such as loyalty and accountability are primarily to the community as a whole and its members. Baker-Zwerenz et al. (Chapter 14) also assert that Greeks often experience separateness from the life of the larger university community in which they coexist. When transgressions or norm violations do occur, there are often internal systems for addressing these issues. Consequently, most Greek organizations are well equipped to "police themselves" when the violation involves members of their own community. This creates some interesting challenges when the same violation has wider repercussions, say, on the larger university community. While the issues of secrecy, honor, tradition, and ritual do bind the Greeks to one another internally, these same characteristics may also present barriers to recognizing the relationship of Greeks to the larger university community. We are not suggesting that there are any easy solutions here. It is simply best to be mindful of any cultural dynamics (racial/ethnic, economic, organizational, etc.) that may exist as you proceed.

7. Design a System for Managing the Post-Conference Agreements

A critical stage in any restorative justice circle is the follow-up stage in which the reparative agreements are actually completed. As noted earlier, this situation presented some logistical challenges at this stage as well. Again, the wisdom of hindsight informs us that having a single individual charged with the responsibility of overseeing 30 agreements may prove problematic. We can turn to the UCLA experience to inform us as to how to effectively manage multiple agreements (Chapter 17). In that instance, we formed a post-conference agreement team to work with the ten offending students in ensuring that the agreements were clearly understood by the offending students and managed effectively by the designated university staff. The UCLA post-conference workload was shared by eight staff members who worked as a team. In our sorority case, it may have also been wise to create a temporary structure or team to maintain communication with sorority officials and provide ongoing support for Amy as well as for all of the sorority women involved in the offense. The education process of restorative measures is best viewed as an ongoing process that does not stop at the closure of the circle. The use of a restorative transition team following the intervention could also be viewed as a tool for integrating the sorority within the larger university community and, in effect, lessen the appearance of insulation we encountered among the sorority members.

References

Fraternity Executives Association. 2003. *Statement of Position on Hazing and Pre-Initiation Activities.* http://www.fea-inc.org/hazing.htm.

Owen, Harrison. 1992. *Open Space Technology: A User's Guide.* Potomac, MD: Abbott Publishing.

Chapter 16

THE OFF-THE-FIELD DEVIANCE OF COLLEGE ATHLETES: PROBLEM OR HYPE?

Jeffrey O. Segrave

The off-the-field behavior of college athletes has attracted widespread attention in recent years. Of late, public awareness of the deviant behavior of athletes on college campuses has been heightened by the sustained media coverage given to a wide variety of high-profile cases involving allegations of rape and sexual assault, lying to a grand jury, falsification of reports to investigators, drug abuse, shootings, the fraudulent use of telephone credit cards, and deceitful educational practices. In the process, numerous reputable colleges and universities have found their reputations severely tarnished. For many commentators, the deviant off-the-field behavior of athletes has spiraled out of control to the point that the benefits of an intercollegiate athletic program no longer outweigh its liabilities (Sperber, 2000).

The extensive publicity given to the off-the-field antics of college athletes has also come with the recognition that intercollegiate athletic programs, especially at the NCAA Division I level, have become increasingly professionalized, commercialized, and corporatized, and athletes themselves have become increasingly privileged, pampered, and protected. Often separated, even segregated, from the rest of campus life, athletes are sometimes viewed as entertainers rather than students, and the pervasive cynicism that surrounds athletics has led to the charge that the characterization of the college athlete as a student-athlete is at best an anachronism and at worst a self-serving oxymoron. Furthermore, because athletic participation has traditionally been justified as a character-building experience, allegations of impropriety have contributed further to the perception that college athletes lack self-discipline and self-control and are a problematic rather than a positive presence on campus.

The purpose of this chapter is to review the recent literature on the off-the-field behavior of college athletes, especially as it compares to that of nonathletes; address the theoretical problems associated with understanding deviant behavior among athletes; and focus on the ways in which colleges and athletic associations are responding to the deviant behavior of intercollegiate athletes.

THE OFF-THE-FIELD BEHAVIOR OF COLLEGE ATHLETES

Systematic and comprehensive studies of deviant behavior among college athletes are, in fact, quite rare. It is only recently that independent researchers, athletic organizations, and colleges and universities themselves have actually sought to determine and understand the nature and scope of both on-the-field and off-the-field athletic deviance. My focus here is not on the on-the-field deviance of athletes, which would include breaking rules and regulations, unsportsmanlike behavior, fighting, and playing with excessive violence. My focus rather is on the off-the-field deviance of college athletes, including academic integrity, alcohol use, drug use, gambling, hazing, and violence—topics that have received the most attention in the media.

Academic Integrity

The topic of academic integrity among college athletes has garnered widespread attention because of several highly publicized cases involving prominent universities. In 1994, for example, the NCAA placed Baylor University on 5 years of probation having found that coaches were conducting correspondence work for players. An FBI investigation also resulted in mail and wire fraud convictions against several assistant coaches. More recently, in 1999, in the wake of a $1.5 million investigation conducted by the University of Minnesota and the NCAA into a system of academic misconduct involving the athletic department and the men's basketball staff, two high-level administrators, as well as the head coach, were forced to resign. But despite these, and several other highly publicized cases, the charge that college athletes are more likely than other students to engage in academic cheating has never been thoroughly examined.

What we do know is that cases of academic fraud among college athletes are more likely to garner national attention than incidents of academic impropriety among the general student body; that athletes, unlike nonathletes, are subject to the pressure to abide by published standards of academic eligibility; that athletes, from a relatively early age, can be swept up in a widespread culture of institutional deviance; and that, like all students, athletes operate in a climate where cases of academic dishonesty in general are on the rise across college campuses (see Chapter 12). Furthermore, what comprehensive studies do show is that while college athletes in general graduate at slightly higher rates than nonathletes, college athletes in big-time men's football and basketball in particular do not perform as well academically as other athletes or as other members of the general student body: their grades are lower, they are more likely to be registered for an easy course load in less demanding majors, and they are much less likely to graduate (Eitzen and Sage, 2003, pp. 119–122). The data most recently published by the Department of Education show that 53 percent of Division I football players and 44 percent of men's basketball players graduate within 6 years compared to 59 percent of the overall student body. The rates for African-Americans athletes in these two sports, while improving, are still nonetheless lower (NCAA, 2003).

In other words, the greatest likelihood for academic impropriety occurs within institutions that house big-time, revenue-producing athletic programs in football and basketball. It is in this environment, as Eitzen and Sage (2003) aver, where athletes "are more likely than other athletes and other students to receive grades fraudulently (e.g., "shady" correspondence courses, "friendly" professors, surrogate test takers or term paper writers)" (p. 121). However, it is hard to make definitive conclusions across all institutions about the differences between the academic actions of athletes and nonathletes until further sustained research has been conducted (Coakley, 2004, pp. 179–180).

Alcohol and Spit Tobacco

Unlike the topic of academic integrity, the subject of alcohol consumption among college athletes has received increasing research attention, partly because the misuse of alcohol has become one of the preeminent social problems in higher education today, and partly because both the promotion and the consumption of alcohol has long been an easily identifiable component of the college athletic scene. Alcohol is often on display around athletic fields, at tailgate parties, or during commercial breaks, and is readily associated with post-game celebrations and off-the-field team bonding at parties. Despite the fact that athletic success depends in part on physical and mental health, and despite the fact that athletic programs have long rationalized their place in higher education on the basis of the ideology that athletic participation promotes good character and models a healthy lifestyle, college athletes in fact routinely use alcohol at higher rates than nonathletes.

In a national study of varsity athletes, the NCAA (2001) found that nearly 80 percent of athletes report alcohol use within a 12-month period. Research also indicates that athletes tend to drink in seasonal cycles. One recent study at a large private university found that athletes increase their alcohol consumption by approximately 50% in the off-season. In season, 42 percent of men and 26 percent of women report that they drank alcohol at least once a week in season, and 60 percent of men and 41 percent of women report weekly alcohol consumption during the remainder of the year (Selby, Weinstein, and Bird, 1990).

Moreover, data collected during the 1990s show that both male and female athletes are at greater risk for alcohol use, abuse, and binge drinking than the rest of the student population (Naughton, 1996). In their national study of college student drinking, Nelson and Wechsler (2001) found that athletes have significantly higher rates of heavy drinking than nonathletes. Among male intercollegiate athletes, 57 percent reported heavy drinking in the two weeks prior to the survey compared to 49 percent of nonathletes. Among women, 48 percent of athletes reported heavy drinking compared to 40 percent of nonathletes. Wechsler and Weuthrich (2002) also report that athletes are more likely to say that getting drunk is an "important reason" for drinking than nonathletes. "There is no doubt," Wechsler and Weuthrich state, "that college athletes are at a statistically higher risk for alcohol abuse and exposure to its second hand effects than nonathlete students" (p. 55).

It is also worth noting that male athletes are far more likely to use spit tobacco than other members of the general student body. In their annual national survey, the NCAA (2001) found that 41 percent of baseball players and 29 percent of football players use spit tobacco compared to a national use rate among college men of 17 percent (Anderson, Albrecht, McKeag, Hough, and McGrew, 1991). Although the use of spit tobacco among women athletes is generally rare, the NCAA found that 18 percent of women collegiate skiers report usage. Several studies have also found significant racial and ethnic differences in spit tobacco use (NCAA, 2001; Walsh, Hilton, Ernster, Masouredis, and Grady, 1994). A survey of varsity baseball and football players at 16 California colleges, for example, found that Native American athletes (48%) were the highest users of smokeless tobacco, compared to whites (44%), Hispanics and Asians (33%), and African-Americans (11%) (Walsh, Hilton, Ernster, Masouredis, and Grady, 1994).

Hazing

Hazing, rites of passage that take the form of initiation rituals or ceremonies, has long been and remains to this day a prominent aspect of college athletics (Kirby and Wintrup, 2002). Hazing can involve a variety of practices, including coercing rookies to steal, drink excessively, shave, harass others, appear nude in public, and endure various forms of beatings, brandings, and sexual denigration (Hawes, 1999). Several high-profile cases have exposed the dangers associated with hazing in college athletics, including the well-publicized ice hockey scandal that racked the University of Vermont and ultimately resulted in the program's suspension (Eitzen and Sage, 2003, pp. 144–145; Wechsler and Weuthrich, 2002, p. 157). As the Vermont Attorney General stated after his investigation, the hockey team's hazing practices "violated both criminal statutes and laws of common decency" (quoted in Weiberg, 2000, p. 1C).

The most comprehensive study of hazing in athletics consisted of a survey involving 325,000 athletes at more than 1,000 NCAA colleges and universities (Eitzen and Sage, 2003, p. 144). Conducted at Alfred University on behalf of the NCAA, the study found that two-thirds of the athletes surveyed had been subjected to humiliating and denigrating experiences, including being forced to wear embarrassing clothing or being deprived of sleep, food, or personal hygiene; three-fourths experienced some form of hazing as an entrée into a college athletic team; one-fifth had been subjected to dangerous and potentially illegal behavior, including being tied up or being forced to destroy property; and one-half were required to take part in drinking contests or other alcohol-related activities. The study also found that women were more likely than men to be involved in alcohol-related activities rather than other forms of hazing and that football players were most at risk for dangerous and potentially illegal hazing.

Drug Use

Athletes now have within their grasp a vast cornucopia of designer drugs that have quickly and effectively found a well-publicized niche in the world of highly competitive sport. Whether recuperative or additive, recreational or performance-enhancing, drugs have revolutionized the world of sport and have transformed performances in sports as diverse as gymnastics and football, swimming and tennis, softball and skiing, causing numerous critics of sport to claim that substance abuse by athletes is epidemic in scope.

The extent to which drugs are used in college sports is difficult to assess accurately because it is not easy to collect valid and reliable data on an activity that is illegal. Numerous individual testimonies have claimed that drug use among college athletes is rampant. University of Oklahoma football player Brian Bosworth, for example, has boasted that drugs "were about as common as Anacin" in the Sooner locker room (Bosworth and Reilly, 1988, p. 20). More formal studies indicate that the level of drug use among athletes is actually much less. When the University of Southern California began its drug testing program in 1985, 10 percent of athletes taking it failed; in 1998, only 2 percent failed (Leonard, 1998, p. 153). The most recent NCAA national survey (NCAA, 2001) found that the drugs most commonly associated with sport—steroids—were not widely used among male college athletes at all (approximately 1%), although 3 percent of football players report steroid use. Nonetheless, the rate of steroid use among male college athletes is three times higher than the national norm for nonathletes (Cal Poly Pomona Student Health Services, 2001). Male athletes also report significantly higher rates of amphetamine use than nonathletes (Green, Uryasz, Petr, and Bray, 2001).

Among women collegiate athletes the most commonly used drugs are diet pills, laxatives, and diuretics. In their study of drug use by female athletes, Rosen and Hough (1988) found that 62 percent of female college gymnasts had used at least one extreme weight loss method, including 24 percent who had used diet pills, 12 percent who had used diuretics, 7 percent who had used laxatives, and 26 percent who had induced vomiting, significantly higher rates than among female nonathletes (Heatherton, Nichols, Mahamedi, and Keel, 1995).

Recreational drug use among college athletes is also higher than among the general student population. Although the use of cocaine, crack, heroin, marijuana, and speed among athletes pales in comparison to the use of alcohol, studies indicate that as many as 17 percent of male and 7 percent of female intercollegiate athletes acknowledge cocaine use, which is well above published norms for the general student body (Eitzen and Sage, 2003, p. 151).

Although difficult to generalize, the data suggest that college athletes are more likely than nonathletes to use drugs, certainly in response to the demands of high-performance sport, but also as a part of their everyday life habits. While male athletes are more likely to be drawn to those drugs that promote muscle growth, women are more susceptible to those drugs that facilitate weight control. Both groups, however, are prone to recreational drug use, which, coupled with the behavioral side effects of performance-enhancing drugs—violent behavior among men and eating disorders among women—places athletes at a much higher level of risk than nonathletes within the overall campus culture.

Gambling

A growing consensus of research reveals that the scope of pathological and problem gambling is higher among college students than among any other segment of the population. A comprehensive analysis of problem gambling by Harvard Medical School's Division on Addiction, for example, shows that the rate of "disordered" gambling among college students is 4.7 percent, almost three times higher than the adult rate of 1.6 percent (Gose, 2000). With the massive increase of spectator interest in college sports in recent years, there has been a corresponding explosion in gambling on sports on college campuses, and student-athletes appear to be at even greater risk than other members of the student body. In 1998, a study conducted by the University of Michigan revealed that 35 percent of college athletes reported gambling on sports while attending college and more than 5 percent admitted wagering on games in which they played, providing inside information for gambling purposes, or accepting money for performing poorly in a contest (NCAA, 2000). A study by the University of Cincinnati of 648 Division I men's football and basketball players found that 72 percent had gambled in some form, 25 percent had wagered money on other college sports events, and 4 percent had placed money on a contest in which they had played (Eitzen and Sage, 2003, p. 157; Gose, 2000).

The advent of the Internet has precipitated even greater access to gambling opportunities for college students, a development that has precipitated an ever-deepening concern among college officials and college athletic organizations. In 1999, the National Association of Student Personnel Administrators, so alarmed by the escalating dimensions of gambling on campuses, created a task force of college deans, athletic directors, and mental health experts to study the problem of student gambling—and the possibility that students are increasingly at risk for online gambling addiction. The NCAA, which has recently suffered several point-shaving scandals at member institutions, not only has acknowledged that illegal sports gambling is rampant among students but also has backed congressional legislation to remove the "Nevada loophole," a legislative anomaly that permits Nevada to be the only state to conduct legal gambling on college sports.

Violence

While the violent behavior of athletes may well once have been carefully safeguarded from public scrutiny, the accumulating literature, including biographies, interviews, and empirical research, have presented powerful evidence to the contrary. Furthermore, numerous highly publicized cases of theft, property destruction, assault, sexual assault, rape, gang rape, and even murder involving college athletes have raised the issue of whether the college athletic culture may actually encourage a propensity toward violent and antisocial behavior among athletes (Benedict, 1997).

To some extent empirical research does support the notion that college athletics harbors what Sanday calls a "rape culture" (1981). For example, in their study of victims of sexual aggression at a large midwestern university, Fritner and Rubinson (1993) found that male athletes were disproportionately represented in reports of sexual abuse, abuse, and intimidation. Although men on sports teams comprised less than 2 percent of the total male population on campus, male athletes made up 23 percent of the attackers in sexual assaults and 14 percent in attempted sexual assaults. Many other studies based on official reports, self-report data, face-to-face interviews, and anonymous surveys have found a positive relationship between athletic participation and the incidence of sexual aggression (Crosset, 1999). Research has also demonstrated that gang rapes on college campuses are most likely to be perpetrated by men who participate in intensive male peer subcultures, such as intercollegiate athletics and fraternities, subcultures that tend to foster rape-supportive behaviors and attitudes (O'Sullivan, 1991). There is also some evidence that men on intercollegiate, revenue-producing sports teams, especially football and basketball, are more likely to be involved in sexual assault cases than both nonathletes and other athletes (Crosset, 1999).

In contrast, other studies suggest that athletes are no more violent toward women than nonathletes. For example, Schwartz and Nogrady (1996) found no significant difference between college athletes and nonaffiliated students on a variety of variables associated with sexual assault. And Crosset, Benedict, and McDonald (1995) found no differences between athletes and nonathletes in reports of violence to campus police. While the results of quantitative research are in some ways limited, in the final analysis, and after an extensive review of all the published research on the subject, Crosset (1999) concluded that male intercollegiate athletes, in particular, are more likely to be involved in sexual assaults than other students and other athletes.

In order to more fully understand the relationship between athletic participation and violent behavior, several researchers argue that we need to embrace more interpretative models if we are not to overlook significant cultural, ideological, and situational factors that help account for male collegiate athletes' violent propensities. In either case, the college campus remains an environment in which women and property are to some extent at risk from college athletes and the behavior of collegiate athletes remains as much a personal problem as a public issue.

FACTORS UNIQUE TO THE DEVIANT BEHAVIOR
OF THE COLLEGE ATHLETE

Before addressing how colleges are seeking to respond to the problem of the off-the-field behavior of athletes, it is worth briefly noting the ways in which deviance among college athletes is unique and different from the deviant behavior of other students (cf. Coakley, 2004, pp. 138–141).

First, as my review of the literature demonstrates, the deviant behavior of college athletes is multiple and varied, ranging from hazing rookie team members to betting on sports, from turning in papers written by someone else to committing sexual assault, from destroying property on a road trip to taking drugs. In each case, athletic and college officials have to respond in distinctly different and diverse ways.

Second, what is condoned in athletics is often punished in society. Athletes are commonly allowed, even encouraged and rewarded, to behave in ways that could be defined as criminal in other cultural settings. For example, violence is encoded into the rules of many sports, especially the quintessential male collegiate sports of football, wrestling, and ice hockey, sports that by their very nature rely on controlled rage and reckless abandon, and athletes learn behaviors that, if carried over into the everyday, could be subject to civil, even criminal, litigation.

Third, deviant behavior among college athletes is often the result of over-conformity to commonly endorsed norms and expectations, not the rejection of them. This type of "overdoing it deviance," as Coakley calls it (2004, p. 141), is grounded in athletic experiences—both on and off the field—that involve a potent amalgam of exhilarating experiences and powerful social processes, which facilitates, even encourages extreme forms of behaviors. In other words, athletes are particularly vulnerable to over-conformity deviance, and the social dynamics that underpin this type of deviance are often very different from the dynamics that produce the antisocial behavior of alienated youth.

Fourth, as in professional sports, training and performance in college sports have become medicalized. Discussions and debates about athletic success, most especially at the big-time Division I level, are now invariably framed against the backdrop of the efficacy and desirability of a high-powered sports pharmacology. For athletes in particular, the line between technologized training and deviant behavior has become increasingly blurred.

Finally, it is worth noting that college athletes, especially those at the NCAA Division I level who compete in the high-profile, revenue-producing sports, have to operate in what some have characterized as a culture of institutional deviance. In other words, the pressures placed on coaches and college administrators to perpetuate a tradition of success and economic gain have resulted in the institutionalization of questionable values and practices that normalize, even condone, deviance not only among athletes but also among coaches, administrators, team managers, agents, boosters, and sports medicine professionals.

HOW COLLEGE CAMPUSES ARE RESPONDING

In response to the off-the-field deviance of athletes, college intervention practices have typically employed either punitive measures—the deterrence approach—or normative changes—consciousness raising through educational programs. Both approaches, however, tend to emphasize individual choice, and more recently, especially with regard to male athletes' assaults on women, researchers and administrators are advocating attention to the structural and situational features that constitute the lives of intercollegiate athletes as the most likely and effective way to combat deviant behavior.

The Deterrence Approach

Simply stated, the deterrence approach is grounded in the imposition of rules and sanctions. Policies and procedures are established and violations result in punishments. For example, following then-Secretary of the U.S. Department of Health and Human Services, Donna Shalala's call for a complete severance between college sports and drinking, numerous colleges and universities have institutionalized polices and procedures that prohibit the use of alcohol by student-athletes during the playing season. Violators are punished accordingly. According the NCAA's most recent Drug-Education/Testing Survey (2001), 68 percent of 372 responding colleges also indicate that they have established a zero-tolerance policy toward the use of alcohol during student-athlete recruitment trips. Likewise, governing bodies, as well as individual colleges, have routinely mandated prohibitions with regard to hazing, gambling, and, perhaps most notably, drug use.

Along with the International Olympic Committee and the National Football League, the NCAA has taken the lead in mandatory and random drug testing. Although legally complex and still under scrutiny, NCAA athletes are currently obliged to submit drug-testing consent forms, and predicated on published lists of banned drugs—both performance-enhancing and recreational—athletes acknowledge the punitive consequences, both for themselves and for the institution, of testing positive for drug use. Beyond the practices of the NCAA itself, 49 percent of member colleges, including 93 percent of Division I programs, currently utilize a drug testing program for their own athletes (NCAA, 2001). Moreover, 95 percent of these programs are mandatory.

The Educational Approach

Unlike the deterrence approach, which penalizes athletes for inappropriate behavior, the educational approach seeks to combat deviant behavior through the promotion and inculcation of prosocial values and norms. As a result, educational programs for athletes are now common on college campuses. The NCAA (2001) reports that 66 percent of colleges currently operate drug/alcohol educational programs for athletes and that 74 percent sponsor outside speakers for special presentations on drug and alcohol abuse. Largely in response to the Clery Act, colleges routinely offer rape prevention programs, rape awareness sessions, and date rape seminars to their male athletes; some specifically target football players. In some programs, athletes themselves serve as rape prevention educators, peer educators on sexual harassment, and mentors to other athletes (Nelson, 1994, pp. 156–157; Parrot, Cummings, Marchell, and Hofher, 1994).

Given both the reality of and the publicity focused on the off-the-field behavior of athletes, colleges have also turned to a wide variety of educational programs sponsored by sports organizations, private organizations, and even individuals. The NCAA, for example, sponsors publications, seminars, presentations, guest speakers, grant opportunities, and a host of educational programs in an effort to provide colleges with information, programmatic support, and expertise. Among the most well known NCAA programs are CHOICES (a grant program for alcohol education), the Betty Ford Professional-in-Residence program, the Champs/Life Skills Program, and the Sports Sciences Speakers Grant. According to the NCAA, 48 percent of colleges sponsor the Champs/Life Skills Program (NCAA, 2001), and grants totaling more than $2.5 million have been awarded to colleges since the CHOICES program was initiated in 1991 (NCAA, 2003). One of the NCAA's most recently heralded programs, the Student-Athletes Taking Active Responsibility Roles, is based on the social norms approach and uses facts about alcohol use and other issues to reduce misconceptions and help students make more responsible decisions (Rosenberg, 2003),

The Structural/Situational Approach

While both the deterrence and the educational approaches seek to change how athletes act, the structural/situational approach centers on changing how athletes think. Within this paradigm, discussions focus on athletic deviance as structurally encouraged and situationally appropriate. The role of research is to determine why some teams, programs, or sports are prone to committing specific types of deviance and the role of intervention is to change the structural features and situational dynamics that predispose athletes to deviance. Some colleges, for example, have restricted the housing of athletes to on-campus mixed dormitories or have discouraged the construction of potentially unsafe parties and celebrations. Speaking specifically about male athletes' propensity toward violence against women, Crosset (1999) argues that intervention programs should also address "men's hostile attitudes toward women, expose male privilege, and inform men of the potential consequences of their beliefs and actions" (p. 254).

CONCLUSION

In this chapter, I have reviewed the research on the off-the-field deviance of college athletes. While it is difficult to be definitive about the findings, partly because colleges accommodate such a wide variety of programs—

ranging from NCAA Division I scholarship programs that often sponsor pseudo-professional teams to Division III programs that offer no scholarships based on athletic ability and where programs are decidedly educational in priority—and partly because systematic research is relatively scarce, the data nonetheless suggest that the deviant rates of athletes may be higher than they are for comparable peers, especially in the case of drinking, drug abuse, gambling, and certain types of assault. Some forms of deviance also appear to be growing rapidly, especially those facilitated by technology, such as Internet-based gambling. Colleges are responding to these problems in a variety of ways and are employing a combination of approaches, including those that rely on traditional deterrence-based measures, those that offer educational programs, and those that seek to change the environment that constitutes and determines the lives of college athletes.

References

Anderson, W. A., R. R. Albrecht, D. B. McKeag, D. O. Hough, and C. A. McGrew. (1991). "A National Survey of Alcohol and Drug Use by College Athletes." *Physician and Sportsmedicine* 19:91–104.

Benedict, Jeffrey. (1997). *Public Heroes, Private Felons: Athletes and Crimes Against Women.* Boston: Northeastern University Press.

Bosworth, Brian, and Rick Reilly. (1988). *The Boz: Confessions of a Modern Anti-Hero.* New York: Doubleday.

Cal Poly Pomona Student Health Services. (2001). National and Cal Poly Pomona Core Alcohol and Other Drug Survey. Cal Poly Pomona.

Coakley, John. (2004). *Sports in Society: Issues and Controversies.* New York: McGraw-Hill.

Crosset, Todd. (1999). "Male Athletes' Violence Against Women: A Critical Assessment of the Athletic Affiliation, Violence Against Women Debate." *Quest* 51:244–257.

Crosset, Todd, Jeffrey Benedict, and Mark McDonald. (1995). "Male Student-Athletes Reported for Sexual Assault: Survey of Campus Police Departments and Judicial Affairs." *Journal of Sport and Social Issues* 19:126–140.

Eitzen, D. Stanley, and George Sage. (2003). *Sociology of North American Sport.* New York: McGraw-Hill.

Fritner, M. P., and L. Rubinson. (1993). "Acquaintance Rape: The Influence of Alcohol, Fraternity Membership, and Sports Team Membership." *Journal of Sex Education and Therapy* 19:272–284.

Gose, Ben. (2000). "A Dangerous Bet on Campus." *Chronicle of Higher Education,* April 7. (http://www.chronicle.com/weekly/v46/i31/31a00101.htm)

Green, G. A., F. D. Uryasz, T. A. Petr, and C. D. Bray. (2001). "NCAA Study of Substance Use and Abuse Habits of College Student-Athletes." *Clinical Journal of Sport Medicine* 11:51–56.

Hawes, K. (1999). "Dangerous Games: Athletics Initiation—Team Bonding, Rite of Passage, or Hazing?" *NCAA News,* September 13, pp. 14–16.

Heatherton, T. F., P. Nichols, F. Muhamedi, and P. Keel. (1995). "Body Weight, Dieting, Eating Disorder Symptoms Among College Students, 1982 to 1992." *American Journal of Psychiatry* 152:1623–1629.

Kirby, S. L., and Wintrup, G. (2002). "Running the Gauntlet: An Examination of Initiation/Hazing and Sexual Abuse in Sport." In C. Brackenbridge and Kari. Fasting (Eds.), *Sexual Harassment and Abuse in Sport: International Research and Policy Perspectives* (pp. 65–90). London: Whiting and Birch.

Leonard, Wilbert. M. (1998). *A Sociological Perspective of Sport.* Boston: Allyn & Bacon.

Naughton, Jim. (1996). "Alcohol Use by Athletes Poses Big Problems for College." *Chronicle of Higher Education* 43:A47–A48.

NCAA. (2003). "Alcohol-Education Grants Awarded to 11 NCAA Schools." *NCAA News,* May 26. (http://www.ncaa.org/news/2003/20030526/awide/4011n13.html)

NCAA. (2001). The NCAA Study of Substance Use Habits of College Student Athletes. Presented to the NCAA Committee on Competitive Safeguards and Medical Aspect of Sport. June 2001 (www.ncaa.org).

NCAA. (2000). Testimony of Robert J. Minnix, Associate Athletic Director, Florida State University, Before the House Judiciary Subcommittee on Crime. In Internet Sports Wagering: Supplement to 2000 NCAA Regional Seminars.

Nelson, Mariah Burton. (1994). *The Stronger Women Get, the More Men Love Football: Sexism and the American Culture of Sports.* New York: Harcourt Brace.

Nelson, Tobin, and Henry Wechsler. (2001). "Alcohol and College Athletes." *Medicine and Science in Sports and Exercise* 33:43–47.

O'Sullivan, C. S. (1991). "Acquaintance Gang Rape on Campus." In A. Parrot and L. Bechofer, (Eds). *Acquaintance Rape: The Hidden Crime* (pp. 86–99). New York: Wiley.

Parrot, A., N. Cummings, T. C. Marchell, and J. Hofher. (1994). "Rape Awareness and Prevention for Male Athletes." *Journal of American College Health* 42:179–184.

Rosen, L. W., and D. O. Hough. (1988). "Pathogenic Weight-Control Behaviors of Female College Gymnasts." *The Physician and Sports Medicine* 16:141–146.

Rosenberg, Beth. (2003). "Alcohol-Education Pilot Has a Sobering Effect in Division III." *NCAA News,* October 13, pp. 14–15.

Sanday, Peggy. (1981). "The Socio-Cultural Aspect of Rape: A Cross-Cultural Study." *Journal of Social Issues* 37:5–27.

Schwartz, M., and C. Nogrady. (1996). "Fraternity Membership, Rape Myths, and Sexual Aggression on College Campus." *Violence Against Women* 2:148–162.

Selby, R., H. M. Weinstein, and T. S. Bird. (1990). "The Health of University Athletes: Attitudes, Behaviors, and Stressors." *Journal of American College Health* 39:11–18.

Sperber, Murray. (2000). *Beer and Circus: How Big-Time College Sports Is Crippling Undergraduate Education.* New York: Henry Holt and Company.

Walsh, M. M., J. F. Hilton, V. L. Ernster, C. M. Masouredis, and D. G. Grady. (1994). "Prevalence, Patterns, and Correlates of Spit Tobacco Use in a College Athlete Population." *Addictive Behaviors* 19:411–427.

Wechsler, Henry., and B. Wuethrich. (2003). *Dying to Drink: Confronting Binge Drinking on Campuses.* New York: St. Martin's Press.

Weiberg, S. (2000). "A Night of Humiliation." *USA Today,* February 4, pp. 1C–2C.

Chapter 17

CONFERENCING CASE STUDY: APPLYING RESTORATIVE JUSTICE IN A HIGH-PROFILE ATHLETIC INCIDENT— A GUIDE TO ADDRESSING, REPAIRING, AND HEALING WIDESPREAD HARM

THOM ALLENA

This chapter relates the story of one harmful incident that occurred in the Summer and Fall of 1999 at the University of California–Los Angeles and details the steps taken by university officials to come to grips with an athletic scandal that received significant national and local media attention. More specifically, this chapter chronicles the development of a restorative conference that took place in the Fall of 1999 on the campus of UCLA and describes the several relevant steps involved in assessment, planning, facilitating, and follow-up of a large-scale restorative justice intervention.

It is my hope that the process described here can serve as a guide or framework for college campuses in addressing the harmful effects of similar high-profile incidents. This is the story of one such university that took the risk of stepping outside its traditional methods of dealing with student misconduct. It is also a story of courage and growth for the individuals involved and for the university community as a whole.

ASSESSING THE IMPACT OF THE OFFENSE ON THE UCLA COMMUNITY

In July 1999, a time when most university campuses usually rest, the campus community of the University of California–Los Angeles was abruptly awakened from its summer intersession. The Los Angeles media reported one evening on the local news the emergence of a scandal that involved the UCLA football team. Fourteen current and former football team members were named as part of an ongoing investigation in which disabled parking placards had been fraudulently obtained and used on campus. News reports of the incident sent shock waves through the university community. The torrent of media coverage and community outrage took aim at the university athletic program and, more specifically, at the athletes themselves, who were characterized as "self-centered," "pampered," and "privileged." Judging from the extensive media coverage within the Los Angeles area, there appeared to be a collective sense of community outrage (Raouf, Morin, and Ferrell, 1999). In addition to the media coverage, there was a predictably strong response from the disabled advocacy community and a number of related university advocacy groups.

As is often the case in university wrongdoing of this nature, it is quite common to come across the phenomenon of triple and perhaps even quadruple "jeopardy" for the offending student. The multiple jeopardy issue stems from the fact that many university sanctioning mechanisms operate in partial and/or complete independence of one another. The incident we were seeking to address, namely, the athletes' fraudulent obtaining and use of disabled parking placards, had wound its way into the hands of several sanctioning authorities. First, the offense had violated the California Municipal Code. Second, the university athletic department had taken its own action in the matter, suspending the offending players for two games at the start of the upcoming season. Third, student-athlete regulations of the NCAA, the governing body for university athletics, had been violated. Fourth, there was the on-campus student discipline process as administered by the office of the Dean of Students applicable to any campus-related wrongdoing. If you consider additional courts of public opinion—campus media, local and national media, the university community—then you get a sense of the extraordinary amount of attention and energy a high-profile wrongdoing case such as this can and often does receive. Our task was to develop a restorative justice process, in this case a group conference to serve as an alternative sanctioning approach to the traditional judicial affairs process.

The Effects of Exhaustive Media Coverage

I want to give the reader a brief glimpse of the attention this incident received. As we would do in any incident that had received scrutiny in the media, I requested that the university public affairs office forward to me any print or video coverage the incident may have received. What I was not expecting to find in my mailbox was a package that weighed nearly five pounds containing feature stories, follow-up stories, editorials, letters to the editor—nearly

300 pieces that had been collected. Add in one 30-minute videotape of local and national TV news coverage detailing coverage of the incident as well as video coverage of the municipal court proceedings where a number of disabled citizens demonstrated inside the Los Angeles County Courthouse.

To give the reader a sense of the emotional pulse on campus, in addition to the numerous articles written in campus print media, I was also sent a sample "Bruin Jerk Permit" ("Jaded, Egotistical, Reprehensible, Kreep for the physically gifted, mentally disabled, emotionally insensitive, ethically impoverished Bruin Football Player") that had been distributed across campus for purchase as well as matching T-shirts with the words "Bruin Shame" fashionably displayed across the front of the garment.

One might ask at this point what incentive the university might have to want to engage in a restorative process in an environment where significant hostility exists. When this issue was put to Assistant Vice Chancellor of Student and Campus Life, Bob Naples, he explained, "There was such a high profile on this particular situation that I felt it was necessary to reintegrate offenders into the campus community. It is important that that we all walk away with good feelings toward these individuals [athletes]" (McMasters, 1999).

Our research and assessment of the presenting misconduct left us with one unmistakable truth: The UCLA and Los Angeles communities had suffered serious harm as a result of the incident and some affirmative steps would need to be taken to repair that harm. It was only as the planning process moved forward and during the actual restorative justice conference that we would later learn the deeper, more harmful effects experienced by a great number of individuals involved. Another reality we discovered was that large-scale incidents of this nature are indeed complex and require time and thoughtfulness in their planning and execution.

Planning the Restorative Justice Conference

The success of a restorative practice is rooted in its preparation. It has been our experience that poorly planned interventions usually become unsuccessful conferences. In the case of the UCLA incident, a number of pre-conference planning and education tasks were critical to the success of the conference. The magnitude of the incident, the number of people and departments within the university, as well as those outside the campus community who would need to be involved, all created a complexity of issues that warranted a planning process that goes beyond that of a typical restorative conference. Following is a summary of the major pre-conference planning activities.

An additional planning step involved meeting with key university administrators who had a clear stake in the conference process and outcome.

Keeping these individuals apprised and involved in appropriate ways was an important function of the planning process. We also convened a university advisory team consisting of a cross section of university administrators and staff to assist us in identifying conference participants as well as conference co-facilitators who would assist in managing the actual process.

Perhaps the most critical step in the planning process involved what we would call the pre-conferencing stage of the event. It was here that we met with each of the players and described as best we could just what the process would entail. As in most restorative conferences, one of the initial tasks was to meet with the offending athletes to accomplish several outcomes:

1. To explain the nature and process of the restorative justice conference so that each could make an informed choice as to whether he wished to participate;
2. To assist each of the offending students in clearly understanding the role he was playing;
3. To better understand the offending students' version of the offense behavior and how they and others had been personally impacted;
4. To begin exploring ideas as to how to repair the harm arising from the incident and;
5. To identify family and friends who would be interested in participating as a support person for each athlete. The office of the dean of students and the athletic department worked in concert to schedule the pre-conferencing sessions with the athletes balancing their class schedules and practice sessions. In addition, other conference participants were interviewed in person and by telephone to prepare them for the conferencing process.

Our final planning task involved training a team of conference co-facilitators. We realized early on that, given the size of our conference and the complexity of the issues, a team of facilitators would be needed to effectively manage the conferencing process. This team proved helpful in addressing several key areas: assisting with logistical issues involving our site; providing information and support for conference participants; and recording the voluminous data generated during the course of the conference.

The Restorative Conference

Opening the Conference

On November 3, 1999, 46 of us gathered in the early morning at the UCLA Tennis Center. This conference site was chosen because it seemed to suit our process needs in that it was easily accessible but afforded us some

degree of privacy. The room was set in a single large circle as the participants faced each other tenuously as strangers, connected by a much-publi-
cized critical incident that impacted everyone in some way. Our conference
circle contained a diverse cross section of the UCLA community: disabled
students and faculty members, ten players who were the focus of our community concern, family members, coaches, university administrators, students, and alumni. After welcoming people, we moved on to describe our
conference purposes:

1. Create an opportunity for many diverse voices impacted by this incident to be heard;
2. Develop some shared understanding of the impact of the incident on
   the UCLA community;
3. Repair the harm to those individuals impacted by the incident;
4. Restore the university community; and
5. Assist the offending athletes in making better future choices and in
   becoming reintegrated within the campus community.

Storytelling: The Building of Shared Community Understanding

The heart of the restorative circle is storytelling, and it is through the use
of story that transformative change often takes root. After all of the participants introduced themselves, we heard first from the ten athletes. A result of
the process is that people come away feeling validated with regard to their
life experiences. We heard stories of the players' personal use of the disabled
parking placards and the circumstances that gave rise to the incidents. We
learned that the placards were obtained for financial reasons as well as to
accommodate several players getting from classes to practices on time. It was
common knowledge that on-campus parking was difficult for everyone at the
university with considerably more cars than available parking facilities and
was expensive (in excess of $800 per school year). Several players spoke emo-
tionally of the impact their behavior had on their families as well as on their
teammates, whose season was essentially lost as a result of their actions.

Next we heard stories from disabled students and faculty. We listened to
several compelling stories of what life is like for a disabled student or faculty member on the UCLA campus. The participants learned about the hours
spent every day preparing for school, performing tasks that take minutes for
the rest of us. We collectively learned that parking in a disabled-designated
parking space is much more than simply a thoughtless and illegal act. We all
began to understand how this act compounds an already difficult set of circumstances for any disabled person. At the heart of any restorative practice
is the building of a "shared understanding" of all involved parties, and we
were experiencing this by mid-morning of our process.

We then heard from several relatives of the players, who represented yet another layer of impact that few of us had previously realized. One mother spoke of the humiliation of seeing her son's face on the six o'clock news. Another parent learned of the incident as she shopped in her local grocery store, where she saw her son's face on an overhead television as she stood in a checkout line. Another parent, a father as well as a former athlete, spoke emotionally of attending the municipal court hearing for his son and following the hearing, leaving the courtroom and watching as a woman in a wheelchair screamed obscenities at his son and another player. As he related the courthouse incident, the situation had clearly left him demoralized and skeptical of any process aimed at addressing the initial violation.

We learned the following from several school officials, all of whom had been impacted in multiple ways: extensive time devoted to responding to the incident; the constant reminder of the humiliating effects of the incident reading the newspaper, listening to the radio, or watching the evening news on television; and the social impacts outside the workplace when they were frequently questioned by family, friends, and acquaintances about the incident. We also listened to stories from other students, an athlete from another university program, coaches, the police officers involved, and alumni, all of whom seemed to have similar themes of concern and disappointment.

As we concluded our conference storytelling process, one of the participants expressed concern about the credibility of several of the offending students' explanations for their misconduct, specifically the issue of not having the financial resources to pay for on-campus parking. This participant challenged the offending students, observing that many students are faced with similar financial hardships yet they do not resort to illegal means to resolve the issues. The athletes, this participant suggested, had made some bad choices regarding their financial priorities. This individual went so far as to challenge several players about their stated financial deprivation. He questioned one of the offending students directly about both the gold neck chains and what appeared to be some fairly high-priced athletic shoes he was wearing. The tone of the conference was rapidly shifting. Several of the athletes expressed concern about these comments and wanted to respond to them. Clearly, some underlying perceptions and judgments were beginning to surface at this point, and the conference process was beginning to take an unexpected turn. The issue being raised was moving beyond the scope of the offense behavior and the larger issue of the daily lives of student athletes was being questioned.

During our lunch break, the facilitation team explored our options as to how to best address the issues now being raised. We concluded that the issues needed time and space for exploration otherwise the process would likely suffer a loss of credibility. The decision to pursue this path seemed risky but necessary. We realized that attempting to address this issue would take time, and we were running the risk of losing the focus of our conference. It was not until later in the afternoon that the decision would pay off when the level of authenticity of the conference dialogue deepened. We were now confronted with the underlying issues of power, difference, and class that existed on the UCLA campus.

After lunch, we plunged into these difficult issues, beginning with the response of the offending students. One after another, the athletes spoke of what it was like to be a student athlete at a major university and challenged the prevailing myth as portrayed in the media and in the minds of a number of our participants. As they told their deeper stories of the difficulties they faced as student athletes, the constant pressure to succeed on the field, of "being used" by the university to enable millions of dollars of revenue that came with television coverage and bowl game payouts, we began to see a shift in perceptions around the circle. Most notable was the response of several disabled community members who seemed to identify with the daily pressure experienced by the players. One disabled community member remarked that after listening to their stories, she had more in common with the players than anyone else in the circle. This led to an unanticipated development as we moved toward our agreement stage of the conference. It was suggested that as a way to repair the harm resulting from this incident the disabled community and the athletes would actually partner to collectively raise awareness and educate the entire university community about the issues that disabled students, staff, and faculty faced on campus (Lee, 1999). Another request was made by a disabled community member: "Could we no longer refer to the athletes as 'offending students' as this label no longer seemed appropriate." She wanted these students fully restored to the university community.

Repairing the Harm: Achieving Consensus on Sanctions

Our group began to explore sanctioning options and met the following criteria, which had been identified prior to the conference:

1. Repair the harm to the disabled community, the university community, and the athletes themselves;
2. Promote healing and partnership between the disabled and athletic communities on campus;
3. Provide education to the UCLA community on issues affecting the disabled community; and
4. All sanctions needed to be accomplished by the end of the school year.

Our conference participants then brainstormed a series of ideas that could potentially meet the preceding criteria. We then narrowed the suggestions and arrived at a consensus on the following four sanctioning ideas:

1. The athletes and disabled community would collaborate in making a video about campus disability issues, and this video would be produced through the UCLA Film School.
2. The athletes and disabled community would address every freshman class on campus about existing disability issues.
3. The athletes and disabled community would sponsor a campus booth where they could interact with and provide information to the larger university community.
4. Each athlete would participate in a disability awareness presentation on campus presented by a former UCLA athlete, Ken Kilgore, who himself was now disabled.

We then formed a "conference agreement team" consisting of eleven members to meet with the athletes the following week to finalize each agreement. At this point our conference was closed.

Post-Conference Evaluation

As with most restorative practices, we solicited feedback from all of the conference participants through a written conference survey. The conference survey was intended to inform our future processes and provide a personal opportunity for each participant to describe his or her experience. Following is a summary of some of the feedback we received from our participants, including all ten of our offending students.

- 100 percent of the respondents (N = 30) indicated that they were either "very satisfied" or "satisfied" with the overall impact of the conference.
- 83 percent of the respondents (N = 30) indicated that they thought that the students were held accountable and 17 percent responded that they were "unsure."
- 100 percent of the respondents (N = 30) indicated that it was "very important" or "important" that harm to the disabled community was repaired.
- 100 percent of the respondents (N = 29) indicated "yes," that this process would assist the offending students in making better future choices.
- 100 percent of the respondents (N = 30) indicated that it was "very important" or "important" that the harm to the overall community was repaired.
- 95 percent of the respondents (N = 19/excluding athletes) reported that they had either a "very positive" or "positive" opinion of the offending students and one reported feeling "mixed."

- 100 percent of the respondents (N = 30) indicated that they had either a "very positive" or "positive" experience of the conference.

We also asked, "Is there was anything else you would like to say about the experience?" Some of the comments we received included:

- "I thought the experience was extremely positive and as a father, I too learned this offense affected the disabled community."
- "A lot was accomplished today. Offending students were sincere and talking amongst all of us brought out different views and ideas on how the matter should be handled."
- "This was a very good conference. It built upon the family aspects of community. Sometimes a family must discuss and fix difficult problems. That is what was done today. The UCLA family grew today. . . ."
- "It was a positive experience for both the players and the disabled community."

In conclusion, the participant feedback seems to strongly suggest that our conference objectives had been met. During our conference process we had achieved the following outcomes:

1. Many diverse voices impacted by the incident had been heard;
2. Shared understanding of the impact of the incident on the UCLA community had been developed;
3. Harm to those individuals impacted by the incident and the university reputation had begun to be repaired;
4. The athletes had been assisted in making better future choices and were being reintegrated into the campus community.

Conference Follow-Up

The week following our conference, our agreement team was convened and the final agreement was finalized for each and signed, with each of the athletes agreeing to participate in at least two of the proposed activities. Copies of our agreement were subsequently forwarded to all of our participants.

We later learned that in the ensuing months, all of the athletes completed their agreements, although some concern was addressed about whether one individual had actually fully completed his agreement. *The UCLA Parking Violation Video* was produced through the UCLA Film School and was screened across the UCLA campus community.

KEY LESSONS LEARNED

Recognizing the Complexity in Issues of Campus Misconduct

There is no question that this process had been time- and labor-intensive, the most common reason we have heard for not using restorative practices in university and other community settings. We found the presenting issues were themselves complex and the residual effects of the misconduct were equally so. This process gave the university a forum for addressing a set of complex issues that a typical fact-finding approach would not have been capable of achieving. The restorative approach, I believe, allows for a more systemic understanding of misconduct rather than a simple cause (student misconduct) and effect (breaking of university policy) model. The process gave us a lens for understanding misconduct as both an individual act as well as seeing it in the context of a community.

Healing as a Adjudication Goal

One of our most important lessons seemed to focus on the need for healing, particularly in cases in which significant harm had been experienced. Healing, we discovered, comes from unusual places and takes unexpected shapes. The process took us beyond understanding and healing to participants actually wanting to collaborate with one another. Also, the questions we ask in a restorative practice determine what we hear. Asking questions that focus us on issues of understanding harm, responsibility for the repair of harm, and restoration tend to invoke healing responses. Healing victims, the university community, and the offending students are all achievable outcomes of a restorative practice.

The Value of Whole System Participation

Misconduct is often viewed as a violation of some campus policy or norm, yet, as earlier discussed, the impact of the offense is usually much wider and deeper than we might imagine. Bringing more voices to the process allowed us a fuller understanding of this incident, more face-to-face accountability of the offending students to their community and more creativity to the sanctioning process. The process also encouraged each of us to think more systemically and beyond our sometimes limited understanding of how situations affect others beyond ourselves.

Trusting the Process

As a facilitator, this conference presented a series of logistical and process challenges. Providing a balance of structure and the ability to address issues as they surface is probably more art than science. Yet for most of us who were involved in this conference either as a participant or as a facilitator, there were several points where direction seemed uncertain and answers just did not exist. In these moments there was no manual or code of conduct to consult for the answer. Trusting that the "wisdom of the community" would evolve required that we let go of the notion that any one of us had *the* answer, especially myself in my role as lead facilitator.

Accountability to the University Community

Most university discipline processes hold students accountable to a process that does not allow for our students to face the people they have affected. Hence, the accountability is largely to a system or protocol and not directly to the harmed parties. As result, the awareness students receive centers around not breaking the rules rather than the need to repair and restore relationships. This restorative practice went beyond this expectation to actually build relationships when relationships previously did not exist.

Building University and Individual Capacity for Shared Understanding and Problem Solving

By the end of the conferencing process, it was apparent that the collective capacity of the forty-six participants to resolve issues had been increased. We had spent eight hours together listening and speaking respectfully in a way that is often not part of a university experience. In my most optimistic reflection of that day, I see a university community now better equipped to deal with harmful incidents they would face in the future. Here are comments of three of the athletes who participated in the conference, which seem to reflect this expanded capacity for understanding:

- "I learned a lot about the people I affected and I felt confident that others respected my opinions."
- "There are some experiences you remember and some you forget. The experience I had today was one I will remember. . . ."
- "It was a great learning experience where we were able to express our feelings face-to-face with other people who were affected."

References

Lee, Cynthia. "Athletes, Disabled Join Together to Heal." *UCLA Today*, December 14, 1999.

McMasters, Joy. "Justice Circle Promotes Healing in Parking Case." *The Daily Bruin*, November 18. 1999.

Raouf, Neda, Monte Morin, and David Ferrell. "UCLA Football Players' New Opponent: The Disabled." *Los Angeles Times*, July 10, 1999.

Chapter 18

HATE CRIMES AND BIAS-MOTIVATED HARASSMENT ON CAMPUS

Stephen L. Wessler

INTRODUCTION: DANNY'S STORY

Danny was a sophomore at a small northeastern college. He had a work-study job that required him to spend three or four nights a week in the campus center, a small facility containing a couple of pool tables, a couple of ping-pong tables, some couches, and a TV set. His duties were to sign students in and to keep the facility clean and in good order. He also was "out" on his campus as a gay student. On this particular Thursday night, late in the fall semester, Danny came to work at 6:00 and by 8:45 not a single student had come in to use the student center. Danny was getting a significant amount of course work done as a result. At exactly 8:45 two male students entered the room. Both of them immediately picked up pool cues and started playing. Neither of them signed in. Danny politely asked the two students to sign in. One of the students gave him an intimidating stare while the other ignored him. In another 30 seconds Danny repeated his request and received the same response. After a third request with a similar result, Danny went over to a telephone on a table in the far corner of the room to call someone from Student Affairs to find out what he should do. The number that he tried to call was a four-digit intracampus extension.

Danny was able to press only three of the four buttons before he was lifted bodily into the air. One of the two students had come up behind, held both hands around his neck, and was big enough and strong enough to lift Danny two to three inches off the ground while choking him and yelling antigay slurs interlaced with death threats. The student continued choking and shaking Danny for approximately 30 seconds and then threw him down on the desk. After several seconds, the student again picked Danny up by the neck, lifted him completely off the table, and began choking and shaking him while yelling the same slurs and threats. At this point Danny was having trouble breathing and had turned red in the face. The student again threw Danny down on the table and after a few more seconds picked him up a third time, continuing the attack. At that point, another student entered the room to use the facilities, saw what was going on, and his mouth fell wide open. The student immediately yelled something and ran to get help. While Danny's attacker did not come to his senses, the entry by another student was enough to cause him to stop the attack. He realized there would be a consequence to his conduct.

When the presenters began investigating this case with the assistance of student affairs staff at the college, they quickly learned that this incident did not begin at 8:45 in the evening late in the fall semester. Rather, the incident began on the first day that students moved into their residence hall in early September, when students routinely began using antigay slurs, without any particular target. Then, at about the two-week mark of the semester, someone "outed" Danny. From that point on, the routine use of degrading language about gays changed to highly focused and derogatory slurs directed at Danny personally. Over the fall semester, the harassment, which was led by the student who eventually attacked Danny, increased in frequency and in the severity of the language used. Finally, the harassment exploded into life-threatening violence close to the end of the semester.

Not many campuses experience life-threatening hate violence. However, every campus experiences the verbal harassment that, if unchecked, can escalate into hate crimes. Understanding the nature of the problem of bias-motivated harassment in colleges and universities requires an understanding of this process of escalation from the routine use of bias-motivated language to increasingly serious language, to threats, and finally to violence.

HATE CRIMES

The Laws

As of 2002, the federal government, 41 states, and the District of Columbia had adopted hate crime statutes. Because these statutes differ in their approaches, definitions, and penalties, there is no one description of a hate crime. However, a workable definition is:

> A hate crime is a criminal offense committed against persons, property or society that is motivated in whole or in part, by an offenders bias against an

individual's or a group's race, religion, ethnic/national origin, gender, age, disability or sexual orientation (Turner, 2003).[1]

Most criminal hate crime laws provide for an enhancement of the sentence if the criminal conduct was motivated by bias against particular groups that are covered by the jurisdiction's hate crime statute. In addition to criminal statutes, a number of states enforce civil laws that authorize the State Attorney General to obtain restraining orders against individuals who perpetrate bias-motivated violence, threats or property damage.

How Pervasive Are Campus Hate Crimes?

It is difficult to determine with any degree of precision how pervasive hate crimes are on college campuses. This is because hate crimes within colleges and universities are significantly underreported for several reasons. First, many students, faculty, and staff are unsure of what incidents should be reported, when to report them, and to whom they should be reported. Consequently, even individuals who are willing to report hate crimes do not report because of lack of information. Second, it is likely that some university administrators are reluctant to report hate crimes because of fear that their campus will become known as a place where hate crimes occur. Finally, and most significant, victims of hate crimes are often reluctant to report incidents to police or campus administrators because they fear retaliation from the perpetrators, because they minimize their own experiences, or because they believe that campus officials will not take the incident seriously. Additionally, gay, lesbian, bisexual, and transgender individuals who attend schools in states with hate crime laws that do not cover sexual orientation likely will be discouraged from reporting. For these, as well as other reasons, reliable statistics on the extent of hate crimes on campus are hard to develop. Nevertheless, three important sources of data on the extent of hate crimes on campus exist: (1) the Federal Bureau of Investigation (FBI) Annual Report on Hate Crimes, (2) the U.S. Department of Education's Campus Security Statistics, and (3) the International Association of College Law Enforcement Administrators (IACLEA) Annual Survey on Campus Crime Statistics.

- *U.S. Department of Education Data, collected pursuant to the Clery Act.* The Clery Act required colleges and universities to report campus crimes, specifically including crimes that appear to have been motivated by bias. In the most recent data from the Clery Act, approximately 6,000 schools reported a total of 1,910 hate crimes.

---

1. The particular types of bias that are included in any particular hate crime statutes vary significantly between jurisdictions.

- *The FBI Uniform Crime Report on Hate Crimes Statistics.* The 2002 FBI Report on Hate Crimes Statistics is based on reports from 103 colleges and universities from 34 states. The FBI Report indicates that 112 incidents were motivated by bias based on race or ethnicity, 99 incidents were motivated by bias based on sexual orientation, and 49 incidents were motivated by bias based on religion.
- *IACLEA Survey.* The IACLEA Survey is based on an annual survey of college campuses. In 1998, the last year that IACLEA collected data, 411 campuses were surveyed. Of these campuses, 88 reported at least one hate crime on their campus. In fact, these colleges and universities reported an average of 3.8 hate crimes for 1998, yielding a total of 334 incidents. The IACLEA Report indicates that 80 percent of reported hate crimes on college and university campuses were motivated by bias based on race and sexual orientation.

None of the three reporting sources described here is comprehensive. Only a limited number of colleges and universities report hate crimes to each source. Nevertheless, the reports from these campuses indicate that hate crimes on colleges and universities are a significant problem.

What Kind of Conduct Is Involved in Campus Hate Crimes?

Hate crimes occurring within colleges and universities involve a range of criminal conduct from graffiti, to e-mail and written threats, to bombings, and, finally, to violent physical assaults. Hate crimes occur at every type of college at the university and in every part of the nation. Perpetrators include current students, former students, and nonstudents. Following is a description of a sampling of federal and state hate crime enforcement actions involving hate crimes occurring on college campuses (Wessler and Moss, 2001).

- *United States v. Samar.* James Samar, a college student, was indicted on three counts of using threats of force to interfere with the federally protected rights of three college students attending a small Massachusetts college. Samar used anti-Semitic slurs, threatened two fellow students, and threatened to kill one fellow student. In addition, he delivered photographs of holocaust victims to one student and stated, among other things, that the photographs were "a reminder of what happened to your relatives because they too made a mockery of Christianity." Samar entered a plea agreement.
- *United States v. Machado.* A former student was convicted of disseminating an e-mail containing racially derogatory comments and threats to 59 college students, nearly all of whom were of Asian descent.

- *State v. Tozier.* A student at a small college in Maine yelled antigay slurs and threats at a fellow student who was working in a student lounge and, in three consecutive attacks, violently choked the student. The defendant signed a consent decree in a civil rights case brought by Maine's Attorney General.
- *United States v. Lombardi.* A nonstudent was charged with detonating two pipe bombs on the campus of a primarily African-American public university in Florida. After each of the bombings, violent racist telephone calls were made to the local television station.
- *State v. Masotta.* Three white students at a university in Maine left an anonymous racist and threatening message on an African-American student's answering machine. The message ended with the following:

  > I wonder what you're gonna look like dead? Dead. I wonder if when you die you'll lose your color. Like the blood starts to leave your body and you're gonna . . . start deteriorating and blood starts to leave your skin . . . You get the picture? You're *** dead.

  The defendants signed consent orders in a civil rights case brought by Maine's Attorney General.
- *United States v. Little.* The defendant, Robert Allen Little, was charged with igniting a homemade pipe bomb in the dorm room of two African-American students on a small campus in Utah. The letters "KKK" were painted in red fingernail polish on the bomb's firing device. The bomb caused extensive damage to the building and destroyed the belongings of both students. After the bombing, Little returned to the dorm and left a threatening and racist note on the door of another African-American student. Little was sentenced to 12 years in prison, fined $12,000, and ordered to pay restitution.

BIAS-MOTIVATED HARASSMENT

Every college and university in the United States experiences multiple incidents of bias during the year. Bias incidents involve conduct motivated by bias against a victim because of race, religion, ethnic/national origin, gender, disability, or sexual orientation but which does not involve criminal acts. Bias incidents can involve the use of slurs, degrading language, and jokes; written comments that are offensive and degrading; graffiti that does not damage property; and offensive and prejudiced skits.

Based on input from college students received through workshops, conferences, and informal interviews and readings, the use by students of degrading language, slurs, and jokes based on race, gender, ethnicity, and sexual orientation occur with disturbing frequency on college campuses. Students report that they hear fellow students use sexually degrading and homophobic words, often with no particular specific target, multiple times per day; and they hear far more focused and degrading comments aimed at particular students on a regular but less frequent basis.

Bias incidents often have the same emotionally destructive impact on students as hate crimes do. But bias incidents can do even more damage; the routine use of degrading language and slurs aimed at students of color, women, and gays, and lesbians can create an environment in which degrading language and slurs can escalate to serious, and even life-threatening, violent acts. The sequence of events related earlier in "Danny's Story" unfortunately is not an exception. Campus administrators and police see this same pattern, where the use of degrading language and slurs escalates over time to more serious bias-motivated conduct or crimes. A U.S. Department of Justice study (Lockwood, 1997), analyzing middle school violence found that

> [i]n the largest proportion of violent incidents, the "opening move" involved a relatively minor affront [usually involving "minor slights and teasing"] but escalated from there.[2]

Unfortunately, when students, staff, or faculty do not interrupt the use of degrading language and slurs, the powerful, but unintended, message is sent that this kind of language is acceptable. The result is that some students who used or heard the slurs may think that it is acceptable to engage in similar, and sometimes more serious, behavior. This process ultimately can move from degrading language, to graffiti, to threats, and finally to violence.

IMPACT OF HATE CRIMES AND BIAS INCIDENTS

Hate crimes and bias incidents on college campuses can have deep, destructive, and long-lasting emotional impacts, not only on the students who are specifically targeted but also on other members of the campus community. Some students react with fear, sometimes fear that can become paralyzing. Other students become angry. Some feel isolated. Whether students are experiencing fear, anger, or isolation, it can be very hard to focus on academics. Professor Jack McDevitt and colleagues compared the victim impact of bias-motivated assaults with the impact of all other assaults and concluded that hate crime victims suffer greater levels of fear, more job loss, and more significant health issues than victims of non–bias motivated assaults (McDevitt et al., 2001).

---

2. The experience in middle schools differs little in this regard from the campus experience.

Victims of hate crimes or bias incidents and other members of the campus community who learn of the incident can be adversely impacted when campus administrators appear not to take an incident of bias or a hate crime seriously. This process is what victims services professionals refer to as secondary victimization—when individuals believe that the greater community minimizes or fails to respond adequately to their victimization.

Secondary victimization of the targets of hate crimes or bias-motivated harassment on college and university campuses can occur in a number of ways:

- The failure by campus administrators to respond in any way to the incident;
- The suggestion by campus administrators that the incident was not particularly serious;
- The failure of administrators to meet with the student and inform him or her that they are sorry the incident occurred and to inquire whether the student is "okay"; and
- The suggestion by campus administrators that the incident was an anomaly when the targeted students and others believe that the incident was just one of many.

In all of these examples the message received by the targets of bias or hate is that the campus does not think the incident is important or the campus is seeking to minimize the incident for its own purposes. The result is that students feel rejected, humiliated, and angry.

The impact of secondary victimization is felt not only by the particular victims of bias or hate. Students, staff, and faculty from the same ethnic, racial, religious, sexual orientation, or gender group as the victims may also suffer similar feelings of rejection, humiliation, and anger. Moreover, individuals from other groups that historically have been targeted with hate and violence may experience some of these same emotions. Individuals from these groups may suspect that the college or university's response to a future hate crime against a member of their group will show the same indifference and lack of empathy.

EFFECTIVE RESPONSE AND PREVENTION

Effective Response to Hate Crimes and Bias Incidents

Reporting

No campus can effectively respond to bias-motivated incidents or hate crimes unless students, staff, and faculty report incidents to campus police and to campus administrators. Effective reporting, however, does not occur spontaneously. Rather, those campuses that have the most effective reporting broadly disseminate literature on reporting hate crimes and bias incidents; train campus police on identifying and reporting incidents; and train student affairs professionals, athletic staff, and other key employees on the importance of reporting.

Responding to Incidents

The initial response to hate crimes and bias incidents focuses on the victims and the perpetrators. Campus police and student affairs staff must begin investigating who was responsible for the incident while at the same time addressing the physical and emotional trauma of the victims.

Subsequently, those individuals responsible for the crime or the bias incident can be subject to campus disciplinary proceedings and/or criminal prosecution. The sanctions, whether administrative or judicial, are usually punitive rather than restorative.

Effective response to hate crimes or serious bias incidents on campuses, however, goes well beyond addressing the needs of the victims and identifying and punishing the perpetrator(s). Many colleges and universities respond with a public condemnation of bias and violence through campus-wide meetings or letters from the president to the campus community. These efforts both help calm those students, staff, and faculty who feel that their safety has been compromised and increase their trust in campus administrators.

Effective Prevention

Responses to hate crimes or incidents of bias are by their nature reactive. Colleges, universities, and civil rights organizations are expending increasing resources on proactive prevention programs. These prevention programs include:

- Training for student affairs staff, campus police, athletic staff, and student leaders on understanding the destructive impact of bias incidents and hate crimes and practical skills for intervening to stop slurs and degrading comments before they escalate;
- Campus dialogue groups through which students learn skills for discussing emotionally charged issues involving bias and prejudice; and
- Student-led civil rights groups that advocate for the rights of traditionally targeted groups.

CONCLUSION

The potentially fatal experience of Danny, whose story was told in the introduction, is not the norm on American campuses. While life-threatening hate crimes are relatively rare, assaults, threats, property damage, and degrading incidents of bias and prejudice are far too common. The challenge for colleges and universities is to develop effective prevention programs to reduce both the prevalence and the destructive power of bias incidents and hate crimes.

References

Lockwood, Daniel. 1997. *Violence Among Middle School and High School Students: Analysis and Implications for Prevention.* Washington, D.C.: United States Department of Justice.

McDevitt, J., J. Balboni, L. Garcia, and J. Gu. 2001. "Consequences for Victims: A Comparison of Bias- and Non-Bias Motivated Assaults." *American Behavioral Scientist* 45:697–713.

Turner, Nancy. 2003. *Responding to Hate Crimes: A Police Officer's Guide to Investigation and Prevention.* International Association of Chiefs of Police. http://www.theiacp.org.

Wessler, Stephan L. and Margaret Moss. 2001. *Hate Crimes on Campus: The Problem and Efforts to Confront It.* Washington, D.C.: United States Department of Justice.

Chapter 19

POLICY CASE STUDY: RESPONDING TO HATE SPEECH—THE LIMITATIONS OF SPEECH CODES AND THE PROMISE OF RESTORATIVE PRACTICES

BEAU BRESLIN

Schools looking for a shortcut through the First Amendment toward the difficult goal of fighting intolerance forget the obligation to foster a climate of acceptance and open debate. In fact, such a shortcut is an abdication of this responsibility, a white flag that says, muffling the worst about and among us is the best we can do. *The People for the American Way* (1991, p. 25)

THE PROBLEM OF HATE SPEECH

Imagine the following events occurring on a college or university campus: A white student ritually shouting "my parents own you people" whenever he sees a particular female black student; fliers declaring "open hunting season" on all blacks; posters referring to blacks as "saucer lips, porch monkeys, and jigaboos"; a fraternity displaying a 15-foot caricature of a black man complete with a bone in his nose; an anonymous e-mail message sent to a faculty member of Middle Eastern descent that states, "Death to all Arabs! Die Islamic scumbags"; a poster that encourages the reader to shoot all "homos" on sight.

Now ask yourself, how should that imaginary college or university react to these events? What is the proper administrative and academic response to such incidents of hatred and bigotry? Should the students responsible be thrown out of the institution, or should the institution somehow attempt to educate and rehabilitate them? Should the college or university take long-term, drastic measures to combat the possibility of such occurrences repeating themselves, or should that institution look the other way in the name of free expression? Finally, on a more personal level, how should individual members of the academic community respond? Are faculty charged with a responsibility to discuss these incidents in class? Should administrators speak out publicly in favor of free expression and/or against prejudice? Should parents get involved? Should students?

As troubling as it may sound, these incidents have all recently occurred on college and university campuses across the United States. In fact, they are but a small fraction of the examples of hatred and bigotry that now pervade institutions of higher learning. As colleges and universities attempt to increase the presence of minorities (broadly defined) on campus, it seems they are finding it more difficult to handle the tensions that often accompany a push to diversify.

Almost every college and university in the United States has at one time or another confronted the problem. Stephen Wessler observes that despite the tendency to underreport incidents, "hate crimes on colleges and universities are a significant problem" (Chapter 18). And often the response from college and university administrators is all too predictable: They condemn the specific incidents while simultaneously celebrating the general principle of free expression. In response to a racially motivated event on the University of Michigan campus, for example, the president of the university issued a statement "condemning the racist acts" and reaffirming the university's commitment not only to diversity but also to freedom and liberty.

This chapter explores the interplay between the needs of a college or university to be open to the free exchange of ideas and the claim that intolerance is disruptive or deleterious to the academic mission. It begins by sketching the chain of events that inevitably transpire in response to the growing incidence of hate speech on America's campuses. The chapter thus first describes the trend by both public and private universities to curb hateful messages by instituting "campus speech codes" aimed at punishing offenders and deterring future incidents (Earle and Cava, 1997).[1] Inevitably, however, what follows is a legal challenge to the speech codes themselves, and that, I argue, has consequences for the resolution of *future* episodes. Finally, I consider how the use of courts—institutions that are obviously far removed (both literally and figuratively) from the academic setting—impedes the possibility of long-term solutions to the problem of bigotry and hate in America's institutions of higher education. In the end, the simple argument I wish to make is that the use of traditional legal channels to resolve issues of free speech on college campuses invariably results in a too narrow conception of campus discipline. Litigants are accustomed to arguing cases in a particular way, while judges are used to resolving cases in a similarly specific way, and neither litigants nor judges are likely to rec-

---

1. Colleges and universities have many labels or names for their speech regulations. Typically, however, they are called either "campus speech codes" or "anti-harassment codes."

ognize the distinctions that characterize the college and university experience. The result is that once the case enters the courtroom, there is little or no room for alternative models of dispute resolution. I suggest that another model—a restorative model—might be better suited to handle the serious business of hate and prejudice on America's college and university campuses.

THE EMERGENCE OF SPEECH CODES

The college or university setting has long been considered the paradigmatic environment for the free exchange of ideas (Golding, 2000). Both students and faculty alike continue to work in America's institutions of higher learning under the assumption that what they have to say—however bold or controversial—will likely be protected, even if not altogether celebrated. What is the purpose of higher education, many ask, if not the unfettered exchange of ideas? Shouldn't the college or university, more so than perhaps any other distinct community, be the ideal place for the dissemination of all ideas, both noxious and innocuous?

The answers to these and other questions, of course, depend on a number of factors. The official response from all but a few colleges and universities is that America's collective educational environment is freer than ever. We are constantly reminded that most classroom discussions focus on debates about both mainstream and unorthodox ideas, while faculty hiring, tenure, and promotion decisions are largely decided in reference to the quality of academic instruction and inquiry. Indeed, it should come as no surprise to the world at large that the principle that all are engaged in the careful and critical pursuit of the truth lies at the very foundation of the entire academic experience.

Yet many are equally quick to remind us that such a perception often runs counter to the reality. Critics like Alan Kors and Harvey Silverglate have increasingly challenged the very notion of America's colleges and universities as havens for academic freedom. "In the shadow university, [the] precondition of informed change—free and unfettered debate among free individuals—is precisely what has been replaced by censorship, indoctrination, intimidation, official group identity, and groupthink" (Kors and Silverglate, 1998, p. 5). And they are not alone (Craddock, 1995; Sedler, 1992). Critics of the recent development in America's institutions of higher learning suggest that this country's colleges and universities have been co-opted by the rising tide of political correctness, and that such a phenomenon is tantamount to a new and silent form of intellectual tyranny. The left wing progressives, critics contend, have overrun our institutions of higher education and managed to "assert absolute control over the souls, the consciences, and the individuality of our students" (Kors and Silverglate, 1998, p. 4). These "liberal" academics have succeeded in entrenching themselves within the walls of the academy and are now professing their wisdom, oftentimes at the expense of liberty itself. The freedom to think and speak, Kors and Silverglate argue, is pervasive on the college or university campus, so long as one thinks and speaks in a particular way.

At the center of the debate are the twin forces of free expression, manifested on college campuses in the form of academic freedom, and tolerance, a principle that often overlaps in important ways with policies aimed at maximizing diversity and multiculturalism (Hodulik, 1991).[2] The issue of academic freedom, of course, is as old as some of the oldest colleges and universities in the United States, and yet the genesis of speech codes can be traced back only to the very recent past when America's institutions of higher learning responded to episodes of racism, anti-Semitism, homophobia, and so on (O'Neill, 1997, pp. 7–11). Leading universities like Stanford and the University of Michigan introduced speech codes in the mid- to late 1980s. A number of other public and private institutions followed, and by the early 1990s close to 300 campuses across the country had adopted some form of hate speech regulation (Wilson, 1995).

Two specific examples are legendary. The Universities of Michigan and Wisconsin each introduced speech codes during the initial wave of restrictions, and each, in its own way, became emblematic of the problems associated with campus restrictions on free expression. Michigan's flagship university instituted a speech code after a series of incidents that occurred in the winter of 1987. Timothy Shiell describes the events:

> On January 27, 1987, a group of black female students found a pile of handbills in a dormitory lounge declaring "open hunting season" on all blacks (whom it referred to as "saucer lips," "porch monkeys," and "jigaboos"). Shortly thereafter—on February 4, 1987—a disc jockey for the campus radio station encouraged listeners to call in and tell racist jokes on the air (Shiell, 1998, p. 18).

As a result, the university crafted a broad-based regulation in which "behavior that creates an intimidating, hostile, or demeaning environment for educational pursuits, employment, or participation in University sponsored activities"[3] was prohibited.

In designing the regulation, the university divided the campus into three levels, or "tiers," for the purpose of assigning differing degrees of restraint

---

2. Hodulik was the lawyer representing the University of Wisconsin in the late 1980s when the university's speech code was challenged as violative of the First Amendment. She noted that the code was an effective way to balance the principles of free speech and equality.

3. *John Doe v. University of Michigan*, 721 F. Supp. 852 (1989).

to separate constituencies.[4] The first "tier," which was largely immune from restriction, included the student newspapers. What that meant was that stories and editorials that were part of the two major student newspapers were exempt from the restrictions; those newspapers, in other words, were free to print whatever they wanted.[5] The second "tier," in contrast, covered the "public" parts of the university—the public spaces, dining halls, dorms, and so on. Michigan's speech code mandated only limited restrictions on speech in these "public" spaces. Certain messages would not be tolerated in these "public" spaces, while other messages would.

The third "tier," however, involved the academic nerve center of the institution. Classroom buildings, libraries, study centers, laboratories, and other related locations were viewed by the writers of the code as central to the mission of the university, and thus regulation of speech in these areas was far more severe. The pertinent parts of the code read, in part, that individuals were subject to punishment for

1. Any behavior, verbal or physical, that stigmatizes or victimizes an individual on the basis of race, ethnicity, religion, sex, sexual orientation, creed, national origin, ancestry, age, marital status, handicap, or Vietnam-era veteran status, and that:
   a. Involves an express or implied threat to an individual's academic efforts, employment, participation in university-sponsored extracurricular activities, or personal safety; or
   b. Has the purpose or effect of interfering with an individual's academic efforts, employment, participation in university-sponsored extracurricular activities, or personal safety; or
   c. Creates an intimidating, hostile, or demeaning environment for educational pursuits, employment, or participation in university-sponsored extracurricular activities.
2. Sexual advances, requests for sexual favors, and verbal or physical conduct that stigmatizes or victimizes an individual on the basis of sex or sexual orientation where such behavior:
   a. Involves an express or implied threat to an individual's academic efforts, employment, participation in university-sponsored extracurricular activities, or personal safety; or
   b. Has the purpose or reasonably foreseeable effect of interfering with an individual's academic efforts, employment, participation

---

4. According to officials at the University of Michigan, the main purpose behind dividing the campus into three "tiers" was to maximize the impact of the code without significantly interfering with the right of free speech.

5. Obviously, the University of Michigan is a public university, and so the extent of its tolerance toward all views is regulated by the First Amendment.

in university-sponsored extracurricular activities, or personal safety; or
c. Creates an intimidating, hostile, or demeaning environment for
educational pursuits, employment, or participation in university-
sponsored extracurricular activities.

It was clear to many that officials at the University of Michigan were
attempting to curb hateful and bigoted speech, while at the same time trying to maximize the degree of free speech on campus (Johnson, 2000).

The University of Wisconsin speech code, implemented two years after
the University of Michigan code, covered the same general ground. It
resembled the Michigan code in that it prohibited speech or action that
stigmatized or victimized individuals. Wisconsin's regulation, however, went
a bit farther by including guidelines meant to provide context to the vague
provisions of the text. The ordinance noted, for example, that a student
would be in violation if:

(a) He or she intentionally made demeaning remarks to an individual
based on that person's ethnicity, such as name calling, racial slurs, or
"jokes"; and
(b) His or her purpose in uttering the remarks was to make the educational environment hostile for the person to whom the demeaning
remark was addressed.

Continuing, the regulation also mentioned that a student would be in
violation if:

(a) He or she intentionally placed visual or written material demeaning
the race or sex of an individual in that person's university living quarters, or work area; and
(b) His or her purpose was to make the educational environment hostile
for the person in whose quarters or work area the material was
placed.

Perhaps fearing that the courts may not look favorably on their efforts,
officials at the University of Wisconsin admitted to drafting the narrowest
policy possible. Indeed, the university defined inappropriate speech as
"racist or discriminatory comments, epithets, or other expressive behavior directed at an individual or creating an intimidating, hostile, or
demeaning environment for education." Yet despite their cautious
approach, in the end, their fears about the reticence of the judiciary were
well founded.

THE LIMITS OF CAMPUS SPEECH CODES

To be sure, both codes sparked debate. All sectors of the university communities discussed the merits of such speech regulations. But, not surprisingly, what they did not do was eliminate or stifle tension (Schweitzer, 1995). Their effectiveness, in other words, was dubious. At various satellite campuses of the University of Wisconsin system, incidents of hate continued long after the regulation was implemented. Timothy Shiell notes that the "total number of complaints filed under the policies [at both Michigan and Wisconsin] was not high," but complaints were steady (Shiell, 1998, p. 28). Students continued to engage in the activity that gave birth to the regulations in the first place. What was different now was that the courts were being asked to comment on the deeper, more fundamental issues.

The first case to test the parameters of free speech on campus occurred as a result of the University of Michigan's attempt to curb hateful expression. Fearing repercussions from freely discussing controversial biological theories in class, a graduate student challenged the constitutionality of the school's prohibition on First Amendment grounds. He maintained that the speech code was vague and overbroad and that, if enforced, it would likely infringe on constitutionally protected speech. The language of the ordinance, he argued, was not precise enough to give him (or any other person) proper guidance as to what was acceptable speech and what fell outside First Amendment protection.

The District Court for the Eastern District of Michigan agreed.[6] The school's speech code was defined by the District Court as both vague and overbroad. In trying to outlaw admittedly obnoxious and hurtful utterances, the code trampled on areas of expression that have long been protected under the blanket of the First Amendment. Words that "stigmatize" and "victimize," the Court concluded, are used every day, both inside the academy and out, and they are typically protected in America's courtrooms. All members of the University of Michigan community, the Court argued, should be confused by the details of this ordinance; what remains constitutionally protected and what exists outside of these protections are altogether unclear.

Furthermore, the District Court scolded university officials for constructing a speech code that was entirely content-based. The motivation for implementing such a policy was to eliminate certain messages from the college environment, messages that were deemed by most as offensive and hateful. In response to this point, the Court reminded the University of Michigan that "under our Constitution the public expression of ideas may not be pro-

---

6. *John Doe v. University of Michigan,* 721 F. Supp. 852 (1989).

hibited merely because the ideas are themselves offensive to some of their hearers."[7] The very spirit of the First Amendment requires us to tolerate speech that offends our very soul and challenges our self-restraint. The District Court for the Eastern District of Michigan thus ruled that the university's speech code was unconstitutional.

Not surprisingly, a similar case arose as a result of the University of Wisconsin speech code. In writing the code, administrators at the university were influenced by the decision in *Chaplinsky v. New Hampshire*, 315 U.S. 568 (1942), in which the Supreme Court categorized "fighting words" as outside the domain of First Amendment protection. The ruling in *Chaplinsky* stated unequivocally that certain messages—fighting words, in this case—were of such little value that they could be prohibited without violating the First Amendment. Most speech would still receive crucial constitutional protection, the majority in *Chaplinsky* opined, but remarks that were deleterious, were directed at other individuals or groups, and were likely to spark violent reactions, would not be defended. The University of Wisconsin recognized that if it could anchor its speech code to the precedent set in *Chaplinsky*—that is, if it could ground its policy in the "fighting words" doctrine—it stood a better chance of winning the constitutional battle. Hate speech, the school argued, was a close relative of speech intended to cause a fight; both contributed very little to the marketplace of ideas, and thus both could be outlawed.

Despite the school's valid effort to work within the definitional boundaries set by the judiciary in prior cases, the Federal District Court in Wisconsin upheld the constitutional challenge to the university's speech code.[8] The Court was not persuaded by the argument that the code was permissible because it could be located within the parameters of the "fighting words" doctrine. Racist and demeaning utterances would not necessarily result in violent reactions, the Court noted, and thus they did not warrant the type of restriction placed on them by the state. Tying all of the principles together, the District Court concluded:

> The problem of bigotry and discrimination sought to be addressed [by the University of Wisconsin] are real and truly corrosive of the educational environment. But freedom of speech is almost absolute in our land and the only restriction the fighting words doctrine can abide is that based on the fear of violent reaction. Content-based prohibitions such as that in the UW Rule, however well intended, simply cannot survive the screening which our Constitution demands.[9]

---

7. *John Doe v. University of Michigan*, 721 F. Supp. 852 (1989).
8. *The UWM Post, Inc. v. Board of Regents of the University of Wisconsin*, 774 F. Supp. 1163 (1991).
9. *The UWM Post, Inc. v. Board of Regents of the University of Wisconsin*, 774 F. Supp. 1163 (1991), at 1181.

In the end, advocates of free speech hailed the victory in the Wisconsin case as marking the functional end of speech codes on America's university campuses.[10]

In both cases, the federal courts were quick to point out that the college and university setting is distinct. It is in the academic institutions of this country that we must be most vigilant of the right to free expression, they said. Colleges and universities rest almost entirely on the principle that ideas must be aired and that debate must be free. Speaking directly to officials at the University of Wisconsin who had argued that diversity on campus would be *enhanced* with a speech code, the District Court noted the inherent irony: "By establishing content-based restriction on speech, the rule *limits* the diversity of ideas among students and thereby prevents 'the robust exchange of ideas' which intellectually diverse campuses must provide."[11] Speech codes are inherently ironical: they seek to limit speech in the name of fostering greater freedom of speech. In addition, they aim to stifle deliberation by legislating what can and cannot be said. And, finally, the logical consequence of introducing speech codes is an invitation to resolve conflicts, not within the confines of the particular community affected, but rather in the courts, institutions that are not analogous in their aims and purposes to that of colleges and universities.

In fact, no one stopped to ask if the courts themselves are the most appropriate venue for tackling the thorny issue of speech codes. Parties to each case felt violated by the provisions of the codes, and thus they rushed headlong into court to seek relief. But are courts the best place to handle the more fundamental issue at the heart of all speech codes? Are courts the most effective institution to help us out of this cycle of hatred? Some would certainly say so, and yet one might argue that America's courts are *not* properly equipped to recognize, much less provide, the essential needs of most colleges and universities. That is to say, they are designed—programmed, in fact—to resolve disputes in an adversarial way, and that model for dispute resolution is often incompatible with alternative practices that may be *more* effective in the insular setting of a college or university campus. One thing is certain: Our adversarial legal system is dramatically different from a system based on the principles of restorative justice. That difference, I believe, makes a difference.

Undoubtedly, America's judiciary *can* be useful in solving any number of educational issues, but when it comes to the problem of hate speech, it

---

10. The case of *Dambrot v. Central Michigan University* 839 F. Supp. 477 (E.D. Mich 1993) in which the District Court for the Eastern District of Michigan upheld a challenge to Central Michigan's speech code probably marks the actual end of speech codes in the country.
11. *The UWM Post, Inc. v. Board of Regents of the University of Wisconsin,* 774 F. Supp. 1163 (1991), at 1176 (emphasis added).

seems as if the old methods of legal maneuvering simply mask the central problem rather than actually helping to solve it. In other words, courts are ill equipped to move us out of any period that includes the use of racist and bigoted speech precisely because they tend to approach these types of cases in a narrow and singular way, a way that rewards defiance and confrontation and not conciliation and compromise. These are hard issues, to be sure; but as long as we ask courts to resolve issues that are framed in terms of our highest priorities—individual rights versus tolerance, or academic freedom versus diversity—we are asking them to do the impossible; indeed, we are asking courts to choose between competing first principles.

The problem is cultural, and it certainly is not unique to America's colleges and universities. We insist that courts do our most difficult work. In other words, we find great comfort in the adversarial system where there is a clear winner and a loser, and where presumably objective and dispassionate arbiters are asked to choose between competing, and often equally powerful, interests. But should we always aspire to have clear winners and losers?[12]

Mary Ann Glendon has much to say about the cultural phenomenon of courts. She insists that our increased reliance on the judiciary to resolve our problems, and especially those conflicts that pit one fundamental right (or first principle) against another, has led to the demise of our most valued social commitments. She has long maintained that once we enter the courtroom, we surrender any hope of resolving these issues through rational dialogue and the art of compromise: "the language of rights," she says, "is the language of no compromise. The winner takes all and the loser has to get out

---

12. The modern judiciary has been deluged with requests to resolve analogous cases outside the academy, and the results have been mostly mixed. *Santa Fe Independent School District v. Jane Doe* 530 U.S. 290 (2000), for example, involved an Establishment Clause challenge to a school district's policy of permitting student-led, student-initiated prayer at football games. Jane Doe's First Amendment position was that the policy violated the Establishment Clause in that the school—and thus the state—was lending its considerable weight to the promotion of religious teachings. By allowing a student to deliver an "invocation or benediction," the school was de facto endorsing the expression of particular religious beliefs. It did not matter what exactly the student said, what was critical was that it was religious in nature and that it had the support of the state. This, Jane Doe's attorneys concluded, was precisely the type of governmental coercion that the Establishment Clause was meant to prevent. Consequently, they sought to end the practice.

In response to the challenge, however, the Santa Fe school district raised equally serious free speech claims. The school insisted that it could not interfere with a student-initiated program because to do so would be tantamount to censorship. The students should be left to exercise their right to free expression regardless of whether the nature of their comments is non-secular. In other words, the school district insisted that if it silenced the students it would be violating the constitutionally protected right to free speech. The dispute, much like the dispute between advocates of free speech and proponents of greater cultural sensitivity on college campuses, seemingly had to be resolved in the courtroom. It's the American way.

of town. The conversation is over" (Glendon, 1991, p. 9). About America's propensity to speak in this language of rights, she further contends:

> The most distinctive features of our American rights dialect are the very ones that are most conspicuously in tension with what we require in order to give a reasonably full and coherent account of what kind of society we are and what kind of polity we are trying to create: its penchant for absolute, extravagant formulations, its near-aphasia concerning responsibility, its excessive homage to individual independence and self-sufficiency; its habitual concentration on the individual and the state at the expense of the intermediate groups of civil society, and its unapologetic insularity. Not only does each of these traits make it difficult to give voice to common sense or moral intuitions, they also impede development of the sort of rational political discourse that is appropriate to the needs of a mature, complex, liberal pluralistic republic (Glendon, 1991, p. 14).

If Glendon is correct, and I suspect she is, our tendency to frame issues in terms that only contemporary courts can understand signals trouble for America's colleges and universities. The academy, after all, is also a "mature, complex, liberal pluralistic" polity. (Indeed, individuals, both inside the academy and out, view institutions of higher education as replicas of the larger political community). Our insistence that we define our most serious differences in the "language of no compromise" actually impedes our ability to identify long-term solutions for the problem. As Glendon argues, the "most distinctive features" of our modern habits are the precise features that prevent us from imagining the type of community we want to inhabit. The same is true for our communities of learning.

RESTORATIVE RESPONSES TO HATE SPEECH

Which brings us back to the central concern of this volume. Prescriptions for change are perhaps beyond the scope of this chapter. But let me propose one simple suggestion: The practice of restorative justice offers one response to the problem of rigidity and inflexibility so central to our adversarial legal system. It may not be the panacea for all racial tension on college and university campuses, and it may not be appropriate for all cases of campus discipline, but it is an idea that rests on the principle of understanding and conciliation. It brings all affected parties together in a way that the standard legal system simply does not. For that reason alone, it may be worth considering.

Stephen Wessler and Margaret Moss have considered its place on college and university campuses. Their research indicates that victims of bias-motivated harassment and other hate crimes experience considerable trauma as a result of these incidents. They write: ". . . bias incidents can have a traumatic impact on students, staff, and faculty. Members of a campus community often experience fear when they are on the receiving end of degrading language or slurs or see graffiti that targets groups in which they are members. This fear can interfere with the ability of students to fully focus on their academic work" (Wessler and Moss, 2001). Wessler and Moss further insist that victims require institutional support to help them cope with the trauma. To them, and many others, restorative practices can provide the type of support needed.

For example, evidence suggests that victims of bias-motivated crimes want to be heard. Advocates of restorative justice note that when individuals are victimized, they often seek an audience; they want the opportunity to tell their story and to ask questions. In fact, victims insist that they often need to engage in dialogue primarily with the offender; they need to hear the offender speak in his or her own words about the incident, and to answer the many questions that plague them. For that reason, conferencing is well suited to respond to some of the initial needs of victims.

Restorative practices are also useful insofar as serious acts of hate on college campuses are often preceded by minor—but largely overlooked—incidents (Wessler and Moss, 2001). Too often, Wessler and Moss write, there is a pattern of escalation that begins with relatively minor offenses and ends with more serious crimes. The problem, they say, is that schools often do not take the minor offenses as seriously as they should.

A restorative approach helps solve this problem by responding to the minor incident, thereby potentially alleviating some of the tension or conflict that leads to more serious acts of hate. Restorative practices are particularly good at providing parties with a set of expectations for future behavior. Monitoring arrangements can be agreed upon by all parties, and systems can be put in place to ensure that offenders do not repeat their troubling behavior. In addition, offenders can be assigned tasks that relate closely to the offense itself: they can work for community outreach organizations that specialize in issues of race and tolerance, or they could help educate specific constituencies on campus—fraternities, athletic teams, and so on—that may be more likely to engage in the offensive behavior in the first place. They can participate in sensitivity training, research the origins of hate, or write an essay on how speech can be emotionally harmful to many. If successful, the specific practices of restorative justice should provide campus officers with the means to closely monitor the actions of the offender, as well as the ammunition for future action in the event that the offender does not comply with the original terms. Rather than waiting for an offender to get violent, it seems prudent to begin a dialogue as early as possible. Restorative justice recognizes this urgency.

Consider one example. The University of Michigan responded to the incidents in which separate students were responsible for the racist handbills and the on-air jokes by coming down hard on the offenders. "The nineteen-year-old white student who admitted to distributing the first handbill was evicted from his dorm and barred from university housing, and the disc jockey who encouraged the racist call-ins was dismissed from his job at the radio station" (Shiell, 1998, p. 18). Both cases were adjudicated through the university's normal judicial processes, which, not surprisingly, mirrored in many ways the adversarial structure of our criminal justice system. The consequence of these cases, as we know, was an escalating problem of bigotry and hatred on Michigan's campus, eventually resulting in the adoption of a campus speech ordinance.

Now imagine if instead of isolating and ostracizing the perpetrators, the university embraced a restorative approach and brought representatives of all constituencies affected by the students' actions together for a conference. The individuals injured by the hate speech would be able to confront those who were responsible for their pain. In addition, individuals and groups affected in other ways by the racist incidents could tell their stories as well. The result is no doubt a far better teaching moment than can occur in any adversarial environment where the offender is not exposed to his or her victims. True to the mission of an institution of higher education, the parties to the incident could learn from each other, they could hear about the trauma suffered, and together they could propose ways to remedy the problem. The offender could accept responsibility for the incident and he or she could make amends. The entire educational community could benefit. If we believe that educating the campus about the impact of hate speech can be an antidote for the disease of prejudice and bigotry, it seems as if a restorative approach is better suited to achieving that aim.

Speculation is always uncertain, but perhaps if Michigan had embraced a restorative posture at the first sight of racism, the need for a campus speech code would have been reduced. Indeed, as we stand by and watch more and more of our colleges and universities deal with incidents of prejudice, we need to think about alternative models of dispute resolution. In the end, the real irony is that arguably the *least* educational model—the adversarial court system—is the one most often employed when fundamental principles of America's institutions of higher learning are at stake.

Bibliography

Craddock, Jeanne M. 1995. "Words that Injure; Laws that Silence": Campus Hate Speech Codes and the Threat to American Education." *Fla. St. U. L. Rev.* 22:1047.

Earle, Beverly, and Anita Cava. 1997. "The Collision of Rights and a Search for Limits: Free Speech in the Academy and Freedom from Sexual Harassment on Campus." *Berkeley Journal of Employment and Labor Law* 18:282.

Glendon, Mary Ann. 1991. *Rights Talk: The Impoverishment of Political Discourse.* New York: The Free Press.

Golding, Martin P. 2000. *Free Speech on Campus.* Lanham, MD, Rowman & Littlefied.

Hodulik, Patricia. 1991. "Racist Speech on Campus." *Wayne State Law Review* 37:1433.

Johnson, Catherine B. 2000. "Note: Stopping Hate Without Stifling Speech: Re-examining the Merits of Hate Speech Codes on University Campuses." *Fordham Urban Law Journal* 27:1821.

Kors, Alan Charles, and Harvey A. Silverglate. 1998. *The Shadow University: The Betrayal of Liberty on America's Campuses.* New York: HarperCollins.

O'Neill, Robert M. 1997. *Free Speech in the College Community.* Bloomington, IN: Indiana University Press.

People for the American Way. 1991. Hate in The Ivory Tower: A Survey of Intolerance on College Campuses and Academia's Response. Washington, DC: People for the American Way.

Sedler, Robert A. 1992. "The Unconstitutionality of Campus Bans on Racist Speech: The View from Without and Within." *University of Pittsburgh Law Review* 53:631.

Schweitzer, Thomas A. 1995. "Hate Speech on Campus and the First Amendment: Can They Be Reconciled?" *Connecticut Law Review* 27:493.

Shiell, Timothey C. 1998. *Campus Hate Speech on Trial.* Lawrence, KS: University of Kansas Press.

Wessler, Stephen, and Margaret Moss. 2001. "Hate Crimes on Campus: The Problem and Efforts to Combat It." United States Department of Justice, Office of Justice Programs. http://www.ncjrs.org/txtfiles1/bja/187249.txt (December 16, 2003).

Wilson, John K. 1995. *The Myth of Political Correctness: The Conservative Attack on Higher Education.* Durham, NC: Duke University Press.

Chapter 20

CRIME AND SEXUAL VICTIMIZATION ON COLLEGE AND UNIVERSITY CAMPUSES: IVORY TOWERS OR DANGEROUS PLACES?

BONNIE S. FISHER, KRISTIE R. BLEVINS,
SHANNON A. SANTANA, AND FRANCIS T. CULLEN

The civil unrest on American campuses during the 1960s tarnished the image of the college campus as an "ivory tower" where students could further their education in a serene environment protected from the realities of the "real world." Over the next two decades, progress was made to restore the ivory image of college campuses. During the late 1980s and early 1990s, however, college students, their parents, faculty, staff, and campus administrators called the ivory tower image into question as they became increasingly aware of and concerned with campus crime and security-related issues. Today both issues remain salient among college students' parents and the campus community.

In the fall 2000, there were 15,312,299 students enrolled in degree-granting institutions in the United States (U.S. Department of Education, 2002). Given the sheer number of college students and their property, the campus is an important social domain that may be ripe for personal and property victimization. Research has shown that (1) the routines of the campus environment can provide opportunities for victimization (Fisher and Nasar, 1995), and (2) college students have several characteristics that are associated with increased risk of victimization (Fisher, Sloan, Cullen, and Lu, 1998). First, campuses typically have an ebb and flow of educational, social, and recreational activities that allow open access to their buildings, facilities, and green spaces 24 hours a day, 7 days a week, by the campus community and visitors with a variety of purposes (e.g., delivery people, ticket holders to an athletic or cultural event, guests of enrolled students) (see Fisher and Sloan, 1995). Second, college students are young, with a substantial percentage being between the ages of 18 and 21 years old. Third, most students possess many attractive property targets (especially portable electronic devices such as cell phones, CD/DVD players, or laptop computers). Fourth, many students routinely use alcohol and drugs as a form of recreation while a large percentage binge drink (see Harvard School of Public Health, 2002). And last, despite the risk of victimization, very few students use crime prevention measures while on campus (Fisher, Sloan, Cullen, and Lu, 1997).

The empirical research revealing a positive association between college students' characteristics and victimization provides a ripe opportunity to investigate whether campuses are ivory towers that are safe havens from crime or dangerous places that are hot spots for crime. In this chapter, we address the questioning of the ivory tower image of the campuses. The first section examines the events that led to the discovery of campus crime and its rise on the policy agenda of campus administrators and Congress. To separate the myths of on-campus crime from the reality of on-campus crime, we then devote a section to an overview of the extent and nature of on-campus victimization. Here we begin with a discussion of official crime statistics and their limitations and provide research results from college student self-report victimization studies. Continuing with the myth versus reality theme, in the third section we turn our attention to on-campus rape and sexual victimization. We discuss measurement issues surrounding rape and sexual victimization estimates as the backdrop to presenting estimates from (1) official rape and sex offense statistics, and (2) national-level studies of on-campus rape and sexual victimization among college students, primarily college women. Next, we turn our attention to the extent and nature of stalking among college students, particularly college women. We end the chapter by revisiting the nature of campus crime and the reality that the vast majority of such victimizations—including sexual assaults—are never disclosed to campus or law enforcement officials. The implications of these findings for restorative justice are briefly explored.

THE "DISCOVERY" OF CAMPUS CRIME

Several events raised the concerns of college students, their parents, the campus community, and policy makers about on-campus crime and security and fueled their demands for safer campuses. First, in the early 1980s, Mary P. Koss and her colleagues published results from the first-ever national-level study of the sexual victimization of college women. Their research established that sizable proportions of college women had experienced attempted and completed rape, sexual coercion, and unwanted sexual contact within the past year (Koss, Gidycz, and Wisniewski, 1987). Their results quickly became a rallying point for the feminist movement to substantiate their claims that the sexual victimization of college women, heretofore rendered invisible, was rampant.

Second, Howard and Connie Clery, whose daughter was brutally murdered in her dorm room at Lehigh University in 1986, founded Security-On-Campus, Inc. (SOC), a "non-profit grass roots organization dedicated to safe campuses for college and university students" (Security on Campus, Inc., 2002). One of SOC's accomplishments was to successfully elevate campus crime and safety issues on the agendas of Congress and numerous state-level legislatures during the late 1980s. At present, SOC actively engages in lobbying efforts and maintains a web site (see Security on Campus, Inc., 2002) containing campus crime-related resources and information to continually educate current and prospective students and any interested parties as to campus crime and security issues.

Third, through SOC, the Clerys orchestrated a movement to publicize nationally violence on campus as a widespread social problem in need of federal legal intervention. Their actions invoked the passage of state-level legislation to address college student victimization. In 1988, Pennsylvania passed the first campus security reporting law; 16 others states have similar laws (Fisher, Hartman, Cullen, and Turner, 2002). In 1990, *The Jeanne Clery Disclosure of Campus Security Policy and Campus Crime Statistics Act* (20 USC § 1092 (f)) as part of the Higher Education Act of 1965 (the Clery Act)[1] became federal law. Among its mandates, the Clery Act requires private and public institutions of higher education that participate in federal student financial aid programs to publicly disclose and publish information about selected crime statistics on and around their campuses and their security policies. This information must be disseminated annually to all students and employees while prospective students and employees may request this information. Prior to the passage of the Clery Act, colleges and universities did not have to publicly report their crime statistics; the sole source of campus crime statistics, calculated from crimes reported and recorded by law enforcement, was the FBI's Uniform Crime Report (*UCR*) (see Fisher et al., 2002). Research revealed that only a very small percentage of schools reported their crime statistics to the *UCR* in any given year and even fewer schools consistently reported over any length of time (Fisher, 1995).

Fourth, during the 1980s, several crime victims or their families brought civil lawsuits against colleges and universities (including the Clerys, who eventually settled out of court) (Fisher, 1995). The premise behind these lawsuits was that institutions were negligent in not providing a safe campus for students. The courts found in several cases that the schools in question

---

1. The Clery Act was originally enacted by Congress and signed into law by President George H. W. Bush in 1990 as the *Crime Awareness and Campus Security Act of 1990*, Title II of Public Law: 101-542 (see http://www.securityoncampus.org/congress/cleryhistory.html).

were liable for the victimization, mainly because they did not take steps to prevent "foreseeable" crime or offer sufficient security for students and school employees (Smith and Fossey, 1995).

Fifth, campus disciplinary processes for breach of the student code of conduct exist in some form on nearly every campus. A national-level study of 2,438 randomly selected Title IV-eligible postsecondary schools reported that 71.9 percent of these schools mentioned having disciplinary, judicial, or adjudication procedures for a breach in the respective school's code of conduct (Karjane, Fisher, and Cullen, 2001). Originally institutionalized to adjudicate charges of cheating and plagiarism, these campus disciplinary proceedings are now commonly investigating on-campus violent crimes such as rape and assault (Bohmer and Parrot, 1993). Recently, critics have questioned if these proceedings should be handling serious crime, especially in light of research that suggests these proceedings are less than fair to all parties and allegations that schools grossly mishandle cases (Gose, 2000; Karjane et al., 2001; Kors and Silverglate, 1999).

Finally, the media routinely spotlights heinous crimes on or near campuses (see Security on Campus, Inc., 2002). Along with publishing timely articles focusing on student safety issues, *The Chronicle of Higher Education* has made claims of rising violence, arson, hate crimes, and arrests for drug law and alcohol law violations on campus in their annual report based on their survey of campuses with more than 5,000 students (*The Chronicle of Higher Education*, 2000).

Notably, many of these claims about the extent and nature of crime on campus were made without the benefit of reliable or valid data. Nonetheless, the claims, coupled with anecdotal stories of atrocities on campus, led some commentators to dub college and university campuses as "dangerous places" rife with violence and disorders where students were not only carrying books but also carrying guns (Fisher et al., 1998; Smith and Fossey, 1995).

SEPARATING MYTH FROM REALITY: OFFICIAL CRIME STATISTICS AND RESULTS FROM A NATIONAL COLLEGE STUDENT VICTIMIZATION SURVEY

Outside the obsessive media coverage of violence on campuses, two main sources of data are used to estimate the extent of crime on campuses: (1) official crime statistics, and (2) self-report victimization surveys. Official statistics can be found in one of two sources: (1) the U.S. Department of Education which, under the Clery Act, collects statistics from more than 6,000 schools; and (2) the FBI's *UCR*, which includes data for nearly 400 schools in any one year.

The main objectives of the Clery Act are to make students and their parents as well as employees aware of the number and types of on-campus crimes and to help campus administrators enhance campus safety (U.S. Department of Education, 2001). To this end, the Clery Act mandates that Title IV eligible schools publish an annual report every year by October 1 that contains three years of campus crime statistics broken down by four geographic locations: (1) on campus, (2) in campus residential facilities, (3) in noncampus buildings, and (4) on public property such as streets and sidewalks. Schools must report the following types of index crimes as defined by the FBI's *UCR* definitions: (1) criminal homicide [broken down by (a) murder and nonnegligent homicide, and (b) negligent manslaughter]; (2) forcible and nonforcible sex offenses; (3) robbery; (4) aggravated assault; (5) burglary; (6) motor vehicle theft; and (7) arson in their annual security reports. Note that larceny-theft is the only FBI index offense schools are not required to report (a point we will return to later in this section). Arrests or persons referred for campus disciplinary action for liquor law violations, drug-related violations, and weapons possession must also be reported. Schools are also required to disclose data on crimes that are motivated by the offender's bias, in other words, hate crimes (see 20 USC § 1092 (f)).

These campus statistics are compiled by campus law enforcement or security departments or campus officials based on reports of victimization by students and employees (see Security on Campus, Inc., 2003a). The Department of Education, the agency responsible for the implementation of the Clery Act, maintains an electronic campus crime statistics database that the public can search by various criteria (e.g., state, type of institution, size of student enrollment) (U.S. Department of Education, 2003).

Official campus crime statistics can also be obtained from the FBI's *UCR*. Unlike the Clery Act's federally mandated reporting requirement, no such requirements exist for schools concerning reporting to the *UCR*. Their participation is voluntary. This is why only 506 schools have their crime statistics published in the 2001 *UCR*. A second difference between the Clery Act statistics and the *UCR* statistics is that the *UCR* reports larceny-theft and the Clery Act statistics do not include this crime category.

Estimates of campus crime can also be found in studies that have used student or faculty self-report victimization surveys. Almost exclusively, campus victimization studies have been conducted at a single campus (see, e.g., Robinson and Mullen, 2001; Sloan, Fisher, and Wilkens, 1995) with a convenience sample of a limited number of schools and nonrandom selection of student respondents (see, e.g., Mustaine and Tewksbury, 1998) or a subset of respondents from the National Crime Victimization Survey (NCVS) who reported being a college student (see, e.g., Hart, 2003). To date, only one national-level study of college student victimization using a random sample of students has been executed. Fisher and her colleagues (Fisher et al., 1998) developed and administered a telephone survey modeled after the NCVS to 3,472 randomly selected undergraduate and graduate students at 12 randomly selected schools.

The on-campus data sources lend themselves to addressing the issue as to whether college and university campuses are hot spots of crime or ivory towers; that is, do the data from these three sources support the claims that campuses are dangerous social domains? Overall, these data reveal that campuses are not immune from violence. Violent victimization is a rare event, with the exception of rape and other forms of sexual victimization (see next section). For example, based on the 506 schools that reported to the *UCR* in 2001, violent crime accounted for only 2.5 percent of all index crimes. Specifically, there were seven homicides and nonnegligent homicides reported, accounting for 0.28 percent of all violent crimes reported. There were 461 forcible rapes reported, comprising 18.14 percent of reported violent crime. In other words, almost 82 percent of violent crimes reported consisted of robbery and aggravated assault. Additionally, violent crimes made up only 2.6 percent of the total crimes reported. The other 97.5 percent of crime consisted of property crime, with the majority of property crime consisting of larceny and theft (Security on Campus, Inc., 2003).

More evidence refuting the on-campus myths is found in the official statistics collected under the Clery Act. The 2000 data show that 139,218 crimes as mandated by the Clery Act were reported (Security on Campus, Inc., 2002a). Of these crimes, 41,686 crimes or 29.94 percent were reported in the "on-campus (including residence halls)" location. Of these crimes, by far the largest proportion of crime was property crimes (80.59%): 63.67 percent were burglaries (n = 26,543), 13.89 percent were motor vehicle thefts (n = 5,792), and 3.02 percent were arsons (n = 1260). The remaining 19.40 percent of all crimes were personal crimes. Of these 8,091 crimes of violence, less than one percent (0.35%) were murder or negligent manslaughter. Of the violent crimes, 45 percent were aggravated assaults (n = 3644) and 23.9 percent were robberies (n = 1933).

Of all the on-campus personal crimes, 35.24 percent (n = 285) happened in residence halls. The most frequently occurring crime in residence halls was forcible sex offense (45.03%), followed by aggravated assault (38.34%) and robbery (9.86%).

Both sources of official crime statistics show similar patterns of type of crime: Property crimes far outnumber violent crimes. We should note, however, that these two sources of official crime statistics share a common limitation: They reflect only crime reported to and recorded by law enforcement. As to the reporting limitation, research has consistently shown that a large percentage of crimes are not reported to law enforcement. For example, results from nine years (1992–2000) of the NCVS showed that, on average, 52 percent of simple assaults, 45 percent of aggravated assaults, and

43 percent of robberies were not reported to the police (Hart and Rennison, 2003). Similarly, for our interests, two national-level studies of college students show that a large proportion of students do not report their on-campus victimization to campus authorities. First, Sloan, Fisher, and Cullen (1997), in their victimization of college students study, found that 75.6 percent of on-campus personal crimes[2] and 74.8 percent of on-campus thefts[3] were not reported to campus police or other campus officials. Seventy-five percent of the on-campus burglaries were not reported (see also Hart, 2003). Second, Fisher and Cullen (2000), in their violence against college women study, found that 75 percent of the aggravated assaults and 50 percent of the robberies were not reported to campus authorities. Thus, official *UCR* crime statistics and crime statistics mandated by the Clery Act, with the exception of criminal homicide, most likely underestimate the "true" amount of crime on campuses (see Fisher et al., 2002).

Two studies using official crime statistics provide further evidence as to the myth of campuses being dangerous places where crime is rampant. First, Bromley (1992) compared *UCR* index, violent and property crime rates of Florida's nine public state universities to their respective adjacent cities and surrounding counties. He found that the three crime rates for each university were significantly lower than the crime rates of the city or county, respectively. Second, using official statistics from 416 college and universities across 18 years (1974–1992), Volkwein, Szelest, and Lizotte (1995) reported that since 1985 all violent and property crime categories except campus vehicle theft, which remained level, fell through 1992. Related to the reporting limitation of official statistics, Volkwein and his colleagues argued that "the decline in campus crime rates cannot be attributed to declines in the frequency of reporting crime acts by campus victims, and police. In fact, the current environment encourages the reporting of crime . . . to far greater extent than a decade ago" (p. 666). Supportive of Bromley's "campuses are safer" results, Volkwein et al. reported a 27 percent decrease since 1974 in on-campus violent crimes (from 88 to 64 per 100,000), while violence in the nation increased by 41 percent (from 460 to 758 per 100,000). Similarly, they reported that in 1985 the on-campus property crime rate began to decrease as the national property crime rate increased.

Results from victimization surveys of college students and faculty echo results as those reported from official on-campus crime statistics: high rates of property crimes compared to low rates of violence. First, a nationally representative study of victimization among 3,472 college and university stu-

---

2. Personal crimes included rape, sexual assault, robbery, aggravated assault, and simple assault. All were defined as per the National Crime Victimization Survey's definitions.
3. Thefts include personal larceny with and without contact, motor vehicle theft, and motor vehicle burglary.

dents reported that students are not immune to crime while on campus (Sloan et al., 1997). Nearly one-fourth of the respondents had been victimized at least once on campus since the beginning of the current academic term (note that students were interviewed in the spring) (Fisher et al., 1998). Supportive of the results using official crime statistics, theft was by far the most frequently occurring crime on campus. The on-campus theft rate was 114.6 per 1,000 students compared to the on-campus violence rate of 31.7 per 1,000 students. Within the category of theft, the rate of personal larceny without contact, 109.5 per 1,000 students, far exceed the rate of personal larceny with contact, 5.2 per 1,000 students. Within the crimes of violence, simple assault was the most common (12.1 per 1,000 students) on campus. Only one student (0.3 per 1,000 students) reported being robbed on campus and nine students (2.6 per 1,000 students) experienced an aggravated assault.

Second, Fisher and her colleagues' student victimization results are supportive of an earlier study by Campus Crime Prevention Center at Towson State University of 11,000 undergraduates that reported that 37 percent of the students had experienced victimization on campus during their college tenure (see Siegel and Raymond, 1992). The three most common types of victimization reported (in order of frequency) were (1) theft, (2) vandalism, and (3) fights/physical assaults. Third, Wooldredge, Cullen, and Latessa (1992) surveyed full-time faculty at one urban university as to their on-campus victimization experiences over the previous year. Supportive of the student victimization studies, they reported that 27 percent of the faculty reported experiencing property crime and only 5 percent reported experiencing a personal crime.

Fisher et al. (1998) also examined whether college students are at higher risk of criminal victimization while on or off campus. They concluded that there is no easy answer to this question; although some on-campus crime rates are higher than off-campus rates, others are slightly lower. Evidence of this pattern can be seen when comparing theft and violence rates. While the rate of off-campus violent crimes was 1.2 times higher than the rate of on-campus violent crimes, the rate of on-campus thefts was 2.1 times higher than the off-campus theft rate. Thus, students are more likely to experience a theft on campus compared to off-campus. Their conclusion is supported by results from the 1995–2000 NCVS that showed the majority of violent crimes against students occurred off campus. Notably, the number of off-campus victimizations was over 14 times greater than the number of on-campus victimizations (Hart, 2003).

Data from official *UCR* crime statistics, the Clery Act crime statistics, or victimization surveys reveal that crime happens on campuses. These crime data are quite clear that the campus community is not immune to either violent or property victimization. Even so, the portrait of campuses as hot spots of violence is simply not supported by the data.

While college campuses should not be portrayed as inundated with violent crime, it should be noted that there tend to be high levels of alcohol and drug offenses on campuses. As reported in compliance with the Clery Act, in 2000, there were 42,455 arrests for liquor law violations and 124,673 disciplinary referrals for liquor law violations. Arrests and disciplinary referrals for drug violations were somewhat less, yet still substantial totals: 25,351 and 26,596, respectively (Security on Campus, Inc., 2002a). According to Hoover (2003), these offenses have been increasing yearly over the past 10 years. Based on data collected under the Clery Act, liquor law violations increased 4.7 percent and drug law violations increased 5.5 percent from 2000 to 2001. Although these increases may be the result of more rigorous enforcement, rather than increased violations, there were more liquor law and drug law violations reported in 2000 and 2001 than burglaries and motor vehicle thefts combined. This trend is troublesome given that research indicates that many perpetrators of campus crime are students under the influence of drugs and/or alcohol at the time of the offense (Fisher et al., 1998; Hart, 2003; Siegel and Raymond, 1992).

RAPE AND OTHER FORMS OF SEXUAL VICTIMIZATION

Beginning with the work of Kanin (1957), the victimization research suggests that college students, especially women, may be more at risk than men for some types of victimization: rape and other forms of sexual victimization (e.g., sexual coercion, sexual harassment) (see Crowell and Burgess, 1996). These findings are consistent with a routine activities/lifestyle perspective (see Cohen and Felson, 1979; Fisher et al., 1998; Hindelang, Gottfredson, and Garofalo, 1978; Schwartz and Pitts, 1995). College students converge regularly in time and space, often with minimal adult supervision, both on and off campus. Male and female students also often cohabitate in the same building (e.g., coed dormitories, cooperatives, or apartments), socially interact in the evening hours (e.g., studying, dating, attending a party or fraternity-sorority event), consume alcohol and/or partake in drugs together, and retreat to private settings (e.g., residence hall rooms, apartments) where there is an absence of guardianship (see Fisher et al., 1998). To the extent that men are "motivated offenders," college women will be in numerous situations on and off campus where they are exposed to the risk of victimization (see Fisher et al., 1998; Mustaine and Tewksbury, 1999; Schwartz and Pitts, 1995). One contention of feminist scholars is that such motivated offenders are not in short supply: The hegemony of patriarchy ensures that the propensity of males to pursue sexual relationships and, if necessary, to use force against women in this pursuit is widespread (Gilbert, 1997; Messerschmidt, 1993).

Only recently has a substantial literature examining the rubric of "sexual victimization of college women" developed. The 1970s and 1980s saw many inquiries into the incidence and prevalence of sexual victimization of college women, including studies on date and acquaintance rape, sexual assault, and sexual harassment (see, e.g., MacKinnon, 1979; Koss, Gidycz, and Wisniewski, 1987). Assessing the extent to which female college students are in fact sexually victimized is a daunting challenge, since estimates of victimization often hinge on a variety of methodological choices (compare Gilbert, 1997, with Koss, 1992, 1993, 1996; see also Crowell and Burgess, 1996; Fisher and Cullen, 2000). Even so, there is evidence that a substantial proportion of college women experience rape and other forms of sexual victimization during their college tenure. Evidence indicates that between 8 percent and 15 percent of college women have been the victims of forced sexual intercourse (i.e., rape) during their college tenure (see Belknap and Erez, 1995). It is instructive that Fisher et al. (1998) found that the rate of rape victimization in their sample of college students was approximately three times higher than that reported for the 1993 NCVS general population of the same age; the rate of sexual assault in their sample was nine times higher. Koss and her colleagues (1987) reported that 11.4 percent of college women experienced sexual coercion (114.8 per 1,000 college women)[4] in the last year and 27.2 percent experienced sexual contact (278 per 1,000 college women).[5] The estimates for the college women are higher than the percentages they reported for college men: 5.6 percent experienced sexual coercion in the last year (56 per 1,000 college men) and 12.7 percent experienced sexual contact (128 per 1,000 college men).

Researchers have documented that other forms of on-campus sexual victimization (e.g., sexist or degrading remarks, blatant propositions) against women students are commonplace on campuses (see Paludi, 1996). For example, some of these studies reported that one in three women students have experienced sexual harassment by faculty members at least once during their college tenure (see Belknap and Erez, 1995). Recently, Fisher and her colleagues (2000) reported that over half of their respondents (54.3%) were subjected to sexist remarks within an academic year. Just over half of these incidents (50.6%) happened to the respondent while she was on campus.

Although illuminating, most of these studies have not examined the extent of *on-campus* rape and other forms of sexual victimization. Like other forms of campus crime discussed previously, two sources of rape and sexual victimization statistics exist: (1) official crime statistics, and (2) national-

---

4. Sexual coercion was defined as sexual intercourse subsequent to the use of menacing verbal pressure or the misuse of authority.
5. Sexual contact was defined as fondling and kissing that did not involve attempted penetration.

level victimization studies. Beyond the previously discussed reporting limitation of official crime statistics, there are additional limitations with respect to sexual victimization. The *UCR* report only forcible rape. Crime statistics as per the Clery Act include forcible sexual offenses and nonforcible sex offenses. Hence, both sources of official data are limited in terms of the types of sexual victimization that they report.

Looking at the 2001 *UCR* forcible rape statistics for campuses, one can easily come to the conclusion that forcible rape is a rare event on campuses. Sixty percent (60.7%) of the schools reported zero forcible rapes, 19.6 percent reported one forcible rape, and only 19.8 percent reported two or more rapes. A similar conclusion about sex offenses could be drawn when examining the 2,000 forcible sex offenses and nonforcible sexual offenses as per the Clery Act. Of all the personal crimes, 10.6 percent were forcible sexual offenses and 4.1 percent were nonforcible sexual offenses. Murder and negligent manslaughter were the only two crimes that comprised a smaller percent (1.1% and 0.3%, respectively).

Both of these sources of official crime statistics, however, are grossly misleading. Like other types of crimes, rape and sexual assault are both under-reported by college students as shown in the results from three national-level studies. First, Fisher and her colleagues reported that 78 percent of rapes[6] and 83 percent of sexual assaults[7] that happened on campus went unreported to campus law enforcement and other campus officials (Sloan et al., 1997). Second, in their sexual victimization study of 4,446 female students enrolled at 233 randomly selected two-year and four-year schools, Fisher, Cullen, and Turner (2000) reported that of the completed rapes that occurred on campus, none were reported to the campus police or other campus authorities (e.g., dean, professor, or resident assistant). Of the on-campus attempted rapes, fewer than ten percent (9.4%) were reported to the campus police. None of the attempted rapes were reported to other campus authorities. Fisher and Cullen's (2000) findings from their national-level study of violence against college women are consistent with the previous college women victimization research: A large percentage of these women do not report their sexual victimization to any campus author-

---

6. Like in the NCVS, rape was defined as forced sexual intercourse including both psychological coercion and physical force. Forced sexual intercourse means vaginal, anal, or oral penetration by the offender(s). This category also includes incidents involving penetration using a foreign object such as a bottle. Includes attempted rapes, male as well as female victims, and both heterosexual and homosexual rapes. Attempted rape includes verbal threats of rape.

7. Like in the NCVS, sexual assault was defined as a wide range of victimizations, separate from rape or attempted rape. Includes attacks or attempted attacks generally involving unwanted sexual contact between victim and offender. Sexual assault may or may not involve force and include things such as grabbing or fondling.

ity. To illustrate, in the violence against college women study, of those incidents that happened on campus, 60 percent of the rapes and 90 percent of the sexual assaults were not reported to law enforcement.

Estimates of the extent of on-campus rape and other forms of sexual victimization from self-report victimization surveys reveal that these victimizations are more widespread than official statistics would lead us to believe. To illustrate, Fisher and her colleagues' (1998, 2000) study of the sexual victimization of college women reported an on-campus completed and attempted rape[8] rate of 11.1 victims per 1,000 female students for an average reference period of seven months. On a campus with, say, 10,000 female students, there may well be close to 140 rapes in a given academic year (based on an incident rate of 13.7 [n = 61] per 1,000 college women)— nowhere close to the official statistics reported for any one school in either the *UCR* crime statistics or the Clery Act sex offenses statistics. Salient to the focus of this chapter, 30 of the 49 (61%) on-campus rape victims were repeat victims; that is, they experienced more than one on-campus rape incident during a seven-month period.

Fisher et al. also calculated rates of completed and attempted sexual coercion[9], 14.7 per 1,000 female students, and rates of completed and attempted unwanted sexual contact[10] with and without force, 58.2 per 1,000 female students. Repeat victimization was common for both these types of sexual victimization. Thus, all of the women who experienced sexual coercion were repeat victims, with women experiencing, on average, 4.8 incidents of sexual coercion (std dev = 2.4). Similarly, all of the women who experienced unwanted sexual contact with or without force did so repeatedly. These women experienced an average of 8.7 incidents of sexual contact (std dev = 4.0).

---

8. Completed rape was defined as unwanted completed penetration by force or the threat of force. Attempted rape was defined as unwanted attempted penetration by force or the threat of force.

9. Completed sexual coercion was defined as unwanted completed penetration with the threat of nonphysical punishment, promise of reward, or pestering/verbal pressure. Attempted sexual coercion was defined as unwanted attempted penetration with the threat of nonphysical punishment, promise of reward, or pestering/verbal pressure.

10. Completed sexual contact with force or threat of force was defined as unwanted completed sexual contact (not penetration) with force or the threat of force. Sexual contact includes: touching; grabbing or fondling of breasts, buttocks, or genitals, either under or over your clothes; kissing; licking or sucking; or some other form of unwanted sexual contact. Completed sexual contact without force was defined as any type of unwanted completed sexual contact (not penetration) with the threat of nonphysical punishment, promise of reward, or pestering/verbal pressure. Attempted sexual contact with force or threat of force was defined as unwanted attempted sexual contact (without penetration) with force or the threat of force. Attempted sexual contact without force was defined as unwanted attempted sexual contact (not penetration) with the threat of nonphysical punishment, promise of reward, or pestering/verbal pressure.

Fisher and her colleagues also reported from their sexual victimization of college women study results that provide insight into the nature of on-campus sexual victimization. First, in over 96 percent of all types of sexual victimization incidents, the perpetrator was a lone male. Second, supportive of previous research, they reported that most victims knew the person who sexually victimized them. Most often, a boyfriend, ex-boyfriend, classmate, friend, or acquaintance sexually victimized these women—many of whom can be assumed to be a fellow college student. College professors were not identified as committing any on-campus rapes or sexual coercions, but they were cited as the perpetrator in a low percentage of cases involving unwanted sexual contact. Third, the majority of sexual victimization occurred in living quarters, either those of the victim or in another's living quarters on campus. For example, 62.3 percent of the on-campus completed and attempted rapes occurred in the victim's living quarters, and 23 percent of these rapes occurred in another's living quarters on campus. Incidents of sexual coercion and unwanted sexual contact had a similar location pattern.

BEING STALKED: A HIDDEN COST OF COLLEGE?

Researchers have shown that individuals with certain demographic and lifestyle/routine activities are more likely to be criminally stalked than those individuals who do not posses these characteristics (Fisher, Cullen, and Turner, 2002; Tewksbury and Mustaine, 1999; Tjaden and Thoennes, 1998). College students' demographic and lifestyle/routine activities are characterized by high-risk factors identified by the general population stalking research (see Fisher, 2001). First, the majority of the 15 million college students are young, with 82 percent of them being undergraduates. The stalking research has consistently reported that stalking victims are young, with 52 percent of the victims being between the ages of 18 and 29 (Tjaden and Thoeness, 1998). Second, college students are "relational mobile" in terms of dating and intimate relationships as well as platonic friendships (Spitzberg and Rhea, 1999). Research shows that a stalking victim-pursuer relationship typically precedes the pursuit behavior. For example, Tjaden and Thoeness (1998) reported that for female victims, 19 percent of the stalkers were an acquaintance, 14 percent were dates/former dates, and ten percent were a cohabiting partner/ex-partner. Third, in a substantial proportion of stalking cases, this relationship involved acts of aggression, violence, and sexual victimization (Tjaden and Thoennes, 1998). Such brutal acts are not uncommon among college students involved in dating or an intimate relationship, and most relationship aggression, violence, and sexual victimization is committed by a fellow student (Fisher et al., 2000).

For the stalker to engage in a repeated course of conduct or pattern of pursuit behavior, that person must have access to the victim as well as time to engage in pursuit behavior. From a stalker's perspective, access to the campus is relatively unrestricted, especially if this person is a fellow student. Many campuses have permeable boundaries because they are designed like public parks. Campuses typically never close; they are "open" 7 days a week and 24 hours a day to both students and visitors. Many buildings are never locked, or some buildings, such as the library or computer center, are not locked until late at night. Other buildings, such as dormitories, may have no access requirements during certain times of the day. This easy access coupled with students' academic lifestyle of attending regularly scheduled classes every term and social activities, including making new friends and entering into dating relationships, could contribute to being easily stalked. Additionally, students can be readily located when not in their scheduled classes because their campus address, e-mail address, and on-campus employment address can typically be found in an online university website directory. This information can then be used by a stalker to approach the victim outside his or her residence (such as a dormitory) or place of employment, or to contact the victim by sending gifts, making phone calls, or sending e-mail messages. These acts are relatively effortless if the victim lives on campus because many schools use "no-cost" intercampus or intracampus mail and telephone calls to on-campus telephone numbers. Sending an e-mail message requires minimal effort because today's "high-tech" student is assigned an e-mail address when registering and has access to computer labs located throughout the campus (and some campuses now offer wireless access to e-mail).

A limited, yet growing body of research exploring the extent of stalking among college students has been published (see Fisher, 2001). In part, the measurement of criminal stalking is a young enterprise because stalking was not criminalized by all states, the District of Columbia, and the federal government until the early 1990s (Fisher et al., 2002). The measurement of stalking among college students is characterized by two weaknesses. First, much of this research has employed a relatively small convenience sample drawn from a single campus (see Fisher, 2001, Table 9.1). For example, Logan, Leukefeld, and Walker (2000) used 130 students enrolled in an introductory communications class at a medium-sized southeastern university to examine stalking that occurred following a difficult breakup with an intimate partner. Others have opted for convenience samples from psychology courses or from undisclosed classes that enrolled primarily upperclass students (see Fisher, 2001, Table 9.1). As is well known with single-site studies, the generalizability of the results from these investigations is questionable. Second, the majority of studies used a lifetime reference frame when asking about students' stalking experiences. For example, Frenouw,

Westrup, and Pennypacker (1997) performed two stalking studies using a convenience sample of undergraduates enrolled in psychology classes at West Virginia University. They reported that 31 percent of the females and 17 percent of the males had ever been stalked. However, it is difficult, if not impossible, to know from this reference frame the extent to which college students were stalked while attending college.

There is only one source of estimates of the extent to which college student are stalked: self-reported victimization studies. Neither the *UCR* nor the Clery Act report stalking statistics. Two studies, only one national-level study using a random sample of female students, reported estimates as to extent of stalking among college women when the respondents were college students. First, using a convenience sample of females enrolled in introductory sociology and criminal justice courses located at nine four-year and two-year schools, Mustaine and Tewksbury (1999) reported that 11 percent of their female student respondents reported being stalked[11] six months prior to the administration of their survey. Second, using data from their national-level study of the sexual victimization of college women, Fisher and her colleagues (2000, 2002) reported that 13.1 percent of the females (130.1 per 1,000 female students) in the sample had been stalked[12] since the school year began for a period, on average, of approximately seven months. This estimate is similar to the six-month estimate reported by Mustaine and Tewksbury (1999).

Although our understanding of stalking among college students remains limited, some patterns have emerged in this small, but growing, body of knowledge. First, research has consistently reported that females are more likely to be stalked than males (see Fisher, 2001). Second, in a large percentage of the incidents, the victim knew the stalker. For example, Fisher and her colleagues (2002) reported that four of five stalking victims knew their stalker. Of the stalkers who were known, they were most often a boyfriend or an ex-boyfriend (42.5%), a classmate (24.5%), an acquaintance (10.3%), a friend (9.3%), or a coworker (5.6%). Female students were infrequently stalked by their professors or graduate assistants. Supportive of these results, Frenouw et al. (1996) reported that about four of five women knew their stalkers; over 40 percent had "seriously dated" them. Adding further insight into the victim-stalker relationship, Logan et al. (2000) found that 29 percent of the college women reported being stalked after a difficult breakup. Third, stalking is not limited to on or off campus or just one location. Fisher and her colleagues (2002) reported that more than two-thirds of the pursuit behaviors used to stalk college women were exhibited either on

---

11. Stalking was not defined in the paper.
12. Stalking was defined as the same person exhibiting repeated pursuit behavior that seemed obsessive and made the respondent afraid or concerned for her safety.

campus or both on and off campus; only 31.4 percent of these behaviors occurred exclusively off campus. Most often, victims were stalked at their residence. Other common locations for stalking were over the telephone or through e-mail, in a classroom, at work, or going to and from someplace.

Similar to their not reporting sex crimes to the police, victims of stalking rarely reported their experiences to the police. Fisher and colleagues (2002) found that 83 percent of the stalkings were not reported to the police or campus law enforcement officials. They also noted that few students invoked legal interventions against the stalker: In a little less than four percent of the incidents did a respondent seek a restraining order, in only two percent of the incidents did the respondent file criminal charges, and in a little over one percent of the incidents did the victim file civil charges. Female students were also not likely to use formal disciplinary processes available at their respective institutions; only three percent of the incidents involved a victim filing a grievance or initiating disciplinary action. Rather, the two most common responses by the stalking victim were to avoid or try to avoid the stalker (43.2% of incidents) and confront the stalker (16.3% of the incidents) (Fisher et al., 2000).

CAMPUS CRIME, CONTROL, AND RESTORATIVE JUSTICE

It is understandable that previously quiescent media sources, victims groups, and policy makers are prompted by heinous offenses to focus attention on crimes in certain social domains, such as college campuses. If collectively we have been guilty of "looking the other way" for too long, these atrocities serve to puncture our complacency and to teach us that places unthinkingly considered safe havens—like the "ivory towers" of universities—are not beyond the reach of criminal predators. However, the risk in concentrating inordinately on tragically serious crimes is that this voyeurism can lead us to overgeneralize—to portray what is rare (and thus newsworthy) as though it were commonplace. As we have seen in our review of the research on campus crime, serious violence—despite its depiction as a widespread problem ignored by university officials—remains an infrequent occurrence. Murders and vicious assaults take place within the confines of the ivory tower, but they are the exception and not the rule. Most often, illegalities assume a much more mundane quality, with the most frequent offenses being petty thefts and, to a lesser extent, minor assaults.

We have also seen, however, that for many years, one realm of victimization—sexual assault and stalking, especially of college women—was largely overlooked. Feminist scholars and advocate groups have succeeded in calling attention to these issues, but their claims have been disputed as ideologically driven and as based on biased empirical data (see, e.g., Gilbert,

1997). Importantly, recent research confirms that female college students not only are likely to experience sexist remarks and a measure of sexual harassment but also are at risk of being stalked and being subjected to a range of sexually coercive acts, including rape (Fisher et al., 2000, 2002). To be sure, only a small percentage of women in any given year are victimized by rape or attempted rape on campus—or elsewhere. But the risk of such victimization certainly rises when a woman's multiple-year career in college is considered. Furthermore, even small percentages—when calculated over a large population base—can produce disquietingly large absolute numbers of rape and attempted rape victims (see Fisher et al., 2000).

A barrier to preventing sexual assaults and other campus crimes is that only a small fraction of victimizations are reported to campus police, let alone to law enforcement officials in the community. Except for serious offenses or those in which remuneration requires a police report (e.g., motor vehicle theft), victims in general are reluctant to report their victimization to law enforcement agencies. Although rationales can vary somewhat by the type of offense, victims often cite as reasons for non-reporting that the event was "not serious enough," that they did not think that the "police would do anything," that they did not want family members or others to know they were victimized, and that they feared reprisals. Similar statements are voiced by college students when they are asked to explain why they did not report a criminal victimization, including sexual assaults (Fisher, Daigle, Cullen, and Turner, 2003). The other central issue is that most victims of sexual assault and other direct-contract predatory crimes know—to one degree of the other—the perpetrator.

In a way, this finding on non-reporting and the reasons given for not doing so should not be surprising: It suggests that students victimized on campuses act in ways similar to those victimized in the larger society. In another way, however, the modest rate of reporting of victimization—especially of sexual victimization and stalking—is grounds for concern. Unlike the public at large, students are members of a campus community. To report an offense, they do not have to travel to a distant, impersonal police agency "downtown." Rather, this college community has its own justice system, including police officers who are readily at hand and a judiciary or disciplinary system specially established to deal with student transgressions. There also are school counselors and professors who might be consulted. Instead, if students tell anyone about their victimization, it is most likely their friends (Fisher et al., 2003).

Undoubtedly, it is naïve to anticipate that reporting behavior will be transformed quickly or easily. Still, the failure to report victimizations creates "missed opportunities" for college students to help victims and insulate them from repeat victimization, to punish and treat offenders, and to prevent future crimes from occurring. Although research is sparse, if not nonexistent, one potential institutional barrier to reporting crimes is that campus judiciary systems are not seen as effective instruments for remedying the harms students have suffered. There are now an increasing number of accounts of how offenses brought before such bodies frequently leave some party, if not all parties, unsatisfied—victims who believe that justice has not been done, alleged offenders who claim their due process rights have been trampled, and the campus community, which is often split apart over who got the "raw deal" in the proceedings (see, e.g., Bohmer and Parrot, 1993; Gose, 2000).

The potential institutional barriers to reporting and responding effectively to student victims is illustrated in the findings of our project with the Education Development Center, Inc., which examined the policies of post-secondary institutions for handling sexual assault cases (Karjane et al., 2001). Although not the case with many institutions (e.g., junior colleges), most four-year public and private universities have written codes of student conduct as well as published materials, educational programs, and services aimed at helping victims of sexual assault. Despite these important advances and likely good intentions of campus officials, gaps in the institutional policies and practices often exist.

For example, many universities list a telephone number to call in the event of a sexual assault, but do not note whether this number is operating in evening and weekend hours—at precisely the time when sexual assaults are most likely to transpire. A large minority of institutions also fail to make available safety-related materials that do contain instructions to preserve evidence of an assault (e.g., do not shower, do not clean up the location of the offense)—a key consideration in proving a victimization where consensual behavior is likely to be claimed. Furthermore, universities often target residence hall assistants and students working in security positions for training in responding to disclosures of rape incidents, but do not educate the parties most likely to learn of a victimization—those in the general student population who are friends of the victim. Four-year institutions typically have educational programs regarding sexual assault, but less than a third have special orientation programs for those most at risk for victimization—new students entering the school. Few universities, moreover, advise student victims that they will offer them legal assistance if a crime report is made. And if a victim does report an offense, the specifics of the disciplinary process are frequently difficult to disentangle from student codes—assuming a student knows such a code exists and how to access it. It is often unclear how the investigation will be conducted, who will comprise the hearing committee, and what due process rights the accused will, or will not, be accorded. Most institutions usually do not explicitly mention whether victims will be afforded "rape shield" protections—a guarantee that the victims' past sexual behavior will not be introduced and publicized at a hearing (Karjane et al., 2001).

At this stage, it remains unclear whether the current approach to handling campus crimes, especially those involving sexual victimization, can be substantially improved. Some tinkering and more victim-oriented education might make some difference (for suggestions, see Karjane et al., 2001). But the stubborn reality is that students are unlikely to report offenses committed by people they know—typically fellow students—when the result often exacts a cost on them (e.g., time, emotionally) and brings uncertain benefits. Universities also are faced with the daunting challenge of administering a disciplinary system that wishes to avoid becoming fully adversarial and legalistic but that is willing, on occasion, to impose harsh penalties on alleged offenders in the absence of due process protections. It is doubtful that this sanctioning system, especially in sexual assaults and other difficult cases, will ever be capable of consistently serving the interests of victims, offenders, and the campus community.

In this context, restorative justice emerges as an option to the current campus judicial or disciplinary systems that vacillate between leniency and harshness, with little evidence that its way of exercising control prevents offending. To be sure, restorative justice is no magic cure to the problems of fostering justice and safety on college campuses, and this approach may face complicated issues in trying to address serious victimizations like rape (see, more generally, Braithwaite, 2002; Levrant, Cullen, Fulton, and Wozniak, 1999). Even so, restorative justice offers key benefits lacking in most current approaches to student discipline: an opportunity to restore the harm done to victims, to reintegrate offenders into the campus community, and to send an educational message to students and faculty about the boundaries of moral behavior. In the least, this approach warrants vigorous and extensive experimentation as we endeavor to think in fresh ways about how best to respond to crime and other transgressions within the social domain of higher education.

References

Belknap, Joanne, and Edna Erez. 1995. "The Victimization of Women on College Campuses: Courtship Violence, Date Rape, and Sexual Harassment, pp. 156–178 in *Campus Crime: Legal, Social, and Policy Perspectives*, edited by J. J. Sloan III and B. S. Fisher. Springfield, IL: Charles C Thomas.

Bohmer, Carol, and Andrea Parrot. 1993. *Sexual Assault on Campus: The Problem and the Solution.* New York: Lexington Books.

Braithwaite, John. 2002. *Restorative Justice and Responsive Regulation.* New York: Oxford University Press.

Bromley, M. 1992. "Campus and Community Crime Rate Comparisons: A Statewide Study." *Journal of Security Administration* 15:49–64.

The Chronicle of Higher Education. 2000. "A Look at Campus Crime." *The Chronicle of Higher Education*, June 9. Retrieved July 1, 2003 (http://chronicle.com/free/v46/i40/40a04901.htm#1year).

Cohen, Lawrence E., and Marcus Felson. 1979. "Social Change and Crime Rate Trends: A Routine Activity Approach." *American Sociological Review* 44:588–608.

Crowell, Nancy A., and Ann W. Burgess. 1996. *Understanding Violence Against Women.* Washington, DC: National Academy Press.

Fisher, Bonnie S. 1995. "Crime and Fear on Campus." *American Academy of Political and Social Science* May:85–101.

———. 2001. "Being Pursued and Pursuing During the College Years: Their Extent, Nature, and Impact of Stalking on College Campuses," pp. 207–238 in *Stalking Crimes and Victim Protection: Prevention, Intervention, Threat Assessment, and Case Management*, edited by J. A. Davis. Washington, DC: CRC Press.

Fisher, Bonnie S., and Francis T. Cullen. 2000. "Measuring the Sexual Victimization of Women: Evolution, Current Controversies, Future Research." David Duffee (editor). *Measurement and Analysis of Crime and Justice, Criminal Justice 2000, volumne 4.* Washington, DC: National Institute of Justice, U.S. Government Printing Office.

Fisher, Bonnie S., Francis T. Cullen, and Michael G. Turner. 2000. *Sexual Victimization Among College Women: Results from Two National-Level Studies.* Washington DC: National Institute of Justice, U.S. Government Printing Office.

———. 2002. "Being Pursued: Stalking Victimization in a National Study of College Women." *Criminology and Public Policy* 1:257–308.

Fisher, Bonnie S., Leah E. Daigle, Francis T. Cullen, and Michael G. Turner. 2003. "Reporting Sexual Victimization to the Police and Others: Results from a National-Level Study of College Women." *Criminal Justice and Behavior* 30:6–38.

Fisher, Bonnie S., Jennifer L. Hartman, Francis T. Cullen, and Michael G. Turner. 2002. "Making Campuses Safer for Students: The Clery Act as a Symbolic Legal Reform." *Stetson Law Review* 32:61–89.

Fisher, Bonnie S., and Jack L. Nasar. 1995. "Fear Spots in Relation to Microlevel Physical Cues: Exploring the Overlooked." *Journal of Research in Crime and Delinquency* 32:214–239.

Fisher, Bonnie S., and John J. Sloan III (eds.). 1995. *Campus Crime: Legal, Social and Policy Issues.* Springfield, IL: Charles C Thomas.

Fisher, Bonnie S., John J. Sloan III, Francis T. Cullen, and Chunmeng Lu. 1997. "The On-Campus Victimization Patterns of Students: Implications for Crime Prevention by Students and Post-Secondary Institutions," pp. 101–126 in *Crime Prevention at a Crossroads*, edited by S. P. Lab. Cincinnati, OH: Anderson.

———. 1998. "Crime in the Ivory Tower: The Level and Sources of Student Victimization." *Criminology* 36:671–710.

Frenouw, Williams J., Darrah Westrup, and Jennifer Pennypacker. 1997. "Stalking on Campus: The Prevalence and Strategies for Coping with Stalking." *Journal of Forensic Sciences* 42:666–669.

Gilbert, Neil. 1997. "Advocacy Research and Social Policy," pp. 1–79 in *Crime and Justice: A Review of Research*, edited by M. Tonry. Chicago, IL: University of Chicago Press.

Gose, Ben. 2000. "Brandeis Lawsuit Puts Campus Courts in the Dock: Private Colleges Nationwide Now Fear Increased Scrutiny of Their Disciplinary Codes." *The Chronicle of Higher Education*, July 21. Retrieved July 1, 2003 (http://www.chronicle.com/free/v46/i46/46a03301.htm).

Hart, Timothy C. December 2003. *Violent Victimization of College Students.* Washington, D.C.: Bureau of Justice Statistics, U.S. Government Printing Office.

Hart, Timothy C., and Callie Rennison. March 2003. *Reporting Crime to the Police, 1992–2000.* Washington, DC: Bureau of Justice Statistics, U.S. Government Printing Office.

Harvard School of Public Health. 2002. "College Alcohol Study." Boston, MA: Harvard School of Public Health, Retrieved July 1, 2003 (http://hsph.harvard.edu/cas).

Hindelang, Michael J., Michael R. Gottfredson, and James Garofalo. 1978. *Victims of Personal Crime: An Empirical Foundation for a Theory of Personal Victimization.* Cambridge, MA: Ballinger.

Hoover, Eric. 2003. "Drug and Alcohol Arrests Increased on Campuses in 2001." *The Chronicle of Higher Education*, May 16, pp. A38–A39.

The Jeanne Clery Disclosure of Campus Security Policy and Campus Crime Statistics Act (20 USC § 1092 (f)).

Kanin, E. J. 1957. "Male Aggression in Dating-Courtship Relations." *American Journal of Sociology* 63:197–204.

Karjane, Heather M., Bonnie S. Fisher, and Francis T. Cullen. 2002. *Campus Sexual Assault: How America's Institutions of Higher Education Respond.* Newton, MA: Education Development Center, Inc.

Kors, Alan C., and Harvey A. Silverglate. 1999. *The Shadow University: The Betrayal of Liberty on America's Campuses.* New York: HarperCollins.

Koss, Mary P., Christine A. Gidycz, and Nadine Wisniewski. 1987. "The Scope of Rape: Incidence and Prevalence of Sexual Aggression and Victimization Among a National Sample of Higher Education Students." *Journal of Counseling and Clinical Psychology* 55:162–170.

Koss, Mary P. 1992. "The Underdetection of Rape: Methodological Choices Influence Incidence Estimates." *Journal of Social Issues* 48:61–75.

———. 1993. "Detecting the Scope of Rape: A Review of Prevalence Research Methods." *Journal of Interpersonal Violence* 8:198–222.

———. 1996. "The Measurement of Rape Victimization in Crime Surveys." *Criminal Justice and Behavior* 23:550–569.

Levrant, Sharon, Francis T. Cullen, Betsy Fulton, and John F. Wozniak. 1999. "Reconsidering Restorative Justice: The Corruption of Benevolence Revisited?" *Crime and Delinquency* 45:3–27.

Logan, T.K., Carl Leukefeld, and Bob Walker. 2000. "Stalking as a Variant of Intimate Violence: Implications from a Young Adult Sample." *Violence and Victims* 15:91–111.

MacKinnon, Catherine A. 1979. *Sexual Harassment of Working Women: A Case of Sex Discrimination.* New Haven, CT: Yale University Press.

Messerschmidt, James W. 1993. *Masculinities and Crime: Critique and Reconceptualization of Theory.* Lanham, MD: Rowman & Littlefield.

Mustaine, Elizabeth E., and Richard Tewksbury. 1998. "Predicting Risks of Larceny Theft Victimization: A Routine Activity Analysis Using Refined Lifestyle Measures." *Criminology* 36:829–857.

———. 1999. "A Routine Activity Theory Explanation for Women's Stalking Victimizations." *Violence Against Women* 5:43–62.

Paludi, Michele A. (ed.). 1996. *Sexual Harassment on College Campuses: Abusing the Ivory Tower.* Albany, NY: State University of New York Press.

Robinson, Matthew B., and Kenneth L. Mullen. 2001. "Crime on Campus: A Survey of Space Users." *Crime Prevention and Community Safety: An International Journal* 3:33–46.

Schwartz, Martin D., and Victoria L. Pitts. 1995. "Exploring a Feminist Routine Activities Approach to Explaining Sexual Assault." *Justice Quarterly* 12:9–31.

Security on Campus, Inc. 2002. "About Security on Campus, Inc.: Our Mission Is Safer Campuses for Students." King of Prussia, PA: Security on Campus, Inc., Retrieved July 1, 2003 (http://www.securityoncampus.org/aboutsoc/ index.html).

———. 2002a. "College and University Campus Crime Statistics, 1998–2000." King of Prussia, PA: Security on Campus, Inc., Retrieved July 1, 2003 (http://www.securityoncampus.org/crimestats/2000.html).

———. 2003. "College and University Campus Crime Statistics." King of Prussia, PA: Security on Campus, Inc., Retrieved July 2, 2003 (http://www.securityoncampus.org/crimestats/ucr01.pdf).

———. 2003a. "Complying with the Jeanne Clery Act." King of Prussia, PA: Security on Campus, Inc., Retrieved July 1, 2003 (http://www.securityoncampus.org/schools/cleryact/text/html).

Siegel, Dorothey G., and Carlinda H. Raymond. 1992. "An Ecological Approach to Violent Crime on Campus." *Journal of Security Administration* 15:19–29.

Sloan, John J., Bonnie S. Fisher, and Francis T. Cullen. 1997. "Assessing the Student Right-to Know and Campus Security Act of 1990: An Analysis of the Victim Reporting Practices of College and University Students." *Crime and Delinquency* 43:148–168.

Sloan, John J., Bonnie S. Fisher, and Deborah L. Wilkens. 1995. *Crime, Fear of Crime, and Related Issues on the U.A.B. Campus: Final Report.* Birmingham, AL: University of Alabama at Birmingham.

Smith, Michael R., and Richard Fossey. 1995. *Crime on Campus: Legal Issues and Campus Administration.* Phoenix, AZ: The Oryx Press.

Spitzberg, Brian H., and Jill Rhea. 1999. "Obsessive Relational Intrusion and Sexual Coercion Victimization." *Journal of Interpersonal Violence* 14:3–20.

Tjaden, Patricia, and Nancy Thoennes. 1998. *Stalking in America: Findings from the National Violence Against Women Survey.* Washington, DC: U.S. Government Printing Office.

U.S. Department of Education. 2001. "Campus Security: The Statute." Washington, DC: U.S. Department of Education, Retrieved July 3, 2003 (http://www.ed.gov/offices/ope/ppi/secuity.html#statute).

———. 2002. "Fall Enrollment in Institutions of Higher Education." *Higher Education General Information Survey.* Washington, DC: National Center for Education Statistics.

———. 2003. "Office of Postsecondary Education Security Statistics." Washington, DC: U.S. Department of Education, Retrieved July 3, 2003 (http://www.ope.ed.gov/security/search.asp).

Volkwein, J. Fredericks, Bruce P. Szelest, and Alan J. Lizotte. 1995. "The Relationship of Campus Crime to Campus and Student Characteristics." *Research in Higher Education* 36:647–670.

Wooldredge, John D., Francis T. Cullen, and Edward J. Latessa. 1992. "Victimization in the Workplace: A Test of Routine Activities Theory." *Justice Quarterly* 9:325–335.

Chapter 21

PROGRAM CASE STUDY: CAMPUS-BASED SEXUAL ASSAULT SERVICES—ON THE CUTTING EDGE

CONNIE J. KIRKLAND

I never thought it could happen to me. I still don't know how it did. One minute we were sitting there watching a movie; the next minute he was all over me.

George Mason University student

Although sexual assault and related acts of violence have historically been common occurrences on college campuses across the nation, university and community recognition of this phenomenon has only come to the forefront within the past 15 years. Beginning with the high-profile case of rape, burglary, and strangulation of a freshman coed in her dormitory at Lehigh University in suburban Philadelphia, Pennsylvania, campus security became "newsworthy" (Fisher and Sloan, 1995). After the murder trial of Jeanne Clery's assailant and the civil suit against the university in which Lehigh was found responsible for negligence, failure to protect, and failure to warn, the Clery family founded Security on Campus, Inc. in 1989, a non-profit organization dedicated to improving safety and security on America's college campuses (Security on Campus, Inc., 2002).

FEDERAL LEGISLATION ENCOURAGED SERVICES

The federal Crime Awareness and Campus Security Act passed by Congress in 1990 (Title II of Public Law 101-542) is in large measure due to the efforts of the Clery family and the late Frank Carrington, a Virginia lawyer who raised the Congressional awareness level substantially regarding the need for increased security on the nation's college campuses. Carrington, then counsel to Security on Campus, Inc., drafted both the Virginia Campus Security Act and the federal Crime Awareness and Campus

Security Act. His diligence and tenacity, coupled with the passion of the Clerys, resulted in a document that found its way into the hearts and minds of federal legislators.

The Campus Security Act, as this new law came to be known, requires that all campuses report Part I crimes as defined in the Uniform Reporting Handbook of the FBI. An institution must report statistics for the three most recent calendar years concerning crime on campus or in campus-owned and operated buildings. These crimes are not exhaustive, but include homicide, sex offenses, robbery, aggravated assault, burglary, motor vehicle theft, and arson. In addition, arrests for liquor law and drug law violations and illegal weapons possession must be reported. Perhaps more importantly, however, these same statistics must be provided to college students, campus employees, and prospective students and their parents. The Act, which has been amended several times, also requires that each college and university has policies and procedures for intervention and discipline for these major crimes as well as educational programming to help reduce the risks of college students becoming victims by promoting awareness of rape and other sexual assaults.

Although the act, known as the Clery Act since its 1998 amendments, does not require stalking or dating violence statistics or policies, there is little doubt that this legislation has raised the campus consciousness regarding these issues.

> You know, at first, I didn't tell anyone. I thought no one else would understand. I didn't think that anyone I knew had been raped. But one night I did tell one of my friends and she told me that she knew five other people—also friends of mine that had been raped too. I was so sad. She told me to come to see you and then I might feel better.

After the passage of the Campus Security Act, other important legislation addressing the issue of campus sexual assault followed quickly, to include the Campus Sexual Assault Victims' Bill of Rights in 1992 (20 U.S.C. 1092f). This bill became part of the U.S. Department of Education's Higher Education Reauthorization Act in the same year, which included seven areas that must be addressed by institutional policy regarding campus services for victims of sexual assault. This bill has since been incorporated into the Clery Act (34 C.F.R. 668.46).

> When she walked into the office, she seemed so withdrawn and so quiet. She listened, though, to all the rights that she had as a sexual assault victim. "You have rights guaranteed to you under the law!" the advocate told her. You can make a police report and choose to prosecute to try to punish your perpetrator; or you can choose to file a university judicial complaint and have a school proceeding to find the perpetrator responsible and be given academic sanc-

tions; or you can file a civil lawsuit to seek damages for being harmed by your perpetrator . . . or you can do all three! It's your choice. She smiled faintly.

In 1994 the Violence Against Women Act (VAWA) was enacted (P.L. 103-322). This complicated and much needed piece of legislation included funding to increase sexual assault programming and victim services on college campuses, thus paving the way for more campus victim services. Amendments to these and other pieces of legislation have continued through the past 10 years to strengthen the original campus security laws. The U.S. Department of Education is the federal agency with the power to enforce and monitor the effects of these campus-based laws and services. In fact, the U.S. Department of Education commissioned the development of a campus security document in 1994 to assist colleges and universities as they began to develop policies, procedures, and response protocols to victims of crime on their campuses and to fully comply with federal requirements (Kirkland and Siegel, 1994). Of special interest and focus was the high number of campus sexual assaults. As Fisher et al. write (see Chapter 20), acquaintance rape is now and has been one of the most frequent crimes committed on college campuses today. The awakening of college campuses to the need to provide services to their own student crime victims came a couple decades later than within communities, but with the motivation of federal regulations and media attention of campus crime, administrators have begun to understand the value of victim-based services on their campuses.

A CAMPUS MODEL

During the early 1990s, the Commonwealth of Virginia was also assessing the problem of sexual assault on its college campuses. A statewide task force to study the issue of campus sexual assault was created in 1990 by Governor Douglas Wilder. After intense scrutiny by this group composed of faculty, staff, and students from some of Virginia's major universities, it offered findings to Wilder in early 1993. As a result, the governor emphatically recommended that every college and university in Virginia create three positions to address the issue: (1) a victim advocate based within the campus police department, (2) a specialized counselor within the campus counseling center to respond to student victims, and (3) a coordinator for sexual assault services who would serve as "the hub of the wheel" on any given campus to coordinate the many demands related to campus sexual assault both within the boundaries of a campus and its neighboring jurisdictions as well as to collaborate with other service providers throughout the Commonwealth.

George Mason University, a Virginia university of over 28,000 students located just across the Potomac River from Washington, D.C., had been studying this need on its own for some time. Encouraged by Governor Wilder's special attention to campus sexual assault, the university created two new positions that continue to exist today. The first position was a counselor in the university's counseling center to respond specifically to sexual assault. The second position, and one that has been replicated in several other universities around the state and country, was that of coordinator of campus sexual assault services. The university police victim assistance program, developed in 1989 and considered valuable in the response to campus sexual assault, continued.

> The traditional law enforcement emphasis has always been on the offender . . . the victim (had) taken a back seat in our society. . . . The victim had received little or no attention, even though he or she is actually the focal point of the whole system. . . . The victim, as the most important person in the process, is entitled to dignity and respect. Kirkland (1988)

These three offices collaborated vigorously to achieve a comprehensive response on this large suburban campus. The George Mason University Sexual Assault Response System Protocol Manual states that the implementation of services on campus will be overseen by the Sexual Assault Services Coordinator and that continuity of services among departments, such as counseling and police, is the responsibility of the Sexual Assault Services Office. The goal of this protocol is to specify information for each of the university departments that constitute the immediate support network for students involved in a case of sexual assault, to include boundaries of confidentiality, services offered by the department, options and choices available to the student, and statements about services offered by the department (George Mason University, 2003).

For most crime victims, the criminal incident is a life-threatening experience. The victim is a person in crisis, a person whose life has been interrupted by the trauma of crime. Since crime is an unexpected event in one's life and most individuals are not adequately prepared to handle it well, a victim's response is a series of reactions to the stress of the incident. And victims certainly do not react in the same manner. Victims of sexual assault, stalking, and dating violence often experience feelings of despair, denial, fear, anger, guilt, and helplessness (Koss and Harvey, 1991). Assistance to these innocent victims of crime, which was initiated by grassroots organizations in the 1970s, focused on the victims and society's response to victims. The "systems" approach to dealing with crime victims began to evolve. This approach uses an interdisciplinary team, including medical, mental heath, legal, social services, and law enforcement personnel. The victim may come into contact with all of these helpers, and each must be prepared to respond positively to the person in need (Kirkland, 1988).

College students who have been sexually assaulted most often experience effects on their academic functioning. In nearly every case, the victim cannot perform at the usual level. The academic impact may be felt immediately following the incident or may not be recognized until sometime later. But the negative impact is powerful and, at times, prohibitive for continuation of the normal course load. As a victim attempts to return to a normal lifestyle, there may be great difficulty in concentrating. Missing classes becomes commonplace, either as a result of increased general social withdrawal or in an attempt to avoid seeing the perpetrator. Sleeplessness at night due to anxiety may translate into decreased energy and academic motivation by day (Kirkland, 1994).

She went with her female friends to a bar they had gone to many times before. At some point, she left the table and her friends to use the restroom. Because there was a long line at the main floor restroom, she walked up the stairs to a smaller restroom that she knew was there. She didn't notice being followed; all she knew was that there was no one else in line when she arrived. She had barely gotten into the small room when a man unknown to her burst in, blocking her exit and demanding sex. He told her he had a knife and that he would use it. She followed his demands. After the rape ended, he told her to go back to her friends and not to look around for him. He would be watching her.

Just as he had instructed, she did not tell her friends. She did, however, say that she needed to leave and did so. The next day, after a sleepless night, she called her older sister and became hysterical as she told her what had occurred the night before. A resourceful sister looked to the internet and found the number of the victim's university sexual assault advocacy center. She called the number and told the advocate the basics of what had happened and how traumatized her sister, the victim, was. She said she'd have her sister call the center soon. She did make the call.

The rape victim came into the advocate's office that very day; she wanted to make a police report; the advocate facilitated that and the student said she would go directly to the police department. But she did not. She went back to her lonely apartment instead and spent another sleepless night.

The next day the advocate called her to see if the reporting had been traumatic and was told by a very tearful student that she "just couldn't do it, knowing they would ask all those very personal questions." The advocate understood and advised that she really should consider getting a physical examination to check for possible injuries, STDs, and pregnancy. The student agreed to come right into the student health services. She did and she also spoke with the advocate again, explaining that she didn't feel like she could attend classes or return to her work. The advocate made contact with each of her professors, informing them only that the student had experienced a severe trauma and would need a few days before returning to class.

Nearly one month has passed; the student victim has not returned to class nor has she taken the advocate's advice to seek therapy. She has gone back to her job; she needs the money from that job to pay for her classes; she really has no choice. She missed a follow-up medical appointment, has fallen behind in reading and projects for school, has not informed her other family members of her situation. She spends most of her time when not at work simply in her apartment alone, feeling anxious and depressed. She has made an appointment with a community therapist. She believes she will be able to return to her classes next week.

The awakening of college campuses to the need to provide services to their own student crime victims came a couple decades later than within communities, but with the motivation of federal regulations and media attention of campus crime, administrators have begun to understand the value of victim-based services on their campuses.

Although some colleges and universities were quick to see the need for services, many have abandoned these valuable programs, primarily due to lack of available funds and perhaps lack of priority among competing campus needs. At George Mason University, however, the program that was created in 1993 as a result of a governor's recommendation is thriving in 2004 for a a couple of very important reasons—namely, an intense administrative commitment to continue such services, as well as the expansion of this innovative program through federal Violence Against Women Act (VAWA) funding to George Mason University Sexual Assault Services Office, which has been awarded funds continuously since 1997. Supportive services are kept confidential until the victim/survivor requests assistance from other agencies or offices. All services are offered at no expense to the George Mason University community.

Services offered to the George Mason University community by the Sexual Assault Services Office include:

- Comprehensive assistance to reports of sexual assault, stalking and dating violence;
- A resource for students reporting a recent or past incident, including crisis intervention and referrals;
- Information on sexual assault, stalking, and dating violence to survivors as well as to students for research purposes;
- Trained student Peer Companions to provide assistance and support to student survivors;
- Psychological, medical, legal, and judicial support and information;
- Academic intervention;
- Educational programming; and
- Emergency housing assistance.

As a primary resource for a student reporting an incident, the Sexual Assault Services Office provides 24-hour services to students assaulted both on and off campus. With a strong philosophy of empowerment toward students who are affected by campus sexual assault, dating violence, and stalking, Sexual Assault Services overcomes the barriers that might keep students from disclosing an incident and thus from receiving needed services in order to keep them at the university pursuing their education.

BARRIERS TO REPORTING

It is well documented (see Chapter 20) that campus sexual assault victims rarely report their incidents to the police. In fact, the estimate is that only 5 percent of such assaults are reported to police. What, then, are the barriers to reporting for sexual assault victims? One of the biggest dilemmas is reporting someone the victim knows. When exactly does a person become a non-stranger, or an acquaintance? How long does one have to know someone for him or her to be considered a non-stranger? Many non-strangers are introduced through friends or other acquaintances. A certain level of trust is assumed, rightfully or not, because of this common introduction. When this person, known for a day, a week, a month, or a year, chooses to rape, the victim almost always questions herself or himself.

Why didn't I realize what he was going to be like?
Why did I go alone with him?
Why did I invite him to my home?
Why was I so stupid not to recognize what he was planning?

It is always difficult for people to understand why a rape victim would not immediately contact the police and make a formal report, especially when rape causes more trauma than any crime short of murder. What are the factors that might keep that call from occurring? Let's look at what the victims of non-stranger rape are like on a college campus. Most of these victims are traditional students, which means they are between the ages of 17 and 24. This is the age group that believes they are invincible and invulnerable, even though they are also experimenting with alcohol and/or other drugs, dating new-found friends, staying out later in the evening than ever before, living on their own for perhaps the first time, and essentially enjoying their risk-taking years (Warshaw, 1994).

So why don't victims in this category report their incidents to police and want to prosecute the crimes that have occurred to them? They fear they will not be believed. When the media highlights stranger rapes with injury and or well-known men with money (Mike Tyson, William Kennedy Smith, Marv Albert, Kobe Bryant), the question becomes "just who is on trial?" Blaming the victim is widespread; it seems so much easier than believing that a star athlete or political family member could be responsible for the crime. After all, the victim is probably not known well by society at large.

If a victim tells anyone at all, she or he often first tells a friend, a relative, a hotline, a counselor. Often, valuable time is lost for evidence collection, but we must learn to investigate cases even when a forensic examination will produce nothing, when a case "seems cold," when a victim finally realizes that she is not to blame! Barriers must be understood from the viewpoint of the victim in such cases.

> "I was drinking with him . . . and he'll say we just got drunk and had sex."
>
> "I let him give me a ride home from a party . . . and I invited him in for awhile."
>
> "I have been sexually assaulted before . . . I guess I just deserve it."

It must be remembered that being sexually assaulted is a crisis, not just a crime. And what follows causes the victim to lose her or his equilibrium, to not be able to immediately regain normalcy, to not be able to continue her or his routine without difficulty. The response that any victim has to a sexual assault is often affected by one or more of the following factors: intensity of the incident, duration of the incident, or suddenness of its occurrence (Foa and Rothbaum, 1998). Trauma resulting from a rape or other sexual assault is complicated when one decides to report to authorities. At this point the victim must contend with police interviews; medical examinations; physical concerns, such as STDs, HIV, pregnancy, injuries; telling the "story" over and over; and explaining what happened to family and friends, some of whom will believe the victim and some of whom will not.

A SUCCESSFUL PROGRAM

What George Mason University's Sexual Assault Services does, and does well, is to coordinate with participants in the overall response (legal, medical, academic, housing, and psychological), whether on or off campus in order to offer a consistent, timely, and effective victim-centered response. Creating, and reviewing annually, a university sexual assault policy that includes all the options that a student might want and/or need is the beginning. Too many schools have no policy or have not revised their policy to meet today's federal statutes. At George Mason University, the Sexual Assault Services Office (SAS) developed and has chaired since 1997 a "University Sexual Assault Campus-Community Coordinating Council" that not only meets quarterly, but also has the responsibility of reviewing all policies, procedures, programming, and tasks of the Sexual Assault Services Office. This council was instituted as a result of the Violence Against Women Act federal funding that the SAS office received at that time. The Council has, thus far, created the university's stalking policy and protocol and annually revised the university's sexual assault policy. Without the input of this very active council, the SAS office staff would not be nearly as productive or successful.

So, how does one measure success? Since its creation in 1993, the number of incidents reported to SAS has continued to increase. In the past 10 years, reports from students to this office have skyrocketed from 43 in 1994 to nearly 100 in 2003. SAS staff believe that this is indicative of students understanding that SAS is the office to disclose their incidents to rather than a pronounced increase in crime on campus. These disclosures are a mix of sexual assault, dating violence, and stalking cases. SAS has filled the gap for college students who either distrusted other authorities on campus or did not know their reporting options.

> When the mother of a 17-year-old freshman female student called, she first said that she had been referred by Security on Campus, Inc., that she was the mother of a university student from another state, that her daughter had been drugged and raped by five members of one of her university's athletic teams, and that the university was unwilling to help her or her daughter. The university seemed to be trying to push the incident aside to perhaps mask its responsibility, so she believed. This mother was very distraught; she was willing to do anything to help her daughter but the avenues just didn't seem to be open to her. After several conversations and occasions to laugh and to cry, she introduced me to her daughter, first by e-mail, then in person. The daughter was making that change from victim to survivor under the loving guidance of her mother, who was being supported continuously by SAS, a program not even in the state in which the incident had occurred.

George Mason University's Sexual Assault Services Office has marketed itself to students in every possible way, from kiosks in the student unions to monthly myth flyers to presentations in many classrooms to major initiatives that students cannot avoid noticing. The intent of this massive marketing campaign is to flood the university with information about reporting options and services for victims of interpersonal trauma. For instance, this office sponsors a major fall semester initiative during October to coincide with Sexual Assault Awareness Month. It is called "Turn Off the Violence Week" and it has become a regular feature each fall on this campus of 28,000 students. During this week, SAS broadly displays evidence of violence against women to the campus community. The chief methods are via the annual Take Back the Night Rally and March, The White Ribbon Project, and The Clothesline Project. Each of these is modeled after a national project but is tailored to the university community in order to generate more interest and more attendance.

Of the three events, The Clothesline Project has the broadest appeal. Set in a quiet grove of trees in the center of campus, an actual clothesline is strung from tree to tree. On that clothesline are hung T-shirts designed by and for university student victims. The words and the art of each T-shirt reflect the trauma experienced by female victims of violence on the campus.

> When the 35-year-old female student came charging into my office, I wasn't ready for what transpired. She said directly to me, "It's because of you. You are the one responsible. I have had to walk by that clothesline of shirts every day this week, and I can't stand it. Reading those shirts has made me think about my rape that happened 20 years ago when I was just 15 years old. Now what am I going to do?"

This is a prime example of what happens when a survivor of sexual assault is awakened by the Sexual Assault Services Office initiatives. This female senior student, married with two small children, had never come to terms with the assault that nearly decimated her adolescence. But in the past year, with regular meetings with an advocate and referrals to an off-campus therapist, she has begun to understand that she has value, that she is appreciated, and that she is needed, especially by her children.

CREATING A SENSE OF JUSTICE

SAS works closely with many processes to help create a fair sense of justice for the persons involved in any given situation. But what does justice mean? What does it involve? Many processes coexist on campus today, but unless there is an office that can help students become aware of these processes, the advantages and disadvantages of each, and the procedures for involvement in them, the student may be left in the dark and may choose not to get involved at all, thereby extending the traumatic effects of their assaults. Sexual Assault Services' programming efforts target certain subsets of students; these include freshmen, members of fraternal organizations, student athletes, minorities, disabled, and international students. SAS presents information in classroom settings and during individual disclosures about the many processes that are available to George Mason University students. Coexisting processes (George Mason University Student Handbook, 2003) include:

- Police reporting process
- University judicial process
- Housing judicial process
- Athletic department judicial process

- Greek (fraternity/sorority) judicial process
- University Dispute Resolution process

ENGAGING THE CRIMINAL JUSTICE SYSTEM

It is rare that a student has knowledge of all the resolution options that are available to her or him. If a student identifies the incident as a crime, which is not the case in many instances, then, of course, she or he knows that one option afforded is to make a police report. Unfortunately, many students do not even realize that the university *has* a police department. The term *campus security* or even *campus police* just does not sound like "real police," so students do not call them for help. And because they think that making a police report means dealing with a community agency that they are totally unfamiliar with, they choose not to make a report at all. On the other hand, if the student victim knows that the university does have a certified police department, she or he still may opt not to call them based on prior knowledge of the police department, either their own negative circumstances or that of a friend who has passed along some negativity about the department.

When a student comes to the Sexual Assault Services Office, staff members explain what it means to make a police report and that we can facilitate the report making if the victim so chooses. Once an explanation is given and understood, many student victims decide that they, indeed, do want to make an official police report. The office advocate either calls a detective (preferable to a patrol officer) about the new incident and requests that the detective come to our office to meet with the victim; occasionally we must take the victim to the police department itself. But the comfort level that exists within the confines of the Sexual Assault Services Office is much more conducive to a good interview with a victim than the stark interview rooms of any police department. Since the George Mason University student body is primarily commuter-based, most reports of sexual assault occur off campus, necessitating collaboration with community police services.

The criminal justice system, being as unpredictable and uncertain as it is, affords little relief to the already anxiety-ridden sexual assault victim. The detailed interviews, the time lags between points in the process, and the lack of support that a victim sometimes feels from the police department only heighten the trauma existing after the incident itself. As one 18-year-old freshman woman stated, "When the police officer kept saying over and over that she needed to know if I really said 'no' to my attacker, I began to wonder if she believed anything at all that I said to her. I began to wonder why I even made the report."

And when the police officials *do* believe the victim and think that they have enough evidence to take the case forward to prosecution (and the victim wants this as well), prosecution teams may choose not to file a case, not because they do not believe the victim, but because they believe that there is not enough evidence to gain a conviction (Vachss, 1993). This often leaves victims in a depressed state of mind. Support from advocates is extremely important every step of the way in a criminal justice process. Should the case be filed and actually go to court, it often ends with an acquittal. The victim wonders, "How could that be?" The support personnel serve a valiant role of explaining to the victim not only that she or he did the right thing, but also that the judge or jury did not (usually) disbelieve her. Instead the decision maker(s) simply did not find enough evidence to convict.

EFFECTIVENESS OF UNIVERSITY JUDICIAL PROCEDURES

In cases in which both the victim and the perpetrator are students at the same university or college, another legal option for the victim is the university judicial system. Although these processes vary from school to school, they are known to be less formal, less complex, and less time-consuming than the criminal justice process. The most formal end to a judicial process is a hearing, complete with hearing board, judicial administrator, and testimony from both sides. The Foley Amendment, a 1998 Amendment to the Family Educational Rights and Privacy Act of 1974 (FERPA), 20 U. S.C. 1232g, regulates the disclosure of campus judicial hearings while protecting the identity of the victim and witnesses. At George Mason University, the Sexual Assault Services Office plays an integral part in any judicial process.

> The University is committed to supporting students' exercise ofinformed choice among (disciplinary) services and ensuring theanonymity of those students affected by incidents of sexual assault.Off-campus support and judicial services may also play important roles and the University will continue to provide support services to students who choose to seek criminal or civil prosecution as well as disciplinary action under the University Judicial Code. George Mason University (2003)

The victim and advocate usually discuss the entire process before a formal complaint is entered. Once the complaint has been made to the judicial administrator, he must advise the accused (judicial term for alleged perpetrator). The accuser (or alleged victim) has the option of proposing a settlement to which she or he would agree. This agreement is some sanction less than expulsion and does not include a judicial disciplinary notation on the accused's academic record. Sometimes victims, when asked what they want out of the process, respond, "I just never want to see him again." The informal part of the judicial process might then allow for a negotiated settlement.

For example, the accused might agree to leave the university immediately and not return until the accuser (victim) graduates. Part of any such agreement would also include a "no contact" clause and a "no trespassing on the university " clause. The victim is never required to enter into or sign such an agreement unless this is her or his choice. When both parties agree, this negotiation can be considered a form of campus restorative justice as well.

University housing judicial processes, fraternal organization judicial processes, and athletic department judicial processes may run independently or in conjunction with the main university judicial process. As separate processes, these organizational units handle disagreements among members plus minor infractions of both university and organizational student conduct codes. Only the university judicial process passes judgment on major crimes of violence that occur on campus. One last process, that of dispute resolution, exists on some campuses as well. This process uses mediation as a tactic for conflict management and resolution of differences between students and/or organizations on campus. Uses may include roommate disputes, organizational climate concerns, and minor disturbances. Mediation in sexual assault or stalking cases, which our program does not utilize, remains controversial. It is currently used by a few universities for sexual assault cases, but its use in major victimization raises concerns due to the need for offender acceptance of responsibility (which may not easily be accepted) and the face-to face interactions (which the victim may not want) that usually accompany this process (see Chapter 8).

RESOLUTION, RECOVERY, AND RESTORATION

Resolution choices for campus victims might easily include transferring to another school or dropping out of college entirely at the point of victimization or in the semester following the incident. Assisting the student to realize that she or he can remain in school, even after a campus crime has occurred, is one of the duties of any effective campus-based victim advocacy program. We believe that the most important aspect of a student victim's recovery in most cases is to stay in college and continue on the path that she or he had set for her- or himself—that of completing a college education and moving on to one's desired career. Recognition that a criminal act might be a setback, but that it should, in no way, bring one's education to a halt is vital for the recovery of any student victim so that the term *survivor* is, indeed, appropriate.

Restoring justice to a victim can be achieved when a campus community uses a victim-focused system and a victim-centered approach to resolution to victimization. Victim advocates hear common complaints from victims and survivors—the system is not just, victims have no voice, offenders are not held accountable. The inequalities found in both criminal and alternative system practices at times seem unsolvable (Daly, 2002). Restorative justice suggests that crime creates an imbalance in human relationships (Davis, 2003). The challenge of restorative justice in sexual assault cases is whether it can understand the nature of gendered harms and keep the process from revictimizing the victim (Daly, 2002). The restorative justice process on a college campus can at least address the restoration of the victim to normalcy. The victim will never be the person she or he was before the crime occurred, but she or he can be a well-functioning member of society, both on campus and after graduation (Ogawa, 1990).

Campus-based victim services must emphasize to all students that confidentiality is a key component to these services, that the student is in charge of distribution of any information, and that the office will not make decisions for the student victims. Ethics is paramount. Even when the staff may not belong to protected professions, such as licensed counselors or social workers, the victim advocates must understand both ethical decision making and confidential aspects of the helping profession to which they belong. The role of support and crisis intervention cannot be understated. Even if only a small percentage of actual victims come forward for services, those students will continue to need services long after the incident ends and the disclosure has been made. Sexual Assault Services staff, for example, assists their clients on an average of 20 separate occasions. This assistance may take the form of "drop-in times" or formally scheduled follow-ups. The office has been organized in such a manner that students always feel that they are a priority, with or without an appointment. Such an office is a necessary adjunct to a campus counseling center, which must operate on scheduled hourly (50-minute) cycles.

ADVOCACY VS. COUNSELING

Advocacy is not the same as counseling; both are essential for the restoration of students involved in crisis following a sexual assault (Young, 1993). Counseling often takes place after the initial response to the incident has subsided and the victim perceives a need for additional emotional support. The counseling should address the crime that happened and any consequences or issues that arise in the aftermath of this crime, sometimes manifested as the symptoms of post-traumatic stress disorder (PTSD). It may then direct attention to other aspects of the victim's life that are influencing thoughts, attitudes, and behaviors.

Keeping the counseling relationship focused on the crime helps ensure that the victim—with support—confronts the crisis reactions he or she experienced and begins the process of reconstructing their life. Focused counseling lessens the opportunity for long-term denial and repression to keep the healing process from progressing (Young, 1993).

This is not to say that preexisting life problems will be ignored, but once trauma-specific support has been initiated, the counselor will be better able to assist the victim resolve other problems that may have been reflected or indicated during the criminal incident (Foa and Rothbaum, 1998; Young, 1993).

Advocacy really means to help victims and survivors help themselves (Young, 1998). Allowing victims and survivors to prioritize their own goals will help build confidence in an effort to regain a sense of independence—the independence that was lost as a result of the victimization. Crime victimization leaves victims, families, and friends in emotional turmoil. Due to significant loss—financial, physical, emotional, spiritual—the psychological trauma of a victimization may result in long-term stress reactions that an advocate can attend to. The mission of an advocate is to use a philosophy of empowerment to help the victim reach resolution—a sense of healing. Some aspects of advocacy are simple to state—informing victims of their rights, helping them have their rights respected, stating options available to resolve a problem, providing assistance in locating services needed, making referrals, interceding on behalf of a victim or survivor only when they are unable to effect change themselves (Foa and Rothbaum, 1998; Koss and Harvey, 1991). Providing emotional support to the student as she or he navigates whatever system is chosen following an incident of victimization is the paramount work of an advocate. There is no set time limit for this support; it may last years, or it may last weeks or months. The student in need makes the decision about its value and continuity. Victim services, thus, must encompass the needs as long as they exist.

For the past three years, 33 percent of the students reporting an on-campus incident to Sexual Assault Services also have reported the offense to the university police and chose to consider prosecution (usually *following* the disclosure to Sexual Assault Services Office staff). Statistical follow-through to community police is not as high, however. Off-campus services often are not as invested or as understanding of campus victimization, which usually involves alcohol, late-night parties, and acquaintances (George Mason University Sexual Assault Services, 2003).

EMERGING TRENDS IN CAMPUS SERVICES

Sexual Assault Services staff continually collaborate and train university and community medical and legal professionals about the emerging issues related to sexual assault, stalking, and dating violence, thus creating a climate whereby these professionals not only know the newest trends and concerns, but also learn the investigative techniques and procedures related to each.

An example of this is the issue of drug-facilitated sexual assault. The Sexual Assault Services Office began researching this issue in great detail in 1998 because of an increased number of students disclosing the belief that they had been drugged before being raped. Students indicated at disclosure that they could not remember significant portions of the time period when their sexual assault occurred. Many students suggested that they might have been simply more intoxicated than they had expected to be, but others genuinely believed that someone had put a drug into their drink. Students reported that they knew that they were being raped but could not move their arms or legs to resist. Other students reported having flashes of memory of the evening, but not enough memory to be certain of who perpetrated acts against them.

In the year 2000, with the aid of a federal Centers for Disease Control grant, the Sexual Assault Services Office developed a 100-page manual titled "Responding to Drug-Facilitated Sexual Assault: A Reference Guide for Police and Medical Professionals" (George Mason University Sexual Assault Services, 2000). This manual was distributed widely to George Mason University and local community police and medical professionals. The U.S. Department of Justice National Drug Intelligence Center (NDIC) became aware of this document and requested permission to both update and distribute this manual nationally. This publication, jointly completed by NDIC and GMU SAS, was published in May 2003 as the *Drug-Facilitated Sexual Assault Investigative Resource Guide.* Currently in its third printing, copies of this useful manual have been distributed to thousands of law enforcement authorities nationwide (U.S. Department of Justice, 2003).

A final aspect of George Mason University's Sexual Assault Services Office that is both unique and valuable is its three-tiered Peer Support Program. This program was developed in 1997 to establish a network of trained student volunteers to provide information, support, and direct assistance to victims and survivors of sexual assault. Peer Educators provide educational programming to students in classrooms, residence halls, student organizations, and community agencies. Peer Companions provide one-on-one advocacy, referrals, and education, and offer options that enable victims to make decisions for themselves in order to regain control of their lives. Peer Companions work closely with the Sexual Assault Services coordinator and serve as an adjunct to her professional work. The goal of the Companion is to help increase the victim and survivor's effectiveness in coping with the aftermath of an assault by providing a confidential format to explore feelings of isolation. And Peer Advocates, the most highly trained volunteers in the pyramid, provide crisis intervention and accompaniment through medical and police proceedings as necessary in the absence of or as an adjunct to the staff coordinator.

Through ten years of intense collaboration with the recognized victim service providers (law enforcement and medical institutions) and those that are not necessarily considered so—college deans (to seek incompletes and retrowithdrawals), faculty members (to explain the victimization circumstances and to seek extended time for class assignments), and student accounts (to request tuition rollover when trauma interrupts the semester), this campus advocacy office has surmounted many obstacles and challenges by displaying total commitment to victims of campus crime. With reported incidents to Sexual Assault Services averaging 100 per calendar year, the staff is proud of the fact that since its creation, more and more incidents are also being reported officially to either university or community justice processes with the intent of holding perpetrators accountable and alleviating some of the trauma inflicted upon their victims. The support offered by office staff and volunteers, indeed, makes this achievable, thereby creating a campus climate that is both responsible and responsive to its constituents.

References

Coker, Donna. 2002. "Transformative Justice: Anti-Subordination Processes in Cases of Domestic Violence," pp. 128–152 in *Restorative Justice and Family Violence*, edited by Heather Strang and John Braithwaite. Cambridge: Cambridge University Press.

Daly, Kathleen. 2002. "Sexual Assault and Restorative Justice," pp. 62–88 in *Restorative Justice and Family Violence*, edited by Heather Strang and John Braithwaite. Cambridge: Cambridge University Press.

Davis, Sharon. 2003. "The Burlington Restorative Justice Center Panel Process," pp. 65–66, 75–79 in *The Crime Victims' Report*, Vol. 7, No. 5. Kingston, NJ: Civic Research Institute, Inc.

DeKeseredy, Walter S., and Martin S. Schwartz. 1998. *Woman Abuse on Campus*. Thousand Oaks, CA: Sage Publications, Inc.

Drug-Facilitated Sexual Assault Investigative Resource Guide. 2003. Washington, DC: U.S. Government Printing Office.

Fisher, Bonnie S., Francis T. Cullen, and Michael G. Turner. 2000. *Sexual Victimization Among College Women: Rsults from Two National-Level Studies*. Washington, DC: National Institute of Justice, U.S. Government Printing Office.

Fisher, Bonnie S., and John J. Sloan III (eds.). 1995. *Campus Crime: Legal, Social and Policy Issues*. Springfield, IL: Charles C Thomas.

Foa, Edna B., and Barbara Olasov Rothbaum. 1998. *Treating the Trauma of Rape: Cognitive-Behavioral Therapy for PTSD*. New York: The Guilford Press.

George Mason University. 2003. "George Mason University Student Handbook." Fairfax, VA.

George Mason University Sexual Assault Services. 2000. *Responding to Drug-Facilitated Sexual Assault: A Reference Guide for Police and Medical Professionals.* Fairfax, VA.

_____. 2003. "George Mason University Sexual Assault Response System Protocols and Procedure Checklists." Fairfax, VA.

_____. 2003. Client files.

Hitchcock, J. A., 2002. *Net Crimes and Misdeamors: Outmaneuvering the Spammers, Swindlers, and Stalkers Who Are Targeting You Online.* Medford, NJ: Information Today, Inc.

The Jeanne Clery Disclosure of Campus Security Policy and Campus Crime Statistics Act (20 USC 1092 (f)).

Immarigeon, Russ. 2003. "Australian Study Assesses the Strengths of Restorative Justice for Crime Victims," pp. 35–36, 44 in *The Crime Victim Report*, Vol. 7, No. 3. Kingston, NJ: Civic Research Institute, Inc.

Kirkland, Connie J. 1988. "Police Share Responsibility for Victims of Crime," pp. 9–12 in *Virginia Police Chief.* Richmond, VA: Best Communications, Ltd.

_____. 1994. "Sexual Assault: The Academic Impact," in *Matrix*, Fairfax, VA: George Mason University Women's Studies Newsletter.

_____. 1998. "Recommendations to Administrators for Responding to Campus Sexual Assault. Fairfax, VA: George Mason University Sexual Assault Services.

_____. 1999. "Sexual Assault: Peer Support Program at GMU," p. 10 in *The Peer Educator*, Denver, CO: Bacchus and Gamma Peer Education Network.

_____. 2003. "Campus Sexual Assault Programs—On the Cutting Edge," pp. 2,4, 6–7, in *Critical Response: Assisting Law Enforcement in Meeting the Needs of Victims.* Alexandria, VA: International Association of Chiefs of Police.

Kirkland, Connie J., and Dorothy Siegel, 1994. *Campus Security: A First Look at Promising Practices.* Washington, DC: U.S. Government Printing Office.

Koss, Mary P., and Mary R. Harvey. 1991. *The Rape Victim: Clinical and Community Interventions.* Thousand Oaks, CA: Sage Publications, Inc.

Ogawa, Brian K. 1999. *The Color of Justice: Culturally Sensitive Treatment of Minority Crime Victims.* Needham Heights, MA: Allyn & Bacon.

Schwartz, Martin D. and Walter S. DeKeseredy. 1997. *Sexual Assault on the College Campus: The Role of Male Peer Support.* Thousand Oaks, CA: Sage Publications, Inc.

Security on Campus, Inc. 2002. "About Security on Campus, Inc." Our Mission Is Safer Campuses for Students." King of Prussia, PA: Security on Campus, Inc. (http://www.securityoncampus.org/aboutsoc/index.html).

_____. 2003. "Complying with the Jeanne Clery Act." King of Prussia, PA: Security on Campus, Inc. (http://www.securityoncampus.org/schools/cleryact/text/html).

Smith, Michael R., and Richard Fossey. 1995. *Crime on Campus: Legal Issues and Campus Administration.* Phoenix, AZ: The Oryx Press.

Vachss, Alice. 1993. *Sex Crimes: Ten Years on the Front Lines Prosecuting Rapists and Confronting Their Collaborators.* New York: Random House, Inc.

Warshaw, Robin. 1994. *I Never Called It Rape.* New York: HarperCollins, Inc.

Young, Marlene A. 1993. *Victim Assistance: Frontiers and Fundamentals.* Washington, DC: National Organization for Victim Assistance.

Part IV

CONCLUSION

Chapter 22

RESTORATIVE JUSTICE: AN INSTITUTIONAL VIEW

PAT OLES

> The best student discipline program…creates a campus environment of caring and compassion, and . . . deters hateful and destructive behavior by virtue of commitment to community.
>
> Michael Dannells
> *From Discipline to Development*

Dannells (1997) elaborates a worthy, but difficult, goal. How do judicial systems promote caring and compassion and deter hateful and destructive behavior on campus? What approach meets the needs of contemporary students? Over the past four years, faculty, students, and staff at Skidmore College have been thinking about these and related questions while developing a restorative approach to campus discipline, the Integrity Board (IB). This chapter grew out of my involvement in that project and my reading of the chapters included in this volume. The discussion considers the benefits of a restorative approach from a broad institutional perspective as well as continuing challenges. It also considers why a restorative approach is especially sensible in light of the unique needs contemporary students present.

As several of the chapters in this volume reveal, college communities must respond to a wide range of student misconduct, misconduct that is often illegal, with negative consequences for individuals and the community. In formulating an institutional response, colleges must consider questions about values and standards, make decisions about policy, and enforce those decisions. The work requires a careful consideration of institutional mission, goals and pedagogy, student development, and extant empirical evidence, as well as broader social and legal constraints.

In "Contemporary Practice in Student Judicial Affairs: Strengths and Weakness" (Chapter 2), Lowery and Dannells describe how college disciplinary efforts have evolved from the colonial era, when students endured cor-

poral punishment in front of the entire student body, to contemporary practices that emphasize student rights and well-articulated administrative procedures. Their discussion underscores the long-standing concern colleges
have had with student conduct and character development, and it illustrates
how disciplinary systems grow out of an institutional perspective on human
nature, beliefs about personal change, and prevailing public sentiment.
Their discussion calls attention to the many unresolved questions in this area
of practice and how ripe the field is for new and innovative approaches.

RESTORATIVE JUSTICE AT SKIDMORE COLLEGE

Skidmore College is a liberal arts college committed to preparing students for informed, active citizenship. In our view, citizenship requires
knowledge, critical thinking, and interpersonal skills as well as concern for
community well-being. We understand that students do not arrive at college
fully prepared for the responsibilities that attend membership and that we
must teach them about those responsibilities. The primacy of this educational purpose informs our work with students, those who violate community standards as well as the students who work in the IB system.

Consonant with these broader concerns, Skidmore has worked to develop an IB that teaches students about justice, confronts them with opportunities to examine campus problems and consider solutions while also
requiring students who offend to act constructively in the community.
"Introducing Restorative Justice to the Campus Community" (Chapter 1)
summarizes how Skidmore views student misconduct and outlines the
restorative approach we have adopted.

The restorative approach is a good fit with Skidmore College because it
emphasizes student involvement and relies on discussion, interpersonal
encounter, reflection, and problem solving. The IB is part of the formal curriculum (the Law and Society Program) and is part of student affairs. It is a
context wherein students engage difficult problems, do research, and discover and attempt solutions with the support and involvement of faculty
and staff. The restorative program requires participants to learn in a traditional academic context and to enact the active citizenship the college values. The problems the IB confronts—violence, academic dishonesty,
alcohol and drug abuse, and hate crimes—are significant social problems,
problems this generation of students must successfully resolve once they
graduate. The IB is a laboratory, an opportunity for our students to develop
the capacities we want them to bring, as graduates, to the communities they
will lead and serve later in life.

The logic and potential benefits of the restorative approach are compelling, but developing and sustaining a restorative program is actually

quite challenging. Lowery and Dannells describe several problems such as a reliance on procedures, an adversarial process, and a focus on the primary participants that can develop from a misplaced application of a legal analog to work in college judicial affairs. Dejong (see Chapter 10) describes another pernicious challenge, alcohol abuse—a problem especially problematic for the IB at Skidmore because students, even students harmed by alcohol-related misconduct, tend to consider alcohol abuse as normative and the laws and policies regulating availability as illegitimate. Karp (Chapter 1) refers to this problem as dissensus.

The deepening concerns on and off campus about crime, violence, and plagiarism on campus also challenge an institutional commitment to a restorative approach. Many members of our community have confidence in the beneficial effects of punishment; some view membership as a privilege contingent on conduct and argue for using punitive sanctions such as suspension more often. Some members of the community are also concerned that the restorative tasks are too "easy" and that the college must do something more about misconduct. These are serious intellectual and political challenges.

We have little local empirical data confirming the effectiveness of the approach and no data comparing the benefits of the restorative approach to a more traditional approach. Consequently, we cannot resolve the concerns empirically.

On the other hand, because the approach is contrary to some generally held beliefs about the proper response to misconduct, the IB must struggle with the philosophical implications of the approach and communicate regularly with the community. To the staff, many of the problems the IB works on are familiar, but discussions about fundamental concerns keep the process fresh, and the broader discussions support student involvement, nurturing the connection between the board and the community.

Restorative justice is especially responsive to community concern. The approach permits everyone involved in the process to articulate the harm a student's behavior caused and to request some form of restitution. The conferences bring affected parties together with a focus on articulating harm and developing ways to repair that harm. Providing an opportunity for everyone involved to participate in the conference increases community confidence in the process, and it has reduced the number of appeals students and parents launch. This latter is something my office appreciates and, along with low rates of recidivism, has sustained my interest in developing the program.

The conference structure challenges all the participants to think critically and creatively about the impact of the misconduct, the best way to mitigate the harm, and how to reintegrate the student into the community. The process is obviously concerned with the well-being of all the students involved and the community, but the IB is not offended because a student's behavior "is against the rules." The issue is the harm that the behavior causes to the community. Moreover, the board does not permit students to simply "plead guilty" and take their "punishment." Students whose conduct is detrimental to others must articulate the harm, take responsibility for their behavior, and commit to change. Acknowledging responsibility and agreeing to make amends in the interpersonal context of an IB conference is a powerful moment. Bringing all parties into the process, legitimizing their concerns, and working toward a resolution that satisfies all parties builds support for community standards and expectations. The discussion in "Conferencing Case Study: Community Accountability Conferencing with a Recalcitrant Jonathan" (Chapter 11) illustrates how the affective intensity of a conference may be an important part of the process.

The high level of interest among numerous campus constituents also makes service on the IB meaningful. The problems the integrity board wrestles with are difficult. Service on the board is meaningful. When we began our restorative project at Skidmore College, student interest in service on the IB was low. We had trouble scheduling hearings that included the required number of students and appeals of disciplinary sanctions were routine. Several years into the project, there are two boards, recruiting members to serve is routine, and appeals are extremely rare. The process is slow, but the community's capacity to confront problems and work toward resolution is strengthening, and a tradition of student pride in the system is developing.

CONTEMPORARY STUDENTS

It is easy to focus on problems and theory, but what do students bring to the learning context? What prior experiences, strengths, and deficiencies are characteristic of this generation of students? Is the restorative approach sensible given the needs contemporary students present?

In *When Hope and Fear Collide*, Levine and Cureton (1998) argue for a curriculum that generates hope and promotes responsibility, an appreciation of differences, and personal efficacy. A more recent text, *Millennials Rising* (Howe and Strauss, 2003), describes undergraduates as sheltered, possessing high conventional aspirations, and as having a willingness to work hard at succeeding. The work discusses how smaller families and the amount of time current students have spent in well-supervised, organized play have limited student readiness for the interpersonal demands of college.

Overgeneralizing about a cohort of students is risky, but *When Hope and Fear Collide* and *Millennials Rising* resonate with my personal observations. Students are hungry for community, but I fear they think of community as a commodity they purchase from the college, not something they create at the college. Some were active in high school disciplinary systems, but Howe and Strauss (2003) found that most students are unwilling to risk interpersonal confrontation with peers. Instead, they expect college administrators to deal with peers who disturb their experience. Students value community, but they have not been responsible for creating their communities. In some respects, the campus is their first social context where student participation in governance really matters.

Given this very general picture, the restorative justice program is a highly appropriate educational response. It engages students with real community problems and structures the context so that students can acquire the interpersonal skills necessary for mature engagement with community. The program requires offenders as well as students serving on the board to consider the perspectives of other community members in light of their own experiences, and it requires students to develop and implement what they believe are effective responses to misconduct.

We get a sense of these dynamics in *Conferencing Case Study: Kenny's Celebration* (Chapter 6). Sebok describes a student who clearly values community. He is acutely aware of the impact of his behavior on his community and this caring about community motivates his contrition. The conference confronts some issues while also avoiding a student's problematic use of alcohol. As I read about this conference, especially the author's concern about alcohol being omitted from the discussion, I was reminded of the difficulty students will have confronting difficult problems, especially a problem such as alcohol abuse.

The case also illustrates the educational opportunities for board participants in a restorative program as well as the risks involved. For conferencing to work, the process must be genuinely the product of the participants, and that means that some participants will not cover some issues as well, or as completely, as a professional might cover them. Although well trained, students and affected parties may not be comfortable pursuing the issues fully.

The restorative approach helps students remedy the lack of skills described above. Indeed, this is one of the most appealing elements of the restorative approach. The restorative approach provides a structure for teaching students to invest in a community and to take interpersonal risk. As Levine and Cureton (1998) note, this generation of students has volunteered in great numbers, but that service has been at a safe remove from their own problems and limitations. The IB requires courage and critical thinking and choices about values in a context characterized by moral ambiguity.

Reflecting, clarifying, and acting on personal convictions despite doubts and difficulty and making a contribution *is* the stuff of adulthood. The IB structures educational opportunities for students while also improving the quality of community life on campus. The IB is a crucial element of the educational effort in student affairs while also protecting the integrity of the educational environment as well as the rights of the students involved. Every significant group in the community expects the IB to function wisely and well. Faculty offended by plagiarism, students harmed by peers, and parents upset by some aspect of their son or daughter's experience on campus all have an interest in IB decisions. The important role the IB plays in the community makes service meaningful, and it demonstrates to students that involvement in community processes is important.

THE CLASS

Students participating on the board are required to take a class. This class is an especially an important component of the program at Skidmore. The curriculum includes a full consideration of issues such as the tensions between the educational and protective imperatives underlying the IB, the demise of *in loco parentis*, student rights, the implications of civil litigation, a duty to care, and the student learning imperative. It also trains students in the skills required for effective conferencing.

When first proposed, the student government opposed requiring the course. It looked like an effort to control student behavior by training student "narcs." Students celebrating their liberation from the structures of their parental homes are not inclined to replace their parents with college authorities. *Lord of the Flies* is a distant memory and self-governance looks easy from the outside.

The student government conceived of service on the IB as analogous to being a juror. Students were on the board to represent, even protect, their peers from the authoritarian impulses of the administration. It has taken several years of patient discussion and effort to convince students that service on the board, like all citizenship, requires knowledge and thoughtful reflection. The legislative effort with students has proved worth the time. The student government accepts responsibility for meaningful participation in articulating and enforcing community standards, and the required class is now an important part of the program.

One very important benefit of the class is that it provides a context for members of the board to consider the philosophical basis of the program and to resolve tensions over how to respond to misconduct in advance of hearing cases. The issue of punishment, especially as it relates to serious or multiple offenses, and the ways higher education differs from the criminal justice system are two recurring themes in the class.

Hoekema (1994) argues that a permissive stance toward most behavior is especially congruent with the goals of higher education. In his view, rules proscribing behavior and restrictive consequences are defensible only when they are necessary to ensure safety or to prevent harm or exploitation. A tolerant environment permits students to make choices about values and behavior, and we believe that behavior developed in this fashion is more enduring than behavior that is not simply the result of compliance to strict rules and aggressive enforcement.

However, we are challenged by behaviors that are not obviously dangerous and by the problem of dissensus mentioned earlier. Casual drug use and music piracy are two examples of offenses that students do not readily see as problematic. Class discussions provide the students serving on the board with the opportunity to reflect thoughtfully on these kinds of issues and develop a mature opinion before working with peers who violate relevant policies.

The class discussions of philosophical, theoretical, and practical matters are fundamental to the work of the board. Without a full exploration and resolution of the tension between restoration and retribution, the IB could not sustain a restorative perspective in the face of offended parties and a generally high level of confidence in the deterrence value of punishment.

The administration's commitment to student autonomy, faith in educational intervention, and reluctance to resort to punishment unless the case involves issues related to safety and exploitation are not without irony. I have found that students, especially relatively young students, are more inclined toward a punitive stance when confronting the misconduct of peers than faculty and staff.

The social problems on campus—alcohol and drug abuse, violence and plagiarism, for example—are serious; the negative consequences for students and the community are varied and unacceptable. Campus regulations prohibiting various forms of misconduct clearly serve the interests of all community members, but the college must invest the effort necessary to win genuine support for regulations from the students. Without the active support of students, college regulations are a set of "legal" requirements, and violations are a problem for the "courts."

Students are often sympathetic toward students harmed by misconduct, but there is little appreciation for the ways that misconduct diminishes the educational power of the community. If students are not convinced that conduct is detrimental to the community, the responsibility for maintaining the community will fall, by default, to the administration, not the students. This might be efficient, but it is not educational. This is especially ironic given the well-known inclination among college students to resist authority.

The restorative approach requires students—those serving on boards as well as those appearing before a board—to articulate the benefits of college regulations. This rhetorical focus on the impact of behavior rather than the fact of a rule being broken and the beneficial basis for regulations is significant. It changes the discourse and the relationship between all of the parties involved. While fact-finding is an important component of the process, the more important purposes are making amends, repairing harm, and restoring the community. Replacing "getting caught" and "getting punished" with articulating the harm and making amends changes the discourse and focuses everyone's attention on the community.

The consequences and sanctions developed in a restorative process engage students and builds community capacity. The emphasis on making amends and repairing the harm makes the purpose of the specific regulation and the proceedings clear to everyone involved. Clearly articulating the harm and constructing a meaningful restorative task minimizes the negative effects of punishment and builds support for the regulation.

The class also initiates broader discussions among students and staff on-campus. IB members discuss issues with student government, with various campus offices, and in training and orientation meetings for new students and student staff. These broader discussions are critical to building community support for setting and enforcing standards. The result is a well-informed cadre of students seriously engaged with the theoretical, legal, and professional issues working to strengthen community commitment to civil conduct.

LIMITATIONS

Restorative justice is not a panacea. It rests upon the community developing a shared view about values and standards and it assumes good faith. Unresolved conflicts between student culture and the college's expectations undermine the approach.

The abuse of alcohol and other drugs is an example. The restorative approach requires a clear articulation of harm, a sense that the behavior violates community values, and the offender's sincere willingness to change in order to rejoin the community. In the case of drug and alcohol abuse, student culture is in conflict with the law as well as the college's regulations. Ambivalence in the system is considerable. Students on the IB do not disapprove and faculty and staff are conflicted. When alcohol or drug use correlates with misconduct, the board can appropriately focus its attention on the related misconduct. However, alcohol and drug abuse *itself* is increasingly a concern on campus, and the college cannot ignore repeated violations of the alcohol regulations, even when they are not coincidental with other misconduct.

It is not clear to us whether the problem is our inability to articulate the harm clearly enough or the broader social context implicated in alcohol and drug abuse. Nonetheless, we are considering a more assertive administrative intervention with students who violate alcohol and drug regulations.

Student use of P2P technology to steal copyrighted material, especially music, is similarly problematic. Students agree about the moral dimensions of theft and intellectual property rights, but on this issue, student culture does not align with the college.

Students can go to a hearing, say the right things, and "get off" with relatively little "punishment." A student committed to gaming the system in this way may find it relatively easy in the early going. Apologies that do not ring true, tasks that go uncompleted, and redundant misconduct are ultimately unsuccessful. However, students who are not sincere do damage the system. There are urban myths that discourage other participants, and to some extent, diminish the IB's standing in the community. These are meaningful costs to the system.

In our experience, this kind of gaming behavior is not successful in the end. Students who do not participate sincerely are "self-suspended" for their failure to complete tasks or the student comes before the board again and the board holds them accountable, including on occasion suspending the student for the repeated failure to comply with plans developed with the board. In these instances, the community is confident that reasonable efforts had failed and the student left the college because there was no other choice.

There are colleagues on campus who are opposed to investing this much effort with students who violate college expectations. They argue that the college is not a "soft reform school" or a "treatment center" and suggest that the system invites a high level of disrespect for standards. As concern about campus safety mounts, it is a potent argument. If the goal is a tidy campus, they are correct. However, liberal arts colleges aim higher. The goal is educating citizens and leaders capable of strengthening communities and inspiring commitment. It takes effort and patience, a willingness to invest in students, even those whose behavior is not acceptable. The restorative approach provides colleges with the perspective and means to work toward this crucial goal.

References

Dannells, Michael. 1997. "From Discipline to Development: Rethinking Student Conduct in Higher Education. *ASHE-ERIC Higher Education Report* 25(2). San Francisco, CA: Jossey-Bass.

Hoekema, David, A. 1994. *Campus Rules and Moral Community: In Place of In Loco Parentis.* Lanham, MD. Rowman & Littlefield.

Howe, N., and W. Strauss. 2003. *Millennials Go to College.* Washington, DC: AACRAO.

Levine, A., and J. Cureton. 1998. *When Hope and Fear Collide: A Portrait of Today's College Student.* San Francisco, CA: Jossey-Bass.

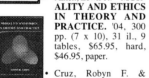

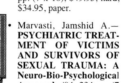
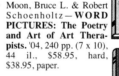
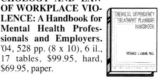

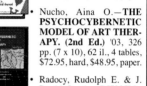